Early Twentieth Century

PHOTOGRAPHY

Identification & Values

COLLECTOR BOOKS
A Division of Schroeder Publishing Co., Inc.

Michael & Susan Ivankovich

Front cover
Top left
Maine lighthouse,
Charles Saywer, $150.00 – 250.00.
Beneath top photo
Prize-winning photograph,
David Davidson, $75.00 – 100.00.
Center
"Zinneas,"
Wallace Nutting, $750.00 – 1,000.00.
Center right
Close-framed snow scene,
Charles Sawyer, $100.00 – 150.00.
Bottom
Sailing ship triptych,
Fred Thompson, $200.00 – 300.00.

Back cover
Top left
Vermont, close-framed bridge scene,
Homer Royce, $75.00 – 100.00.
Center right
"Florida Wilds,"
William J. Harris, $100.00 – 150.00.
Bottom left
Washington DC
close-framed Jefferson Memorial,
Royal Carlock, $50.00 – 75.00.

Cover design ∞ Beth Summers Book design ∞ Erica Weise

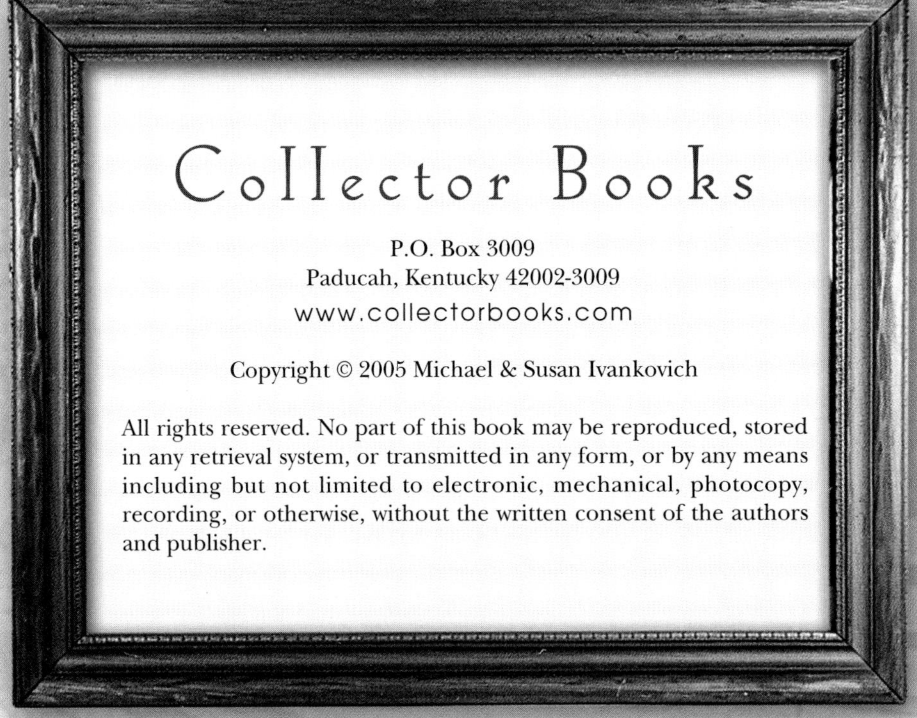

Collector Books
P.O. Box 3009
Paducah, Kentucky 42002-3009
www.collectorbooks.com

The current values in this book should be used only as a guide. They are not intended to set prices, which vary from one section of the country to another. Auction prices as well as dealer prices vary greatly and are affected by condition as well as demand. Neither the authors nor the publisher assumes responsibility for any losses that might be incurred as a result of consulting this guide.

Contents

Preface

Starting with Wallace Nutting pictures in 1973, Michael Ivankovich has been collecting and researching early twentieth century hand-painted photography for more than 30 years. But his first exposure to hand-painted photographs came even earlier than that. While going through a box of mostly black and white family photographs with his sister Lynn during the 1960s, he came across several brightly colored pictures. The first was a hand-colored picture of his mother, Irene, taken when she was a child in around 1931. Apparently, the photographer thought that Irene was so cute that he submitted the picture to a local newspaper, which actually published it. In the same box of pictures, Mike also found a wedding picture of his parents that had been hand-painted by his dad, Metro Ivankovich, an Air Force photographer during World War II. Those two colorized pictures represented Mike's first exposure to hand-painted photography, and little did he know that years later he would be spending a significant portion of his life studying and researching that exact field.

Mike's mom, Irene Ivankovich, hand-painted photo circa 1931

Fast forward to the 1970s, when Mike was decorating the walls of his first house and found himself attracted to the look and reasonable prices of Wallace Nutting pictures. The first pictures he ever purchased were Nutting's "Larkspur" and "Honeymoon Drive." He bought them on the same day, at the Lambertville Flea Market in New Jersey. Those two pictures led to four pictures. Four led to eight. Soon he had accumulated a small collection. And that led to a larger collection that was outgrowing his wall space. Before long, he was forced to become a part-time antiques dealer in order to support his picture-buying habit.

Mike's Dad, Metro Ivankovich, an Air Force photographer during World War II

While employed in management at a major insurance company, Mike became an avid part-time flea market dealer and soon opened an antique shop in a barn behind his first house. Although he sold a wide variety of antiques and collectibles, his primary inventory consisted of Wallace Nutting pictures.

He still remembers buying his first Nutting-type picture, sometime around 1976. It was a David Davidson ("The Porch Beautiful"). The dealer tried to tell him that it was a Hand Handson hand-colored photograph, but he knew better. He knew that although the *D*'s in Davidson's name could sometimes appear to be *H*'s, he was buying a David Davidson picture. He didn't know anything about Davidson, because nothing had been written about him yet. But Mike was certainly ahead of the curve even then. At least he knew it was a David Davidson hand-painted photo.

Mike wrote his first book on Wallace Nutting in 1984, *The Price Guide to Wallace Nutting Pictures*. It was perhaps 50 pages long, it included a few photos, and it was printed at a local offset printing shop. He self published it and had to handle all the printing, advertising, marketing, and warehousing expenses out of his own pocket. No publisher was involved. He expected people to laugh at his first publishing attempt, but surprisingly few did. The book was pretty well received. It even generated some favorable press reviews. That book gave him enough confidence to self publish a second edition of same title. He expanded that book a bit, and added a slicker, two-color glossy cover. It too was pretty well received.

Mike's parents' wedding photo, hand painted circa 1946 by his dad

Sheldon Edgerton, circa 1930

Jean Edgerton, circa 1945

Shortly thereafter, in 1986, he reprinted the *Wallace Nutting Expansible Catalog*, which was Nutting's 1915 saleman's catalog. At the time, in those pre-Internet days, it was the best visual reference book available anywhere on Wallace Nutting pictures. That book was extremely popular with collectors, and a second edition was printed.

Sue entered Mike's life in 1986, and they married in 1988. With their parents, Sue's son and daughter and Mike's twin daughters became one new family. Mike and Sue both enjoyed writing books (Sue had co-written and illustrated two cookbooks prior to meeting Mike). They both loved antiques. They both had an entrepreneurial spirit. And together, they made the decision to leave the corporate world and enter the world of hand-colored photography.

Like Mike, Sue's first exposure to hand-painted photography also came in the 1950s with family photos. Her father, Sheldon Edgerton, was a local physician in Delhi, New York (in the days when doctors still made house calls). And her mother, Jean, was a former World War II army nurse. "Doc" Edgerton was an excellent musician as well, and many of his earlier photos were taken as promo pictures for the various orchestras he played in, and these were colorized by hand to add some pizazz. Little did Sue know that hand-painted photography was going to play a major role in her life as well.

Mike and Sue published their first non-Nutting picture book in 1991, *The Guide to Wallace Nutting–like Photographers*. This self-published book was the first attempt by anyone at documenting the work of Nutting's early twentieth century photographic contemporaries. Information at that time was limited, but what Mike and Sue put together was the best source of information about these photographers. They did the best job that they could at the time, based upon the resources available to them.

Sue & her brother, Paul Edgerton, circa 1954

Now fast forward to today. The World Wide Web, eBay, Internet auctions, Internet stores, Google, other search engines — all types of information available at the click of a mouse, access that few of us dreamed possible in 1991.

Combine all of the advantages of the Internet with nearly 20 years of Michael and Susan Ivankovich auctions and more than 30 years of retail hand-painted pictures passing through their hands. Together, Mike and Sue have handled more than 30,000 pictures through their auctions, certainly more than anyone else in the country. And a large percentage of these pictures were by Wallace Nutting–like photographers of the early twentieth century.

Mike and Sue have talked of finalizing this project for more than 10 years. Throughout this entire time, they have been recording photographs of images, signatures, and paper labels. They have been accumulating any information they were able to track down about the photograpghers. Most of the research they have done themselves, but many of you have contributed to this project as well.

For the past year, Mike and Sue have been putting all of the pieces to this gigantic puzzle together. Gathering letters, notes, photographs, printouts, transcripts from telephone calls, etc., trying to combine it all into a readable and usable resource to help you learn about this rapidly expanding field.

The Ivankoviches have been writing and preaching about Wallace Nutting for 20 years now. Five volumes of Wallace Nutting price guides, other Wallace Nutting reference books, presentations, columns, trade paper articles, television and radio interviews, exhibits at antiques shows – all have been part of the attempt to disseminate information about Wallace Nutting.

The Wallace Nutting Collectors Club has been gathering and publishing information about Wallace Nutting for more than 30 years. When you add in Tom Dennenberg's 2003 *Wallace Nutting and the Invention of Old America* book, frankly, what else one can write about Wallace Nutting that hasn't already been written comes into question.

But the field of early twentieth century hand-painted Photography is wide open and just beginning to become noticed. And here are two very simple reasons why:

1) **Collectors Collect the Name.**
Wallace Nutting, Roseville, Steiff, Heisey, Tiffany, Stickley, etc. To some, the name is more collectible than the object.

2) **Collectors Collect What They Know and What They Understand.**
The more collectors know about something, the more they want to collect it.

Wallace Nutting is a good case in point. Twenty years ago, outside of the Wallace Nutting Collectors Club, most people could have cared less about Wallace Nutting. But the more people learned about Nutting, the more they appreciated him — and the more they wanted to collect his pictures. Today, Wallace Nutting is appreciated in the highest of circles. When organizations such as the Wadsworth Atheneum, the Society for the Preservation of New England Antiquities, and the New York Times speak highly of Wallace Nutting, you know that Nutting has moved from niche to mainstream.

But in the overall field of hand-painted photography, aside from David Davidson, Fred Thompson, and Charles Sawyer, very little been written about the hundreds of other early twentieth century photographers. Until now. We hope that this book opens your eyes to how much knowledge is out there just waiting to be discovered, because we truly believe that we have just skimmed the surface in this area.

Throughout this book, you will notice a major difference between the overall hand-painted photography market and the Wallace Nutting market, which can be summed up in one word, *regionality*.

Unlike the Wallace Nutting market, which has more of a national presence, most of these Nutting-like photographers will be much more highly collectible regionally than nationally. For example, we had never seen a hand-painted picture by a photographer named Craswell until one came through one of our auctions in 2003. It was titled "Fishing Harbor, Prince Edward Island." We checked out our favorite resources and came away with a wealth of information about Cleve Craswell. We learned that Craswell was a photographer who sold hand-painted pictures, taken on Prince Edward Island, Canada, to visiting tourists. A whole web site of information was available. Armed with this information, where do you think Craswell will be more highly valued, Long Island, Staten Island, Catalina Island, or Prince Edward Island? The key to understanding this field is understanding regionality. And this book will help both collectors and dealers better understand and pinpoint the regionality aspect of hand-painted photography.

Enjoy this book. Learn from it. And please, continue to share your new finds with us.

Many of you may have already noticed a change in the terminology we're using in this book. For nearly 30 years, we have been referring to our preferred collectible field as "hand-colored photography." We simply liked the term *hand-colored* over *hand-tinted* or any other variation we had seen. It just sounded more appropriate to us. Well, for several years our friend and co-author of *The Hand-Painted Photographs by Charles Henry Sawyer*, Doug Peters, has been quietly trying to get us to adopt the term *hand-painted photography* instead of *hand-colored photography*. And for years we have steadfastly refused to change. Because after 30 years, why change?

But Doug, being the successful lawyer that he is, has finally made us appreciate his point of view. He has finally convinced us that "hand-painted" is more descriptive of the entire process than "hand-colored." "Hand-painted" leaves nothing to the imagination. Each hand-painted photo is just what the name suggests, a photograph that has been individually hand painted, a one-of-a-kind piece of art.

Hence, the title of this book: *Early Twentieth Century Hand-Painted Photography*.

Congratulations, Doug. You finally convinced us.

And finally, we would like to acknowledge the many individuals who sent us letters and e-mails, or who telephoned us over the past 15 years, telling about their latest finds. You probably thought that we forgot about you. We didn't. We would like to thank the following people for sending us information:

Anders "Andy" Anderson, John Baron, Gary Bicknell, Lisa Calache, Irene Colonna, Jane Crandall, Donald and Alice Davidson, the late Ted Davies, Jim Day, Edward Dennis, Fran Donovan, Tom Driebe, Joe Duggan, Jim and Sharon Eckert, Tracy Elliot, Muriel Everhart, Rhonda Fitzsimmons, Carol Franzoza, Bob Frishman, Ron Gibson, Jim and Claire Graves, Carol Gray, Martha Carlock Green, Michael and Brenda Gridley, Edmond Grof, Larry Hale, Bill and Gretchen Hamann, Don and Nancy Hartman, Jerry Hechler, Kristen Henry, Elmer Funkhouser, Ed and Donna Lanigan, Gary LeBreche, George and Shirley Lovesky, Jorden Kager Meier, Edwin Meyer, Austin Minor, Ed and Hilda Moody, Ed Moore, Harriet Hudson Mullen, Edwin Meyer, Lee and Joan Owen, Doug Peters, Richard Gardiner Roggeveen, Steve Sennert, Barbara and John Snyder, Nancy (Bicknell) Stone, Gordon Struble, Marguerite Sulliva, Freeman Sweetson, Bill Taylor, Richard Turkiewicz, Dick Valentinetti, Glenn at West Pacific, Don and Barb Wiesenberg, and Jim Witham.

If you contributed something to us over the years and we failed to acknowledge you here, please accept our sincere apologies.

Chapter 1

The History of the Hand-Painted Photograph

Ever since the first photograph was developed in 1839, people have been trying to add color to black and white photographs in order to make them appear more realistic and appealing.

Early Daguerreotype, circa 1850

Technically, the first photograph was produced even earlier than 1839. Back in 1826 a French inventor, Joseph Nicephore Niepce, developed a process that enabled him to affix an image to a copper plate with light-sensitive chemicals. Unfortunately, the exposure time was a lengthy eight hours, simply too long for the process to be considered commercially practical or viable.

Several years later, Niepce entered into a partnership with Louis Jacques Mande Daguerre, who had developed a process for affixing an image to a piece of coated copper with an exposure time reduced to 15 – 30 seconds, significantly faster than the eight hours required by Niepce's process. Daguerre named his invention after himself, and *Daguerreotypes* became the most common form of photographs available from approximately 1839 to 1865. Daguerreotypes were direct positives, which means that they had no negatives, and therefore, no additional prints of the same image could be produced. Each picture can be considered a unique piece of art. Daguerreotypes have an almost mirror-like surface. The earliest ones had a silvery look to the image, whereas later ones had a browner tone. Many daguerreotypes were stored in beautiful gutta percha (hard plastic) cases that were often highly decorated in their own right.

COLLECTING TIP

Daguerreotypes were direct positives, unique pieces of art without true negatives.

Almost as soon as the daguerreotype was introduced, a demand arose for "overpainting" to accent the dull black and white images. Lips, hair, cheeks, eyes, gold earrings, watches, other jewelry, and sometimes even flowers were painted to provide a little more color and realism. Because they were fairly expensive, daguerreotypes brought personal photography primarily only to the wealthier classes. The rarest and the best forms of daguerreotypes will normally be found in museums and private collections, but you can still find the more common forms of hand-painted "people" daguerreotypes in today's antiques and collectibles markets.

COLLECTING TIP

People have been "over-painting," or hand painting, photography almost since its invention in 1839.

Calotypes. Around this same time, William Henry Fox Talbot, an Englishman, invented a process whereby a light-sensitive paper could produce a paper negative that could then be used to produce multiple positive prints. He called his invention "photography," and his "negative-positive" process made possible the larger production of calotype photographs. Multiple prints from the same negative could each be colored in a different manner, thereby making identical images appear different. Unfortunately, patent complications prevented the calotype from effectively competing with the daguerreotype.

Ambrotypes were one of the next generations of photographs, and they too were often overpainted by hand. Frederick Scott Archer, another Englishman, invented the process whereby a glass negative was backed with a black paper, black velvet, or some other dark material, and then placed in a daguerreotype-style hard plastic case. The highly reflective ambrotypes were extremely popular with young women during the Civil War years because, supposedly, many young women enjoyed seeing their own images reflecting on the glass over the images of their spouses or loved ones. Perhaps the biggest downside of the ambrotype was that because of the fragile nature of the glass, they were much more difficult to ship. As a matter of fact, most novice collectors today can't differentiate between an ambrotype and daguerreotype. The easiest way to identify the two is to know that the daguerreotype has a more reflective, mirror-like surface than is seen in ambrotypes. Also, because the ambrotype was less expensive than the daguerreotype, it brought photography to the broad middle class. Significantly more ambrotypes than daguerreotypes were produced, and therefore more ambrotypes will be found in today's market. The peak period for ambrotypes was circa 1855 – 1870.

Hand-painted tinytypes

Tintypes were the most popular form of photograph between 1860 and 1900, primarily because they were so inexpensive and could last much longer than other forms. As the name suggests, with tintypes the image was literally transferred onto a piece of tin. Tin was inexpensive and, unlike glass, almost indestructible. Tintypes came in varying sizes and were often framed within an inexpensive paper border. Tintypes could be shipped in a letter without fear of breakage, and tintypes could be quickly and easily hand painted. Tintypes were especially popular with soldiers and civilians on both sides during the Civil War because they could be safely mailed to loved ones in the army or on the home front. Hand-painted people tintypes can often be found in flea markets today and can sometimes be found in large boxes of old photographs priced at $5.00 or less.

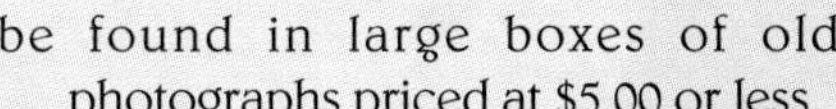

Hand-painted tintype
in oval paper border

Framed hand-painted tintype

COLLECTING TIP

Tintypes were widely popular because they were easily hand painted, inexpensive, and available to the masses.

Nineteenth century photographic prints. Photographic images made from negatives are typically called "prints," and most nineteenth century prints were printed upon paper. Photographic prints are generally classified by finished size and by technique. The following chart lists some of these prints:

Carte de Visite
4¼" x 2½" (circa 1859)

Boudoir Cards
5¼" x 8½" (1860s)

Imperial Cards
6¾" x 9¾" (1860s)

Panel Cards
8¼" x 4" (1860s)

Cabinet Cards
4½" x 6½" (circa 1866)

Victoria Cards
3¼" x 5" (circa 1870)

Promenade Cards
4" x 7" (circa 1875)

Albumen Prints
Various sizes (circa 1850-1910)

Each type of photograph above was widely hand painted.

Hand-painted carte de vistes

Retouching vs. hand painting: Almost as soon as the negative was introduced, retouching followed. Retouching and overpaining are not quite the same process and perhaps need some explanation. Overpainting is simply the process of hand painting a photograph, or adding color by hand. However, in certain instances it was easier for the photographer to change the negative instead of having to change each individual photographic print.

Hand-painted cabinet card

According to Heinz and Bridget Henisch in their book *The Painted Photograph: 1839 – 1914*, retouching was invented circa 1841 by Henry Collen. What this basically means is that almost as soon as the photographic process was invented (1839), photographers felt it necessary to alter some of their work in order to improve upon it. Retouching allowed photographers to eliminate unwanted objects or physical imperfections from photographs, and at the same time allowed them to add almost anything of their choosing. Retouching kits, retouching tools, and retouching machines were all available in the latter part of the nineteenth century, and even Wallace Nutting retouched some of his pictures.

Hand-painted ancestral photo

Hand-painted albumen print, Yellowstone Park, probably early F. Jay Haynes, circa 1895

COLLECTING TIPS

Hand painting and *overpainting* are identical terms, and both refer to the process of painting individual photographs by hand.

Retouching means making physical changes to either the original negative or individual photographic prints.

For example, most Wallace Nutting collectors are familiar with the picture "A Little River." Nutting took this picture along a rocky stream, bordered by a country road, in New Hampshire. The scene is idyllic. Untouched nature at its best. No sign of man. No urban development. No evidence of any technological progress. The way most of us today have never seen America.

Wallace Nutting, "A Little River"

Somewhere around 1894, while serving as a Congregationalist minister in Providence, Rhode Island, Wallace Nutting began to tire after expending significant amounts of personal energy creating, and then delivering, his weekly Sunday sermons. Mrs. Nutting suggested that he buy himself a camera, drive out into the Rhode Island countryside, take some pictures, and relax. Nutting took her advice (except for the relaxing part), and over the next 50 years moved on to become the most successful marketer of hand-painted photographs in the history of the world.

But it didn't happen overnight. Nutting was not the first person to ever experiment with hand painting a photograph. Nor did he invent the process for hand painting photographs. What Wallace Nutting did was perfect the process of hand painting photography. Nutting began his photographic career on a part-time basis between 1894 and 1904. During this period he improved his photographic technique, purchased better equipment, determined the most sellable subject matter, located hired help who could paint the pictures better than he, and then sold a few pictures. As his technique improved, his picture inventory increased, and his sales improved. During this start-up phase, Nutting even published an article on photography, entitled "Photographic Beauties of Objects in Motion" (*Outlook Illustrated*, June 4, 1898).

Nutting's "A Little River" showing areas of retouched car in road and telephone poles

Yet upon closer inspection of this picture, you can see evidence of retouching. What apparently happened is that when Wallace Nutting took the original picture, there was a car in the road and there were telephone poles in the background. Nutting liked the overall look of the image, but didn't like the car and the poles. What to do? Nutting simply sent the original glass negative to a photo retoucher, who deleted the car and the telephone poles from the negative. As a result, each of the literally thousands of black and white platinotype images produced from this original negative had the car and poles already removed. So the next time that you see Nutting's "A Little River," take a closer look. You will see an off-colored splotch in the middle of the road (which is where the car was), and the extremely faint outline of several telephone poles far back on the road.

COLLECTING TIP

Wallace Nutting didn't invent the process of hand-painting photographs. Rather, Nutting perfected the process for producing and marketing commercial hand-painted photographs.

The golden age of hand-painted photography occurred between 1900 and 1940, and that is what this book is about. Up until the mid-1890s, most hand-painted photography involved overpainting personal and family photographs. The public's demand for hand-painted portraits far exceeded its demand for hand-painted landscape scenes until just before 1900. Nineteenth century black and white landscape photographs appeared drab and lifeless, and there was little public demand for them. And because there was so little demand for them, neither photographers nor painters had any success marketing hand-painted landscape scenes to the American public — until Wallace Nutting came along.

After a period of trial and error, Nutting decided that platinum paper was best suited for his work. Although C. J. Burnett had first exhibited the results of his experiments illustrating the use of platinum in photographic prints in 1859, it took another 20 years before platinum paper was introduced commercially. By the mid-1890s, Nutting had settled upon platinum paper as the best medium for his photographs. Even though it was more costly, he preferred it because he was able to obtain maximum tone and it enabled him to bring out as much detail as possible from the negatives that he exposed. Hence, the term *platinotype*, which derives from the photographic paper that he used, best describes Wallace Nutting pictures.

COLLECTING TIP

Platinotype derives from the special photographic paper used by many early 20th c. photographers. The platinum in the paper provided for better photographic tone and effect and produced a longer-lasting image.

By 1900, Nutting apparently sensed that he had hit upon a successful formula. He learned that America didn't want pictures of factories, smokestacks, crowded city streets, or urban tenements. He learned that the public would buy pictures with apple blossoms, birches, spring and fall landscapes, streams, lakes, rivers, hills, mountains, lambs, sheep, and thatch-roofed cottages. America was rapidly changing, and Americans were already beginning to tire of the industrial development around them. Nutting was the one who found the niche, who found that there was a growing market for beautifully hand-painted photographs of America's pristine and picturesque countryside. He would be the one to give them to America.

Wallace Nutting set the standard for all of the other photographers to follow. Platinum paper. Pencil signature lower right beneath the image in the early years, pen signature in the later years. Title lower left beneath the image. Platemark indentation around the picture. Thin wood frame. Watercolors as opposed to oils, and often Windsor & Newton watercolors imported from England. Colors not too bright and not too dull.

Yet throughout Nutting's first 10 years, photography was still a part-time hobby. He was still a full-time minister, with all of the responsibilities that entailed. In 1904, Nutting retired from the ministry citing health reasons, and within only several months opened his first photography studio. Over the next 35 years, he went on to become the best-selling marketer of hand-painted photographs of all time.

And for the hundreds of other photographers during this period, who better to copy than the best? Wallace Nutting set the standard. And nearly all others followed his lead. If it worked for Wallace Nutting, it would work for the rest of them. This book documents more than 300 other American photographers who were selling hand-painted photographs, just like Wallace Nutting, during this 1900 – 1940 golden age of hand-painted photography.

The peak period for hand-colored photography was between 1915 and 1925. By this time, hand-painted photography had become the medium of choice for much of America's middle class. For wedding gifts, shower gifts, holiday gifts, friendship gifts, or pleasant vacation memories, what better way to convey a special message or thought than through a beautiful (and inexpensive) hand-painted photograph? During this time, Nutting sold more pictures than at any other time during his career. And during this same period, there were more photographers selling hand-painted photographs than at any other time in history. Throughout New England, the middle Atlantic states, the Southeast, Florida, the Pacific Northwest, the Southwest, and most of the West, and even in Hawaii, Canada, Bermuda, and the Bahamas, hand-painted photography was certainly in its golden age at this time.

After 1925, sales began to slow down. Fads rarely last 10 to 15 years, and the hand-painted photograph fad lasted longer than most. The crash of 1929 and the subsequent Great Depression of the 1930s severely impacted the sales of almost all photographers. The hand-painted photograph was a middle-class item, and America's middle class was severely impacted financially.

By 1940, the market for hand-painted photography was dead. Although a few studios continued to market hand-painted pictures on a very limited basis, the advent of color film all but replaced hand-painted photography as the standard for colored photography, and the vast majority of any remaining hand-painted pictures were relegated to either the attic, the basement, or even more often, the trash bin.

COLLECTING TIPS

The golden age of hand-painted photography was between 1900 and 1940.

The peak period for hand-painted photography was between 1915 and 1925.

The advent of color film marked the end of the golden age of hand-painted photography.

Hand-painted photography sat pretty much dormant until the mid-1960s, when America's collecting and collectibles craze was born. An extremely limited number of collectors began accumulating hand-painted pictures as they re-entered the market. These pictures were often sold at bargain basement prices by today's standards. As the attics, basements, households, and estates of those households assembled during the 1920s through the 1940s began going to auction, America's new collectors were often able to buy these pictures in large quantities, sometimes for the price of the frames. It was not uncommon during the 1960s for an auctioneer to hold up five or six hand-painted photographs and ask "What will you give me for this lot of frames?" One to two dollars for the entire lot was not an uncommon price.

By 1970, there were enough collectors of Wallace Nutting pictures around for a club to be formed. In 1973, the Wallace Nutting Collectors Club was formed by George and Justine Monro. That club served as a gathering place for collectors. It provided a fountain of knowledge about Nutting, and served as the primary center where collectors were able to buy and sell Wallace Nutting pictures. Today that same club still exists; it has been around for over 30 years, boasts more than 300 members, has an annual convention that is held in a different state each year, and even has its own web page (www.wallacenutting.org).

To the best of our knowledge, no collectors club has ever been formed for any other photographer of this period.

By the mid-to-late 1970s, a very limited number of artists had begun attempting to resurrect hand-painted photography as an art form. Certain artists now try to create a more unusual or subtle quality of work than can be obtained using standard colored photography. These artists feel that hand painting can produce images of a more personal and interpretative nature than can using a straightforward color photo. Of course, an item in this art form usually commands a high asking price due to the creative nature of the one-of-a-kind work.

Let us relate a quick story about contemporary hand-painted photographic art. Several years ago, an entire hand-painted photography exhibition was scheduled to open in our hometown's art museum. Doylestown, Pennsylvania, was the first stop of a five-museum tour focusing on hand-painted photography. We were excited about the concept of such a traveling exhibition, and we were there on opening day. The exhibition turned out to be a major disappointment. In our opinion, it was the most unrepresentative exhibition of hand-painted photography that could possibly have been created. Our recollection is that it consisted of perhaps 10 to 15 images that narrated the history of early hand-painted photography. The exhibition's primary focus was perhaps some 75 to 100-plus pieces of contemporary hand-painted photographic art. A few pieces were attractive; most (in our opinion) were hideous. And throughout the exhibition, there was only one picture representing the entire golden age of hand-painted photography — one single Wallace Nutting picture, and nothing else by any other photographer from this entire 40-year period. The description under the Nutting picture described the work of Nutting and his contemporaries as "mundane," or "pedestrian," or something equally disrespectful. The overall tone of the exhibition was that contemporary hand-painted photographic art was the most important element of the entire 150-plus-year history of hand-painted photography, and the 1900 – 1940 golden age was nothing more than an unfortunate embarrassment to the photographic field. The exhibition was biased, unrepresentative of the field, and in our opinion, a total disgrace. Mike wrote letters to each museum protesting the lack of representation and balance in the exhibition, but to no avail.

It is unknown how many pieces of contemporary hand-painted photographic art are actually sold by the original artists today. However, if there is a strong secondary market for such art, we haven't found it. From what we have seen, almost all of this interpretive art usually sells for far less than the original asking price on the secondary market (if a buyer can even be found).

Why do these newer hand-painted art forms usually drop in value? We give you a very simple answer. Collectors collect the name. And the best, most collectible names in hand-painted photography come from the 1900 – 1940 golden age. So let's now move on and put this entire golden age into better perspective for you.

RECOMMENDED READING

The best reference book we have found on the history of hand-painted photography is *The Hand-Painted Photograph: 1839 – 1914* by Heinz K. Henisch and Bridget A. Henisch. This book is the most complete book we have seen on the subject and is a must-read for anyone interested in developing an in-depth knowledge of the subject.

Chapter 2

Putting It in Perspective: An Introduction

Early twentieth century hand-painted photography, and Wallace Nutting pictures in particular, have become increasingly popular with collectors in recent years. The number of collectors has been growing, and good-quality pictures at reasonable prices have become more difficult to locate.

What's the cause for all this interest in Wallace Nutting and early twentieth century hand-painted photography? Some people call it nostalgia. Young people love these pictures because they show America as it once was, with country roads, rural solitude, no strip malls, no fast-food restaurants — a way they have never seen it. Older people love the pictures because they evoke memories of simpler days past, with no skyscrapers, no telephone poles, no superhighways, no pollution.

A photographer in the field

Some people say the current interest in hand-painted photography is because it is affordable. Others say it is the result of the renewed interest in the Colonial Revival movement. Some say that the high quality of this work is finally becoming recognized, while still others say people are simply trying to cash in on what they perceive to be the low end of a market.

Regardless of the causes for all this interest, the hand-painted photography market has indeed been hot, and Wallace Nutting's work has been in the center of it. What is it that makes these pictures so universally popular with collectors today?

To clearly understand the hand-painted photography market, you must first understand the Wallace Nutting market, and the fact that there are actually three different and distinct segments within the Nutting market. This chapter will attempt to put the overall market of early twentieth century hand-painted photography in perspective, and later chapters will provide more in-depth focus on each of the leading photographers and segments within this market.

Wallace Nutting was best known for his hand-painted pictures. He sold literally millions of his platinotypes between 1900 and his death in 1941, and by 1925, hardly a middle-class American household was without one.

Nutting was an accomplished author who published nearly 20 books between 1912 and 1936, including his 10-volume States Beautiful series, various other books on furniture, photography, and clocks, and his autobiography. He also contributed many photographs to magazines and other books, and as a result of the in-depth research he did for his books, Nutting became widely regarded as the father of American antiques.

Wallace Nutting States Beautiful book

Wallace Nutting, circa 1936.

Nutting also became widely known for his reproduction furniture. His Massachusetts furniture shop reproduced literally hundreds of different furniture forms of clocks, stools, chairs, settles, settees, tables, stands, desks, mirrors, beds, chests of drawers, cabinet pieces, and treenware, most of which were clearly marked with his distinctive paper label or his hard-to-miss block or script signature, which was literally branded into his furniture. Today, Wallace Nutting reproduction furniture is almost universally considered to be the finest bench-made reproduction furniture produced in the twentieth century and is highly collected by all levels of collectors.

A Nutting reproduction tenon armchair

The distinctive Nutting block branded signature and paper label

A typical Nutting exterior scene

Wallace Nutting pictures, Wallace Nutting books, Wallace Nutting furniture: three separate and distinct markets, each with its own group of collectors and enthusiasts. *Synergy* means that the product is greater than the sum of all of its individual parts. This is what places Wallace Nutting as the most collectible of all early twentieth century hand-painted picture photographers. The overall synergy of the Wallace Nutting name has made just about anything Wallace Nutting extremely collectible today. The legion of Nutting collectors has grown significantly in recent years, and today there are more people actively seeking Wallace Nutting pictures than ever before.

COLLECTING TIP

Wallace Nutting was widely known for the millions of hand-painted pictures he sold, for the nearly 20 different books that he published, and for the thousands of pieces of furniture he reproduced.

In very simple economic terms, when too many people are chasing after too few goods, prices have a tendency to rise. This is exactly what has been happening within the Wallace Nutting market over the past 10 to 20 years. Too many collectors and dealers have been chasing after too few pictures, with the net effect being that prices for those pictures remaining in circulation now are often higher than they were several years ago.

A Wallace Nutting & hand-painted photography catalog auction

It's not that the number of Wallace Nutting pictures is decreasing. Rather, as the number of collectors has grown, an increasing number of pictures are being purchased and held in private collections. These are usually the best pictures, in the finest condition, which in effect takes them out of circulation. With fewer pictures remaining in circulation, and more people actively pursuing them, the asking prices on those pictures still in circulation are generally higher than they were five or ten years ago. And because so many collectors are unable to find the rarer pictures in excellent quality, many are paying more for lower quality pictures, while others have slowed down the frequency of their Wallace Nutting purchases.

And as Wallace Nutting pictures have become increasingly more expensive and difficult to find, more collectors have been gravitating to the comparable, increasingly collectible yet generally less expensive, hand-painted photos of other early twentieth century photographers.

What many collectors have now learned is that although Wallace Nutting was widely recognized as the country's leading producer of hand-painted photographs during the early twentieth century, he was by no means the only photographer selling this style of picture. Throughout the country, literally hundreds of regional photographers were selling their own brands of hand-painted photographs from their home regions or travels.

COLLECTING TIP

There were literally hundreds of professional and amateur photographers who were also selling hand-painted photographs on a full-time and part-time basis between 1900 and 1940.

The Inverted Pyramid of Early 20th c. Hand-Painted Photography

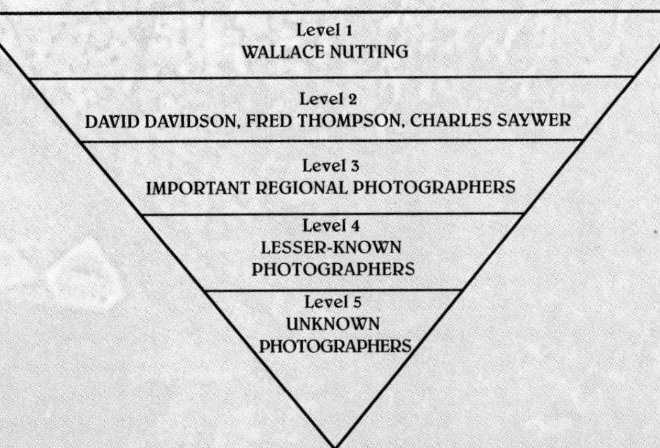

The key to understanding the hand-painted photography market rests upon developing an understanding of the important photographers within this market. The following summaries are designed to provide a very brief overview of each major market segment, while the inverted pyramid graphic is intended to help to visually demonstrate the current interrelationship of the five primary segments within this market.

A typical Wallace Nutting colonial interior scene

Level #1:
WALLACE NUTTING

BACKGROUND

Wallace Nutting was the unquestioned leader within the field of early twentieth century hand-painted photography. He started on a part-time basis in 1894 and worked in Southbury, Connecticut from 1905 to 1912 and in Framingham, Massachusetts, from 1912 until his death in 1941. Although Wallace Nutting did not invent the art of hand-painting black and white photographs, he certainly did perfect the process commercially. Wallace Nutting was the leader, and all of the others followed his lead. Platemark indentations on the mat, signature lower right beneath the image, title lower left, the same subject matter, the same photographic technique — nearly all other photographers trying to sell their pictures on the mass market followed Nutting's lead, to at least some exent.

LEVEL #1 COLLECTING TIPS

* Wallace Nutting pictures are generally the most desirable and collectible of all early twentieth century photographs.

* Wallace Nutting pictures are more readily available to collect than all other Nutting-Like photographers combined.

* There is a larger variety of Wallace Nutting subjects and topics to collect than there is for all other Nutting-like photographers combined.

* Wallace Nutting pictures are typically priced higher than any comparable Wallace Nutting–like picture.

Level #2:
The Next Three Largest Photographers, DAVIDSON, SAWYER and THOMPSON

BACKGROUND

David Davidson, Charles Sawyer, and Fred Thompson each operated relatively large photography businesses and, although not nearly as large or well-known as Wallace Nutting, they sold a substantial volume of pictures that can still be readily found today — often at undervalued prices. The vast majority of their work was photographed in their home regions of New England and sold primarily to local residents or visiting tourists. And it should come as little surprise that each of these three photographers had ties to Wallace Nutting.

DAVID DAVIDSON

Second to Nutting in overall production, Davidson worked out of Providence, Rhode Island, and sold his pictures primarily in the Rhode Island and Southern Massachusetts area. While a student at Brown University in around 1900, Davidson learned the art of hand-colored photography from Wallace Nutting, who happened to be the minister at Davidson's church. After Nutting moved to Southbury in 1905, Davidson graduated from Brown and started the successful David Davidson Studios in 1907, which he operated until the 1950s.

A typical David Davidson picture

CHARLES SAWYER

A father and son team, Charles H. Sawyer and Harold B. Sawyer operated the very successful Sawyer Pictures Company from 1903 to the 1970s. The Sawyer Pictures Company was started in Farmington, Maine, but moved to Concord, New Hampshire, in 1920 to be nearer its primary market of New Hampshire's White Mountains. Charles H. Sawyer briefly worked for Nutting in 1902 and 1903 while living in Farmington. Sawyer's total production ranked third, behind that of Wallace Nutting and David Davidson.

A typical Saywer picture

FRED THOMPSON

Frederick H. Thompson and Frederick M. Thompson were another father and son team, operating the Thompson Art Company from 1908 to 1923 in the Portland, Maine, area. We know that Thompson and Nutting collaborated, because Thompson widely marketed an interior scene he had taken in Nutting's Southbury home. The production volume of the Thompson Art Company ranked fourth, behind the figures for Nutting, Davidson, and Sawyer, in that order.

A typical Fred Thompson picture

LEVEL #2 COLLECTING TIPS

* There are an increasing number of collectors who are focusing their collections on David Davidson, Charles Sawyer, and Fred Thompson pictures.

* There are more Wallace Nutting pictures in circulation than all Davidson-Sawyer-Thompson pictures combined.

* When taken as a group, there are more Davidson-Sawyer-Thompson pictures in circulation than all of the regional, lesser-known, and unknown photographer pictures combined.

* With few exceptions, the prices of Davidson-Sawyer-Thompson pictures are lower than comparable Wallace Nuttings, and are higher than all comparable regional, lesser-known, and unknown photographers combined.

Level #3:
Major Regional Photographers

BACKGROUND

This is actually a new level that we have added to the inverted pyramid graphic in recent years as new information has been gathered about certain photographers. Whereas Nutting was more national in scope, most other photographers worked in a specific region or location. That is where they took most of their pictures, and that is where they sold most of their pictures, usually to visiting tourists who purchased them as take-home memories of a special vacation or trip. Although you won't find as many pictures by these photographers as you will Nutting-Davidson-Sawyer-Thompson pictures, these photographers did produce a significantly higher volume than those in level #4.

The photographers in level #3 include

Esmond .G. Barnhill .... St. Petersburg FL

J. Carleton Bicknell .... Portland ME

Hal Burrowes .... Portland ME

Pedro Cacciola .... Framingham MA

Royal Carlock .... Washington DC

J. Walter Collinge .... Santa Barbara CA

Cleve Craswell .... Prince Edward Island, Canada

Norman Edson .... Vashon Island WA

Emma Freeman .... Eureka CA

H. Marshall Gardiner .... Nantucket MA, Bermuda, Daytona FL

W. H. Gardiner .... Mackinac Island MI, Daytona FL

J. M. Garrison .... CA

Gibson .... Northeastern U.S.

Byron Harmon .... Banff, Alta, Canada

William J. Harris .... Lake Hopatcong NJ, St. Augustine FL

F. Jay Haynes .... Yellowstone Park WY

Jack Ellis Haynes .... Yellowstone Park WY

Charles R. Higgins .... Bath ME

Frederick B. Hodges .... Rome NY

Theo Horydczak .... Washington DC

Fred Kiser .... Crater Lake OR

Kolb Brothers .... Grand Canyon AZ

Lamson Studios .... Portland ME

Wallace R. MacAskill .... Nova Scotia, Canada

Fred Martin .... Palm Springs CA

George Petty .... Chicago IL

Edmond Royce .... St. Albans VT

Harry Standley .... Colorado Springs CO

Joseph L. Stimson .... Cheyenne WY

Florence Thompson .... Portland ME

Stephen Willard .... Palm Springs CA

LEVEL #3 COLLECTING TIPS

- There are an increasing number of collectors who are focusing their collections on pictures by photographers in this newly emerging level.
- When taken as a group, there are more Nutting-Davidson-Sawyer-Thompson pictures in circulation than all pictures by level #3 photographers combined.
- When taken as a group, there are more level #3 pictures in circulation than all of the level #4 and level #5 pictures combined.
- Photographs by these regional photographers are usually in highest demand in the region where the pictures were originally taken.
- Most collecting of these works occurs in New England, Florida, and the western U.S. and Canada.
- Prices on some of the best and rarest pictures by these regional photographers can sometimes surpass $1,000.00.

An F. Jay Haynes Yellowstone National Park scene

Level #4: Lesser-known Wallace Nutting–like Photographers

BACKGROUND

Hundreds of other smaller local and regional photographers attempted to market hand-painted pictures comparable to the ones by the photographers in levels #1, #2, and #3 during the time between 1900 and the 1940s. Some were professional photographers; most were amateurs. Although oftentimes quite attractive, most of these pictures were generally not as appealing or as well marketed as those from the larger and better-known names. As we all know, collectors usually buy the name, and the most famous of all early twentieth century photographers were Nutting, Davidson, Sawyer, and Thompson. However, as the price of pictures by the major photographers has escalated, the work of these lesser-known photographers has become increasingly collectible and is still quite affordable.

COLLECTING TIP

The term *lesser-known photographer* is used to denote any early twentieth century hand-painted picture photographer other than Wallace Nutting, David Davidson, Charles Sawyer, Fred Thompson, or some of the other important level #3 regional photographers whose work is either signed or directly attributable to him or her.

LEVEL #4 COLLECTING TIPS

* The level #4 lesser-known photographers are typically not as widely collectible or desirable as the major photographers.
* Most pictures within this category are collected within the very broad spectrum of early twentieth century photography rather than by the desirability of the individual photographer.
* Price and condition are typically the primary buying motivators within this category. That is, if the price is low enough and the subject matter and condition are good enough, some collectors will want the picture; if the price is too high, or if the subject matter and condition are either uninteresting or of poor quality, few collectors will want it.
* When taken as a group, there are fewer level #4 lesser-known pictures available to collect than there are from level #1 (Nutting), level #2 (Davidson-Sawyer-Thompson), or level #3 (major regional photographers).
* When taken as a group, there are more level #4 lesser-known pictures available to collect than in the entire level #5 unknown photographer category.
* With few exceptions, the prices for works of level #4 lesser-known photographers are lower than the prices for works of photographers from level #1 (Nutting), level #2 (Davidson-Sawyer-Thompson), or level #3 (major regional photographers), but are higher than most pictures by level #5 unknown photographers.

A typical scene by an unknown photographer

Level #5: Unknown Photographers

BACKGROUND

This category is for hand-painted pictures that are not attributable to any specific photographer by a signature, backing label, or any other means. Since collectors typically collect the name, pictures by unknown photographers are the least collectible of all hand-painted photographs. Hence price, subject matter, and condition will be the primary determinants of value. We'll cover unknown photographers in much more detail in chapter 7.

COLLECTING TIP

The term *unknown photographer* is used to denote any early twentieth century photograph that is not attributable to any specific photographer with a 100% degree of certainty.

LEVEL #5 COLLECTING TIPS

* Subject matter typically consists of such topics as people, animals, houses, landscapes, specific places, etc.
* There are fewer pictures by level #5 unknown photographers available than there are pictures from any other level.
* Prices for pictures within level #5 are typically lower than prices for pictures in any other level.

COLLECTING TIP

With very few exceptions (usually relating to subject matter), hand-painted photographs by unknown photographers are the least desirable to collectors.

A typical scene by a lesser-known photographer

Chapter 3

The Process of Hand Painting Photographs

What follows is a very broad and general overview of the process used by many early twentieth century photographers to produce hand-painted photographs. Although the exact process may have varied somewhat by photographer, this summary will provide you with a basic understanding of the overall process of hand painting photography.

COLLECTING TIP
A hand-painted photograph is just what its name implies: a picture that was individually hand painted. Hand painting was a labor-intensive process, and the fact that each picture was an individually painted piece of art is what makes these pieces so different and so interesting to collectors.

Early 20th c. camera

Photographers typically owned their businesses and took their own pictures. They would determine the subject, location, angle, lighting, and positioning of the camera, and would shoot many pictures throughout the day, week, or month.

Upon returning to the studio, the photographer would devlop the newly-shot pictures in the dark room. Glass negatives, typically 5" x 7", 8" x 10", or 11" x 14" in size, were used to print the pictures onto sheets of special photographic paper. Earlier photographers (1900 – 1920) typically used a special paper that contained a higher concentration of platinum. These pictures were called platinotypes. After 1920, the platinum paper became more difficult to obtain, and most photographers switched to a paper having a higher silver concentration. Relatively few collectors today can detect the difference between the earlier platinum and the later silver prints.
The better pictures would be identified, assigned a tentative title, and entered into a studio logbook. Pictures were provided a unique identifying studio number to help identify loose and un-mounted pictures while in the studio, and this studio number was typically written on the back of the picture. Unacceptable pictures were usually discarded.

Titles were created by either the photographer or by a family member or employee. The primary objective of the picture title was not only to provide a descriptive name for the picture, but to help sell the picture. Catchy titles helped sell pictures, and it was not uncommon for the title on certain pictures to change several times before a specific title was finalized.

Once the picture was developed, titled, and entered into the studio log book, the next step was to determine how the picture should be colored. Although the objective was to paint the picture as close to reality as possible, it was not uncommon to add certain enhancements to the picture coloration in order to make the picture appear better than reality. In smaller studios, the photographer was also the colorist; in larger studios, the photographer had colorists to do the actual painting. Once the final coloring was determined, a written set of coloring instructions was made and attached to the model picture to help other colorists color subsequent pictures.

Once the model picture was colored and approved, subsequent pictures were colored following the model picture as closely as possible. Typically, a single colorist would apply all the colors of a picture, rather than each colorist applying

The Process of Hand Painting Photographs

Early 20th c. exposure meter

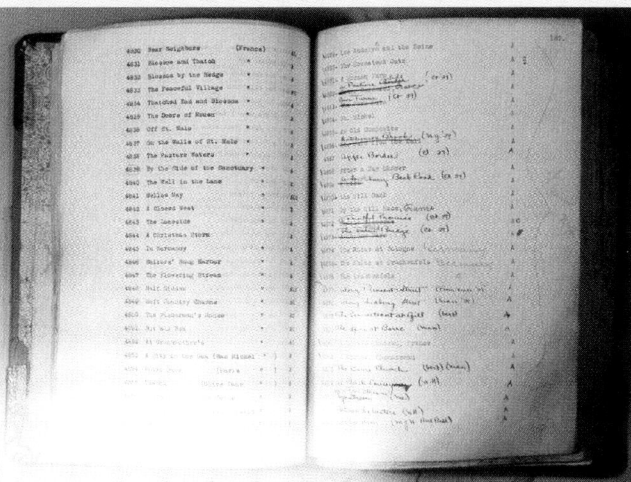
Studio logbook

"Maple Sugaring" model picture

Original glass negative

Ms 167-4   Maple Sugaring

Sugar House (foreground) - Barn red, white trim, black smokestack on concrete and gray rock foundation.
Building (background) - Barn red, snow on roof.
Trees (Maple) - Gray to black.
Sugar Pails - Galvanized.
Horses - Dark brown and white.
Sled - Natural unpainted oak.
Tank on Sled - Oak with galvanized corner pieces and inner tank.
Harness - Black, with gold buttons on bridle and top of harness.
Man - Forest green cap; red, light green and white plaid shirt; forest green trousers; black overshoes.
Clothes on Sled - Red jacket and khaki sheepskin lined coat.
Shed behind Sugar House Filled with Stakced Wood for Firing - Ends light yellow, remainder brown.
Leaf Covered Ground - Brown.
Rocks - Mossy gray.

Colorist's coloring instructions

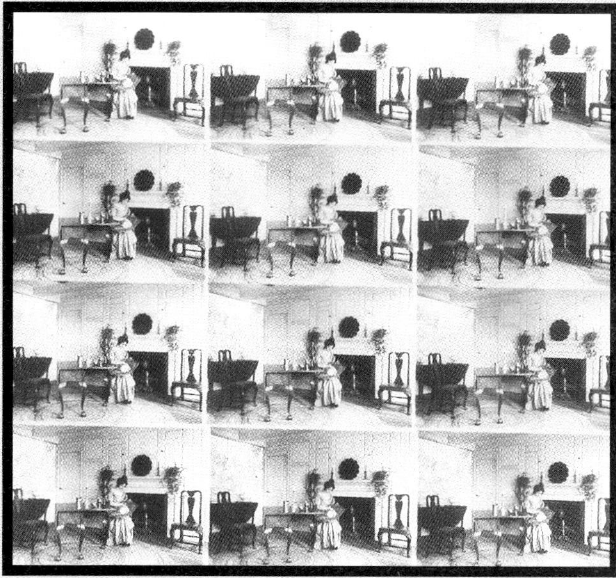

12-picture proof sheet

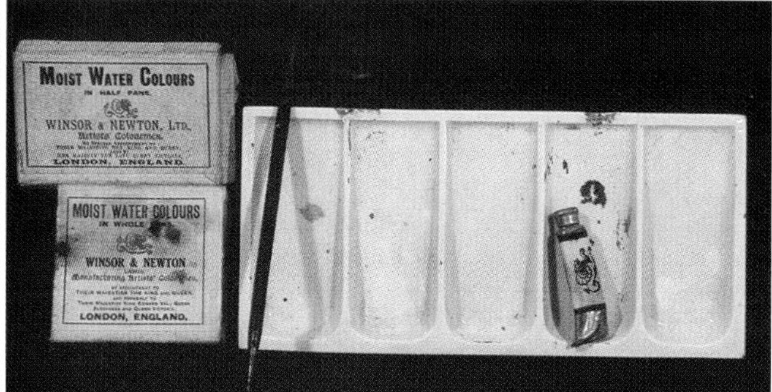

Watercolors & porcelain palette

Colorists

only a single color. Larger pictures would have only a single picture on a sheet; smaller pictures could have up to 20 pictures on a single sheet, all 20 of which would be colored by a single colorist. Larger photographers had a formal studio where colorists worked. Smaller photographers either hand-colored the pictures themselves, or often had a spouse or family member color them. Mrs. Carlock colored pictures at the dinner table. David Davidson even had a colorist who took quantities of pictures to her home on Block Island off the Rhode Island coast in the Atlantic Ocean and, when she returned to the mainland several months later, would return the colored pictures and take another batch of uncolored pictures. Colors were produced by several companies, but the preferred watercolors were often imported directly from the Windsor & Newton Company in England. There were hundreds of different colors and shades available in both tubes and cubes, and each colorist would mix his or her own colors in a porcelain color palette.

Title & signature

In smaller companies, the actual colorists (oftentimes the photographer or spouse) would approve the final picture; in larger companies, either the head colorist (supervisor of colorists) or the photographer himself would approve the final painted picture prior to sale. If the picture was approved, it would be mounted on the matboard; if the picture did not meet the studio standard, it was discarded or destroyed.

Most typically, the picture was mounted on a matboard that had a slight platemark indentation around the entire picture, although other matting variations were used by different studios. Once mounted, the title and photographer's name were added, usually below the picture. Most studios positioned the title below the lower-left corner of the picture, while the photographer's name was placed below the lower right corner of the picture.

The final step was the framing. Frames were sometimes supplied by the photographer's studio; other times, they were selected by the purchaser at the point of purchase. Volume purchasers of pictures, usually department stores or gift shops, purchased their pictures unframed, which enabled them to sell both the picture and the frame. Some customers even framed their pictures themselves. Frames were usually narrow in proportion to the picture, often mahogany or gold/brown in

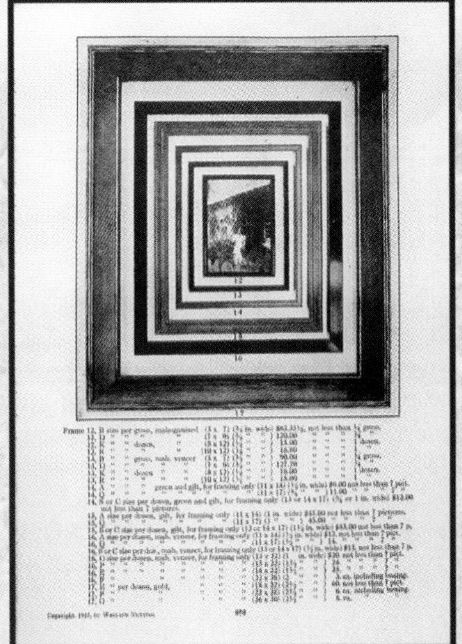

A variety of different frames were available.

color, although other types of frames were used to suit individual preferences and tastes. As a result, you will find a wide variety of frames on early twentieth century hand-painted photography.

SUBJECT MATTER

New England was the home of many early twentieth century photographers of hand-painted pictures, and New England was where most hand-painted pictures were sold. The most popular subject matter of New England photographers was found in pastoral exterior scenes. Apple blossoms, birches, rivers, streams, lakes, ponds, country lanes, hills, and mountains were among the most popular subjects. Photographers sold what the public would buy, and the vast number of basic outdoor scenes remaining today would seem to confirm that outdoor scenes were far-and-away the most popular subject matter of most photographers during the early twentieth century.

A Sawyer exterior scene

However, since hand-painted photographs were oftentimes sold as gifts or vacation memories, many photographers from outside of New England specialized in selling pictures taken in their home regions, with Bermuda, Florida, Colorado, the Colorado Rocky Mountains, the Grand Canyon and other various national parks, the American Southwest, the Pacific Northwest, Nova Scotia, and the Canadian Rockies all being popular picture locations for many photographers.

COLLECTING TIP

Outdoor pastoral scenes were the most common type of picture sold by nearly all early twentieth century hand-painted picture photographers.

Colonial interior scenes were also popular with some photographers. The Colonial Revival movement was in full swing during the early twentieth century, fostered in part by a wave a patriotism brought about by World War I, and for the first time, twentieth century America began to appreciate its colonial heritage. Photographers would re-create a colonial setting, typically with a woman performing an eighteenth century household chore near a roaring fire. Although these interior scenes sold very well for certain photographers, they did not sell nearly as well for others. Some photographers sold foreign scenes as well, with scenes of Europe, Great Britain in particular, usually being the best-selling foreign pictures.

A Davidson interior scene

COLLECTING TIP

Interior scenes were not nearly as popular as exterior scenes, selling only approximately 10% of the number exterior scenes did.

Today, any pictures that fall outside the categories of exterior, interior, and foreign scenes are called miscellaneous unusual scenes. These pictures include such subjects as seascapes, animals, snow, gardens, floral still lifes, churches and cathedrals, bridges, cottages and castles, and pictures featuring children and men, both of which were very poor selling subjects. (For whatever reason, the buying public preferred women over children and men). Relatively few foreign and miscellaneous unusual pictures were produced and, because of their rarity, they are often very popular with collectors today.

This Wallace Nutting English foreign scene, "Within the Close," sold at our March 2004 auction for $2,200.00.

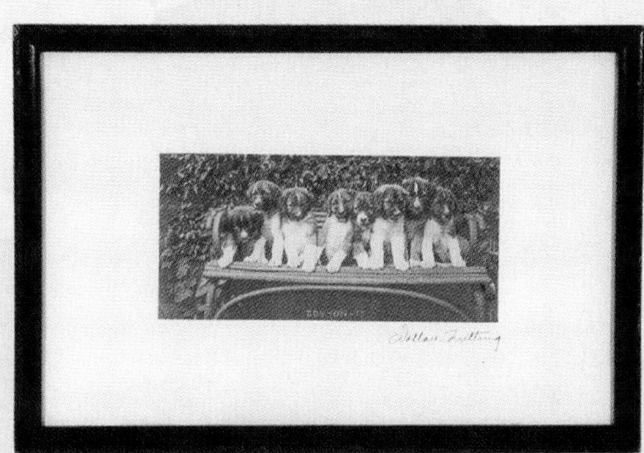

This Wallace Nutting miscellaneous unusual scene, "Dog-On-It," sold at our June 2004 auction for $4,125.00.

Picture sizes could range from 1" x 2" (shown in the center of the very large picture) to 40" x 20".

COLLECTING TIP

Certain foreign and miscellaneous unusual scenes are the rarest today and are often the most sought-after by collectors.

PICTURE SIZE

Just as you can take a negative to a camera shop today and have it developed into many different sizes, early 20th c. hand-painted photography can come in many different sizes, ranging from 1" x 2" to 30" x 50". The general rule of thumb of the larger the picture, the greater the value holds true only to a certain extent. The most popular sized pictures are typically within the 11" x 14" to 16" x 20" sizes. These pictures are large enough to show considerable color and detail, yet small enough to fit most wall spaces.

Pictures (10" x 12" and smaller), although still very popular, often times don't provide the excellent color and detail of the larger pictures and are not as highly valued as the 11" x 14" to 16" x 20" pictures.

Pictures larger than 16" x 20" are sometimes difficult to sell. Although they are rarer, show considerable color and detail, and cost significantly more when originally sold, too few households today offer the ideal wall space for such a large picture. And all too often, such larger pictures were the more popular and common scenes, not the rarities that collectors so highly prize.

COLLECTING TIP

The larger the picture, the more desirable it is to collectors, and the more expensive it will be — up to the 16" x 20" size. Pictures larger than 16"x 20" are oftentimes more difficult to sell because of their extremely large size.

CONDITION

Once you have determined the subject matter and size of the picture, the next step in determining the value is to assess its condition, because condition is the most important determinant of value. Over the past five years, condition has become increasingly more important as astute collectors have developed a better eye for differentiating between good, better, and best pictures. Conversely, some pictures in average to below average condition aren't bringing the prices they did five years ago, because today's collectors have become more discriminating. We'll cover condition in significantly more detail in chapter 5.

COLLECTING TIP

Condition is the most important determinant of value. The rarest picture in poor condition has minimal value; a common scene in excellent condition is still a very desirable piece.

Chapter 4

Are They Pictures or Prints?

Several years ago, we read a letter in a New Hampshire's *Unravel the Gavel* antiques trade paper criticizing the generic term *Nutting-like picture* when used to refer to hand-painted photographs. The writer of that letter was our friend Carol Gray, an authority on Charles Sawyer hand-painted pictures (we have since co-authored a book with Carol on Sawyer pictures). Carol resented having her preferred area of collectiblity always lumped in with Wallace Nutting and published a letter saying so. In our opinion, her resentment was perfectly normal and justified. But since Mike, perhaps more than anyone else in the country, has been responsible for popularizing the term *Nutting-like pictures*, we felt it was up to Mike to defend the appropriateness of the term. What follows here is Mike's rebuttal letter that appeared in *Unravel the Gavel.*

A hand-painted photo

> **COLLECTING TIP**
>
> The term *Wallace Nutting–like picture* is used to denote any early twentieth century hand-painted photograph dating between 1900 and 1940 that resembles the look of and was made with the same process as a Wallace Nutting picture.

For readers to more fully understand why the term *Nutting-like pictures* is probably the most appropriate and descriptive term for early twentieth century hand-painted photography, we should first dissect these very simple words.

1) PICTURES OR PRINTS?

Let's start with the word *print,* which is perhaps the most misused word in the entire antiques and collectibles business. According to *Merriam-Webster's Collegiate Dictionary,* a print is:

"1 a: a mark made by pressure" or

"5 a (1): a copy made by printing" or

"[5 a] (2): reproduction of an original work of art (as a painting) made by a photomechanical process" or

"[5 a] (3): an original work of art (as a woodcut, etching, or lithograph) intended for graphic reproduction and produced by or under the supervision of the artist who designed it."

A machine-produced print

Popular early twentieth century prints (by Maxfield Parrish, Bessie Pease Gutmann, R. Atkinson Fox, Harrison Fisher, Philip Boileau, Howard Chandler Christie, Rolf Armstrong, Haskill Coffin, and so many others) were all machine produced. They were printed in the thousands, and sometimes tens-of-thousands, often in multiple press runs. The publishers sold the maximum number of copies possible, and what they couldn't sell, in many instances they threw out as trash. There was nothing unique or different about these prints. As they came off the press run, each print looked exactly like the ones printed before it and after it. Value today is predicated not upon uniqueness, but upon how many have survived (rarity) and how well they have survived (condition).

Hand-painted photographs on the other hand, whether Nutting, Sawyer, Davidson, Thompson, or anyone else listed in this book, are not prints. They were not produced upon a printing press using printing plates, halftones, and multicolor process printing. And they do not conform to any of the above definitions or any other *print* definition that I have found.

Early twentieth century hand-painted photographs were all individually produced works of art. Regardless of which of the hundreds of photographers listed in this book took the picture, each picture was a unique piece of art, individually hand painted by a human colorist using a brush and watercolors or oils. Granted, some were better than others, and a few were downright awful. Some hand-painted photographs were so popular that thousands of a particular image were sold. Other pictures sold only 100, 50, 10, 3, 2, or 1 copy, making certain pictures extremely rare, and in some instances, totally unique. But regardless of the total number of pictures sold, each photograph was an individually hand-painted piece of art.

It is this individuality of hand-painted photographs that makes them so appealing and so collectible to so many people. And it is the individuality that makes them so potentially increasingly valuable in the long term.

Unfortunately, too many people are guilty of misusing the term *print* when referring to hand-painted photography. When referring to a hand-painted photograph, the correct word is *picture* or *photograph.* The term *print* is inappropriate; it degrades the entire process and should never be used when referring to early twentieth century hand-painted photography.

2) NUTTING-LIKE:

Over the years, we too have struggled to derive an all-inclusive term that covers the entire field of early twentieth century hand-painted photography — in three words or less. We eventually concluded that we could come up with nothing better than "Nutting-like pictures."

When referring to a Sawyer picture, it is certainly appropriate to call it a Sawyer picture. Yet the minute you step outside the immediate realm of Sawyer collectors, most people have no idea what a "Sawyer" picture is. Who was Sawyer? An artist, illustrator, or photographer? Did he produce prints, pastels, photographs, watercolors, oil-on-canvases, or oil-on-boards?

The same holds true for Davidson pictures, Thompson pictures, and all of the other regional, lesser known, and unknown early twentieth century photographers who produced hand-painted pictures. The overall number of collectors is so relatively small that most people have no idea who these individuals were or what they did.

But because of the strength and fame of the Wallace Nutting name, upon hearing "Nutting-like pictures," most people immediately understand what you are referring to: a high-quality, early twentieth century hand-painted photograph, typically an exterior landscape or colonial interior scene, either matted or close-framed, and carrying the photographer's name and quite often the picture's title.

If you are dealing only in Sawyer pictures, Davidson pictures, or Thompson pictures, you don't really have a problem. You can simply refer to your preferred artist.

But in our position of writing about all types of early twentieth century hand-painted photography, whether in our books, columns, articles, or auction catalogs, where we must repeatedly use an all-encompassing term that ties all early twentieth century hand-painted photography into one simple phrase, *Nutting-like pictures* seems to be the shortest and most descriptive phrase that we have been able to come up with. It's not intended to offend any particular group of collectors. Yet based on the way it has caught on, no one else seems to have invented a better catch-all phrase.

We have challenged collectors for many years to come up with a better generic term to described early twentieth century hand-painted photography than *Nutting-like pictures.* And no one has yet proposed a better catch-all phrase.

Do you have a better alternative? If so, we would like to hear from you.

Colorists who personally hand painted pictures

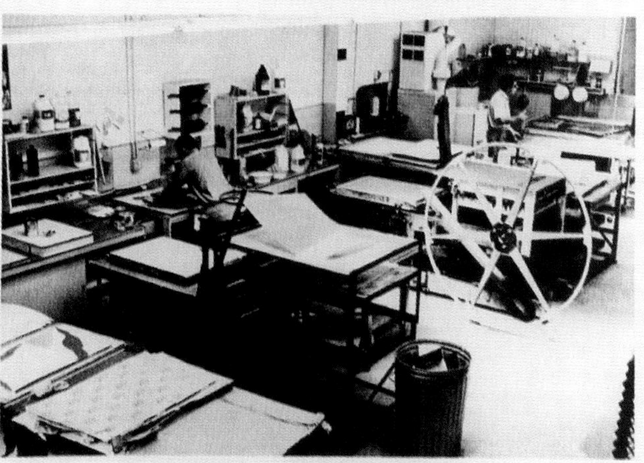

Printing press for creating prints

Chapter 5

Evaluating Condition & Rarity

We've all heard the expression that the value of most real estate is determined by three words: *location, location, location*. In our opinion, the value of most early twentieth century hand-painted photography can be determined by three very similar words: *condition, condition, rarity.* Let's discuss each individual component.

5.0 grading, mint, just out of the box

EVALUATING CONDITION AND CONDITION

We use the word *condition* twice, because having been picture and print collectors and dealers for so long, we have come to one very important conclusion: condition is the most important determinant of value. We have repeatedly seen that, regardless of which early twentieth century photographer created it, the rarest picture, in poor condition, can have relatively minimal value, while a relatively common picture, in absolutely beautiful condition, is still an extremely desirable picture to all levels of collectors. Therefore, condition should be worth twice the next most important value factor.

We don't have to tell you that the vast majority of hand-colored photos readily available in today's retail market are overpriced and in poor condition. It's an unfortunate fact that most general-line dealers who have little knowledge in the area of hand-colored photos have a tendency to set their prices based upon the name of the photographer rather than upon the condition or rarity of the piece.

What typically happens is that a dealer will purchase a picture at auction and price it in one of two ways. He or she may use the name approach and set an asking price based strictly on the name of the photographer without even considering the condition or rarity of the piece. That is, if a picture is Wallace Nutting, it must be worth $100.00 – $200.00. It doesn't matter whether the picture is a $15.00 picture or a $1,500.00 picture, the dealer will still price it at $100.00 – $200.00 because it is a Wallace Nutting. If it is Fred Thompson, it must be worth $50.00 – 100.00, etc.

Or, a dealer may refer to a general price guide. If a guide says that an H. Marshall Gardiner sold for $400.00, this kind of dealer will assume that his or her picture must be worth the same amount or more. Such dealers fail to take into account such extremely important factors as rarity (Gardiner Nantucket vs. Gardiner Bermuda), image size, mat size, type of frame, date of sale, type of sale (i.e., a retail sale to a collector vs. discounted sale to a dealer), method of sale (auction, group shop, individual dealer, etc), sale dynamics (little interest vs. two bidders, neither of whom were leaving without it), or whether it was an actual sale or simply the price guide author's best guess. And of course, they fail to consider the quality of image color, mat stains or blemishes, picture grading, and a host of other condition factors that will all impact the final overall value.

How do you differentiate varying degrees of condition when there are so many different types of hand-colored photos to collect? It's actually quite easy when you recognize that all popular early twentieth century hand-painted photography comes in one of only two forms: matted (the picture is mounted upon a matboard prior to being framed) or close-framed (the picture is framed without any matting whatsoever). And it's even easier if you use this five-point grading system when evaluating both matted and close-framed pictures.

HAND-COLORED PHOTOGRAPHY GRADING AND CONDITION GUIDE

This numerical grading system is something that we developed when cataloging pictures for our hand-painted photography auctions. Pictures are assigned a grading of 1.0 – 5.0, with 5.0 being mint and 1.0 being the worst. In order to arrive at the appropriate numerical grading, we have developed the following guidelines.

We should remind you that this numerical grading system is nothing more than our personal system for evaluating hand-colored photographs. It is not perfect, and it is very subjective. However, we feel comfortable using it and, in the absence of a better system, you are welcome to use it as well.

5.0 Grading

Perfect condition. The mat, image, and frame are perfect. Looks like it came right out of the box.

These are pictures with absolutely no visible flaws:
a) The picture has perfect color and detail.
b) The mat is in perfect condition with proper size and aging.
c) The frame is in near perfect condition and appropriate for the period.

> **COLLECTING TIP**
>
> Very few pictures will ever achieve a 5.0 grading.

4.0 – 4.75 Grading

No damage whatsoever to either the image or the mat.

4.75 Grading

Near mint condition. Looks like is almost just came out of the box. To reach this grading, the image must have near mint color and detail, and the mat must be in near mint condition with practically no aging. The frame must be attractive, appropriate for the period, and just about perfect. We rarely grade things 4.75.

4.5 Grading

Exceptional condition. Exceptional picture, with a mat that is free of any noticeable stains or blemishes. To reach this grading, the image must have exceptional color and detail, and the mat must be in exceptional condition with practically no aging. The frame must be attractive, appropriate for the period, and just about perfect. We rarely grade things 4.5.

4.25 Grading

Excellent condition. Excellent picture, with a mat that is free of any noticeable stains or blemishes. To reach this grading, the image must have excellent color and detail, and the mat must be in excellent condition with practically no aging. The frame must be attractive, appropriate for the period, and just about perfect. We seldom grade things 4.25.

4.0 Grading

Very good condition. Very nice picture with a mat that is free of any noticeable stains or blemishes. To reach this grading, the image must have very good color and detail, and the mat must be in very good condition with practically no aging. The frame must be attractive, appropriate for the period, and in very good condition. We often grade things 4.0.

> **COLLECTING TIP**
>
> Very few pictures will ever be graded a 4.25 – 4.75. Many pictures will be graded 4.0.

3.0 – 3.75 Grading

Mat damage, but no image damage.

3.75 Grading

Very minor mat damage. A very minor mat stain, or a mat that is very slightly dark from age, or very minor foxing, etc. We often grade things 3.75.

3.5 Grading

Minor mat damage. A minor stain, or a mat that is slightly dark from age, or some very minor foxing, etc. We often grade things 3.5.

3.25 Grading

Noticeable mat damage. A noticeable mat stain, or mat that is fairly dark from age, noticeable mat foxing, etc. We often grade things 3.25.

3.0 Grading

Major mat damage or overmat. A major mat stain, or a mat that is quite dark from age, or major mat foxing, or an overmat concealing possible or probable damage to the original mat, or a picture than has been remounted or re-signed. We often grade things 3.0.

> **COLLECTING TIPS**
>
> A picture with a water stain can never be rated a 4.0 or higher, regardless of how large or small the stain or blemish actually is.
>
> An overmatted picture can never be rated higher than 3.0.
>
> A remounted or re-signed picture means that the matting and/or signature are not original. A picture that has either been remounted or re-signed is not a very desirable piece and can never be graded higher than a 3.0.
>
> Most pictures will fall within the 3.0 – 4.0 category.

2.0 – 2.75 Grading

Image damage, and probably mat damage as well.

2.75 Grading

Very minor image damage. A very minor image stain, an image that is very slightly dark from age, very minor image foxing, or a very minor image chip or crease, etc.

2.5 Grading

Minor image damage. A minor image stain, an image that is somewhat dark from age, minor image foxing, a minor image chip or crease, etc.

2.25 Grading

Clearly noticeable image damage. A clearly noticeable image stain, an image that is quite dark from age, clearly noticeable image foxing, a clearly noticeable picture chip or crease, etc.

2.0 Grading

Major image damage. A major image stain, an image that is quite dark from age, major image foxing, or a major image chip or crease, etc.

1.0 – 1.75 Grading

Usually not even worth buying.

Quite frankly, you very rarely see pictures with this grading, because by the time they have reached this level, most have been thrown away. However, occasionally they do turn up. Specifically, pictures that are rated 1.0 – 1.75 have irreparable damage to the image itself. Specific examples would include images with major tears, images with unsightly spotting, images with ink spots, or other major damage making the image irreparable.

> **COLLECTING TIP**
>
> There will be relatively few pictures in the 1.0 – 1.75 categories, because by the time they reach this condition, most pictures have been thrown away.

EVALUATING RARITY

This is actually the hardest part of collecting, and is not something that we can explain in only a few paragraphs. The rarest and most desirable pieces will vary by collectible area, and you must do your homework.

How do you learn about rarity? Here are several suggestions:

* Attend our catalog auctions and follow our free website auction catalogs and post-sale prices and our eBay live auctions and free post-sale prices.
* Scan the general prices guides to see which items are bringing top dollar.
* Study the specialty price guides to see which items are bringing top dollar.
* Attend local auctions to see what people are paying top dollar for.
* Check eBay's Completed Sale Items to see which items have recently brought the top prices.
* Join collectors clubs and subscribe to specialty newsletters.
* Subscribed to specialty dealers' mailing lists to see what they are asking top dollar for.

And finally, attend antiques shows and talk to knowledgeable dealers and ask them why they are asking top dollar on certain items. Chances are, they will tell you that the item is quite rare and in very nice condition.

> **A FEW FINAL COLLECTING TIPS**
>
> Condition is the most important determinant of value. The rarest picture in poor condition has minimal value. A common picture in excellent condition is still a very desirable piece.
>
> Condition depends upon three key components: 1) the image itself, 2) the matting, and 3) the frame. Damage to any of these three components will tend to reduce value.
>
> In today's market, there are more pictures being offered for sale in poor condition than in excellent condition.
>
> The rarest pictures, in the best condition, bring the highest prices. If either factor — condition or rarity — is impacted, the value drops.
>
> Damaged pictures are significantly easier to buy than to sell.
>
> Your profit is made when you buy your picture, not when you sell your picture. If you buy smart, you will most likely make a profit when you sell. If you take a shortcut and buy something with damage, you will most likely have a hard time getting your initial investment back.

One of the hardest parts of being an auctioneer is telling people that they have little chance of recovering what they have paid for some, many, or all of the pieces in their collections. It's an unfortunate fact that all too many collectors have failed to pay much attention to quality when making their purchases over the years. They bought what appealed to them, or the cheapest items they found, without ever intending to sell their collections. Or they relied on the underbidder to comfort them into believing that they hadn't overpaid "If someone else was willing to pay only a few dollars less, I couldn't have overpaid that much." Unfortunately, two determined but unknowledgeable bidders competing for the same item can often result in a significantly overinflated price that does not reflect the true market value of a picture.

And also, unfortunately, for most of us that inevitable day comes when we must part with what we have purchased. Because of death, downsizing, divorce, a change in collecting interests, college education financing, buying a new house or a vacation home, or any other reason, the fact remains that most of us must someday sell what we have purchased. And of course, it is always preferable to sell at a profit than at a loss.

When all is said and done, value is usually determined by those three critical factors, condition, condition, and rarity. If you learn nothing else from this book, I hope it is this: Always buy the best quality that you can afford. You will rarely be sorry in the long run.

4.5 grading
Exceptional condition

4.0 grading
Very good condition, just not mint or exceptional condition

3.75 Grading
Very minor mat damage (e.g., a slightly dark mat)

3.5 grading
Minor mat damage (e.g., clearly noticeable mat foxing)

3.5 grading
Minor mat damage (e.g., mat slightly cropped)

3.25 grading
Noticeable mat damage (e.g., obvious mat foxing)

3.0 grading
Major mat damage (e.g., major mat staining)

3.0 grading
Major mat damage (e.g., overmatted)

2.5 grading
Minor image damage (e.g., image burn resulting from acids in wooden backing)

3.0 grading
Major mat damage
(e.g., re-signed, signature not original)

Wallace Nutting

1.0 – 1.75 grading
Major mat and image damage,
usually not even worth buying

Chapter 6

Known Photographers

MARK ALAN

BACKGROUND
Little background information on MARK ALLAN has been found. The only Mark Alan picture we have seen was taken in Bermuda circa 1925 – 1935.

REGIONALITY
Bermuda

REPRESENTATIVE TITLES & VALUE GUIDE
Untitled Bermuda scene
Estimated value range: $25.00 – 50.00+

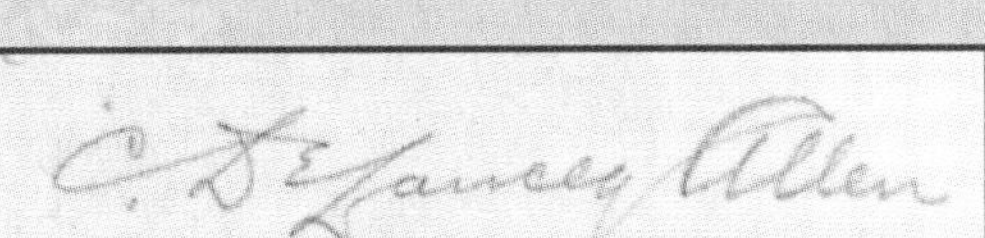

C. DELANCY ALLEN

BACKGROUND
Little background information on C. DELANCY ALLEN has been found. We have seen his pictures signed "C.D. Allen" and "C. Delancy Allen," and we know that he was from Ardsley, Pennsylvania.

REGIONALITY
Pennsylvania

REPRESENTATIVE TITLES & VALUE GUIDE
"Laurel Ledge Drive"
"A Pasture Road"
Estimated value range: $25.00 – 50.00+

C. D. Allen
"Laurel Ledge Drive"

"The Sentinel"

OSCAR ALLEN

BACKGROUND

Little background information on OSCAR ALLEN has been found. We have only seen a few Oscar Allen pictures and each, in our opinion, was taken in New England circa 1920 – 1930.

REGIONALITY

New England

REPRESENTATIVE TITLES & VALUE GUIDE

"The Sentinal"
Estimated value range: $25.00 – 50.00+

American Photo Studios

AMERICAN PHOTO STUDIOS

BACKGROUND

Little background information on AMERICAN PHOTO STUDIOS has been found. We have only two such pictures, and both were different scenes titled "Havana Cuba." Most likely these were hand-painted photographs sold to visiting American tourists circa 1920 – 1930.

"Havana Cuba'

REGIONALITY

Havana, Cuba

REPRESENTATIVE TITLES & VALUE GUIDE

"Havana Cuba" fort
"Havana Cuba" street scene
Estimated value range: $25.00 – 75.00+

"Havana Cuba"

THIS PICTURE was made by STANLEY L. ANDERSON. "Idaho's Leading Pictorial Photographer."

The picture was hand [illegible] in permanent oils on location and [illegible] condition of the scene at the season of the year when it was made.

A frame especially tinted to match the scene can be purchased complete for (..................) through your dealer.

Copyrighted by ANDERSON PHOTO CO.
Rexburg, Idaho.

Western U.S. exterior scene

STANLEY L. ANDERSON

BACKGROUND

STANLEY L. ANDERSON worked out of Rexburg, Idaho, and billed himself as "Idaho's leading pictorial photographer." His pictures were hand painted in oils instead of watercolors, and he operated the Anderson Photo Co. circa 1920 – 1930.

REGIONALITY

Western U.S.; Rexburg, Idaho

REPRESENTATIVE TITLES & VALUE GUIDE

Western U.S. exterior scene
Estimated value range: $25.00 – 75.00+

"Taku Glacier"

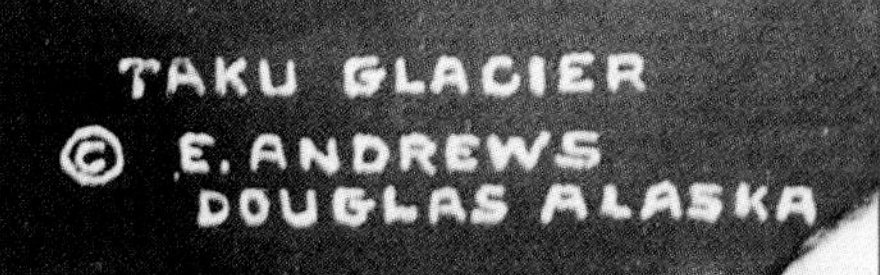

E. ANDREWS

BACKGROUND

E. ANDREWS seemed to work primarily in Alaska circa 1920 – 1930. We have seen very few Andrews photos, and all have been from Douglas, Alaska.

REGIONALITY

Western U.S.; Douglas, Alaska

REPRESENTATIVE TITLES & VALUE GUIDE

"Taku Glacier"
Estimated value range: $50.00 – 150.00+

Exterior scene

J. P. ANTHONY

BACKGROUND

Little background information on J. P. ANTHONY has been found. We have only seen one Anthony picture, and in our opinion, it was taken in New England.

REGIONALITY

New England

REPRESENTATIVE TITLES & VALUE GUIDE

New England exterior scene
Estimated value range: $10.00 – 50.00+

FREDERICK S. ARMBRISTER

BACKGROUND

FREDERICK S. ARMBRISTER was a commercial photographer based in Nassau, Bahamas. He was active circa 1910 – 1920. Armbrister sold both postcards and hand-painted photographs to the Bahamian tourist trade. He also took photographs in North and Central America, the West Indies, and throughout the Bahama nation and island group.

REGIONALITY

Nassau, Bahamas

REPRESENTATIVE TITLES & VALUE GUIDE

Bahamas Palm Trees and Sand
Estimated value range: $50.00 – 75.00+

ASSOCIATED SCREEN NEWS LTD.
CHATEAU LAKE LOUISE
LAKE LOUISE, Alberta

"Lake Louise, Alberta"

ASSOCIATED SCREEN NEWS LTD.

BACKGROUND
ASSOCIATED SCREEN NEWS LIMITED was established in affiliation with the Canadian Pacific Railway Company's photography department. It produced still photographs, newsreels, and travelogues, all featuring the railroad and navigation company. In April 1935 the company purchased the world-famous Notman photographic business in Montreal, along with its 400,000 negatives. We have only seen a few of its hand-painted pictures, and each was taken in Canada. The backstamp on its photos suggests that it worked out of the Chateau Lake Louise, which was a large resort hotel in the Canadian Rockies, Alberta, Canada. Most pictures were probably sold to Lake Louise tourists.

REGIONALITY
Alberta, Canada; Canadian Rockies

REPRESENTATIVE TITLES & VALUE GUIDE
"Lake Louise, Alberta"
Estimated value range: $25.00 – 75.00+

"Old Man of the Mts., NH"

Atkinson

ATKINSON (first name not known)

BACKGROUND
Little background information on ATKINSON has been found. We have only seen a few Atkinson pictures, and each was taken in New Hampshire. All "Old Man of the Mts., NH" hand-painted photographs have seen a dramatic increase in value in recent years, ever since the historic landmark came crashing down in 2003.

REGIONALITY
New England; New Hampshire

REPRESENTATIVE TITLES & VALUE GUIDE
"Old Man of the Mts., NH"
Estimated value range: $25.00 – 50.00+

I. AUSTIN

BACKGROUND
Little background information on I. AUSTIN has been found. We have only seen a few Austin pictures and, in our opinion, each was taken in New England circa 1920.

REGIONALITY
New England

REPRESENTATIVE TITLES & VALUE GUIDE
New England exterior scenes
Estimated value range: $10.00 – 50.00+

"Weare, N.H."

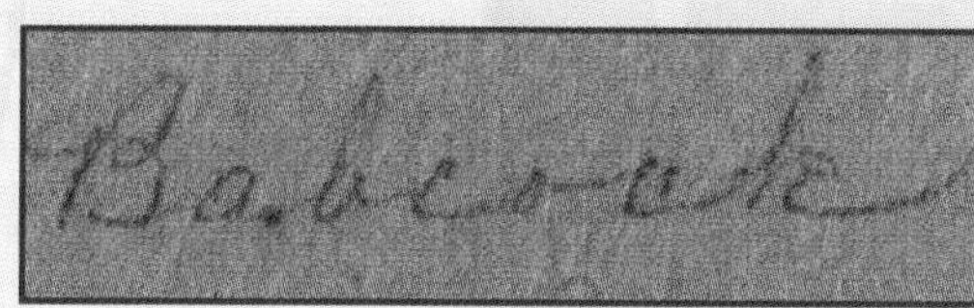

BABCOCK (first name not known)

BACKGROUND
Little background information on BABCOCK has been found. We have only seen a few Babcock pictures, and each was taken in Weare, New Hampshire, circa 1920 – 1925.

REGIONALITY
New England; Weare, New Hampshire

REPRESENTATIVE TITLES & VALUE GUIDE
"Weare, N.H." exterior #1
"Weare, N.H." exterior #2
Estimated value range: $25.00 – 50.00+

BAGNALL (first name not known)

BACKGROUND
Little background information on BAGNALL has been found. We have only seen a few Bagnall pictures, and each was taken in the southwestern U.S. One specific picture was titled "Palmdale, Calif. '35," which suggests that Bagnall worked in the Riverdale, California, area circa 1935.

REGIONALITY
Western U.S.; California

REPRESENTATIVE TITLES & VALUE GUIDE
"Joshua in Bloom, Palmdale, Calif."
Estimated value range: $25.00 – 75.00+

"Joshua in Bloom, Palmdale, Calif."

BAKER ART GALLERY

BACKGROUND
Little background information on the BAKER ART GALLERY has been found. We have only seen one Baker Art Gallery picture and, in our opinion, it was taken in New England circa 1905 – 1910. We do not believe that this company was associated with Florian Baker.

REGIONALITY
New England

REPRESENTATIVE TITLES & VALUE GUIDE
New England exterior scene
Estimated value range: $10.00 – 50.00+

FLORIAN A. BAKER

BACKGROUND

Little background information on FLORIAN BAKER has been found. We have only seen a few Florian Baker pictures, and each was taken in New England. The photograph of the Highland Light lighthouse (built in 1857, also known as Cape Cod Light) was taken on Cape Cod near North Truro, Massachusetts, which suggests that Baker was probably based in Massachusetts.

"Highland Light"

REGIONALITY

New England; Massachusetts

REPRESENTATIVE TITLES & VALUE GUIDE

"Autumn by the Lake"
"Highland Light"
"Inland Beauty"
"Rushing Waters"
Estimated value range: $25.00 – 50.00+

WALLACE BALDWIN

BACKGROUND

Little background information on WALLACE BALDWIN has been found. We have only seen one Wallace Baldwin picture and, in our opinion, it was taken in New England circa 1910 – 1915.

REGIONALITY

New England

REPRESENTATIVE TITLES & VALUE GUIDE

New England exterior scene
Estimated value range: $10.00 – 50.00+

ESMOND G. BARNHILL (1894 – 1959)

Florida sunset scene

BACKGROUND

ESMOND G. BARNHILL specialized in Florida hand-painted photography. Born on March 4, 1894, in Saludi, South Carolina, Barnhill established his first photography business in St. Petersburg, Florida, during 1913, at the age of 19. Specializing in postcards and greeting cards, his photography business remained relatively small, and he basically photographed, published, hand-colored, and distributed most of his work himself. His earliest postcards were printed in Germany, but in later years most of his postcards were printed by the Albertype Co. of New York.

Florida sunset scene

Barnhill expanded into selling hand-painted landscape photographs taken in and around St. Petersburg and, eventually, further into the Florida countryside. All Barnhill views that we have seen are Florida landscapes, some measuring as small as 2" x 3", others measuring as large as 11" x 14". Some Barnhill pictures are mounted on a signed/titled mat board, very similar to those of the other major photographers. However, most Barnhill images we've seen have been either unframed or close-framed in newer frames. Our guess is that a large amount of Barnhill's original unsold inventory has surfaced fairly recently and is slowly being released into today's marketplace. The price of Barnhill pictures is usually higher in Florida than anywhere else in the country.

Apparently Barnhill had always been interested in the culture of the American Indian. At some point he met with Edward S. Curtis, the famous photographer of the American West, when he was in his late teens. While working with Curtis, Barnhill learned the delicate "goldtoning" photographic process using uranium dyes, and he experimented with this process from 1914 until the mid-1920s. It is quite apparent in the color schemes used on a large number of his pictures.

Florida sunset scene

During World War II, Barnhill established an Indian Trading Post at the Wisconsin Dells, which he operated in the summer months until 1959. Several years later he opened the Indian Springs Museum.

Esmund G. Barnhill died in 1987 at the age of 93.

REGIONALITY

St. Petersburg, Florida

REPRESENTATIVE TITLES & VALUE GUIDE

Florida scenes: $50.00 – 200.00+
Florida postcards: $5.00 – 25.00+

Pair of hand-painted postcards

PUBLISHED BY E. G. BARNHILL STUDIO

Moonlight on the Lake Florida

Postcard marking

RECOMMENDED READING

Florida's Golden Age of Souvenirs: 1890 – 1930, by Larry Roberts. This book includes a chapter on Barnhill and Harris Florida hand-colored photographs.

J Bert Barton Seattle

"Mt Rainier–Mirror Lake"

J. BERT BARTON

BACKGROUND

Little background information on J. BERT BARTON has been found. We have only seen a few J. Bert Barton pictures and each was taken in the Pacific Northwest. The Mt. Rainier, Mirror Lake scene with "Seattle" after his signature suggests that he was probably based in Seattle, Washington, and worked primarily in the Pacific Northwest.

REGIONALITY

Northwest U.S.; Seattle, Washington

REPRESENTATIVE TITLES & VALUE GUIDE

"Mt. Rainier–Mirror Lake"
Estimated value range: $50.00 – 100.00+

"Yosemite Falls from Valley Road"

BEAR PHOTO

BACKGROUND

We have only seen a few BEAR PHOTO pictures, and each was taken in the western U.S. A Bear Photo label indicated that its pictures were colored with genuine oils instead of watercolors. The mention of Yosemite National Park in California suggests that the studio worked out of Yosemite National Park or at least in that vicinity. We have seen other California pictures, which have had studio numbers appearing on the images, that we've suspected were Bear Photos.

REGIONALITY

Western U.S.; Yosemite National Park, California

REPRESENTATIVE TITLES & VALUE GUIDE

"Yosemite Falls from Valley Road"
Estimated value range: $50.00 – 100.00+

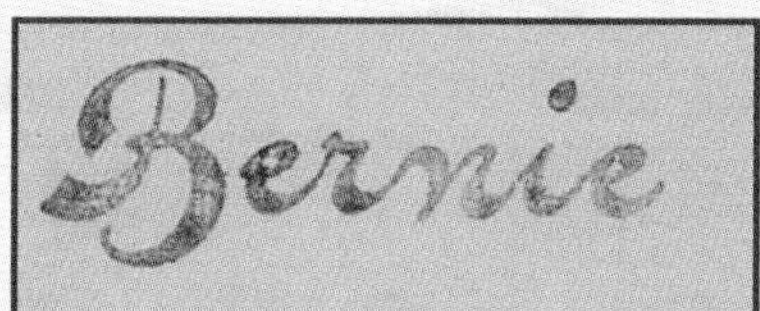

BERNIE (first name not known)

BACKGROUND
No background information on BERNIE has been found. We have only seen a few Bernie pictures, and each was seemingly taken in New England. We have noticed a strong similarity between the style, tone, theme, and coloring of Bernie and Gibson pictures and have wondered whether "Bernie" may have been a pseudonym used by Gibson, but have been unable to confirm this suspicion.

"Spring Blossoms"

REGIONALITY
New England

REPRESENTATIVE TITLES & VALUE GUIDE
"Spring Blossoms"
Estimated value range: $25.00 – 75.00+

Paper label, 16 Pitt St., Portland, Maine, address

Unusual paper label with handwritten title

JOHN CARLETON BICKNELL
BICKNELL MANUFACTURING CO.
BICKNELL PHOTO SERVICE

BACKGROUND
As it has for some of the other photographers, information about J. CARLETON BICKNELL has proved elusive. We have seen pictures signed "Bicknell," "J. C. Bicknell," and "J. Carleton Bicknell." And we have seen unsigned pictures that carry a "Bicknell Mfg. Co." paper label. And we have also learned about a "Bicknell Photo Service." Were all of these photographers the same J. Carleton Bicknell?

Apparently not. According to Nancy (Bicknell) Stone, there were actually two Bicknells in the Portland, Maine, photography business, John Carleton Bicknell and his brother, Edward Alton Bicknell.

From the history and genealogy of the Bicknell family supplied by Nancy Bicknell Stone, we learned that John Carleton Bicknell was born on May 28, 1871, in Madison, Maine. He was the son of John R. and Mary (Moulton) Bicknell. The genealogy, which was published in 1913, made no mention of Bicknell's death. It also stated: "At the age of seven John Carleton came near losing his life, by the falling of a tree, which cost him his right arm. His business education was gained at Skowhegan High School, Somerset Academy, Athens ME, and Shaw's Business College, Portland, ME. He was first an accountant, and later established the Bicknell Mfg. Co., of Portland, ME, in which he and his brother Edward have won merited success as honorable and reliable business men. His home is at Portland, ME."

Typical Maine lake scene

This would tend to confirm that J. Carleton Bicknell worked out of Portland, Maine, circa 1910 – 1930. And it would confirm that both brothers did indeed work together for a period of time. Their business name was Bicknell Mfg. Co., located at 16 Pitt Street, and later at 231 Middle Street, both in Portland. Sometimes John's pictures were signed "Bicknell," "J. C. Bicknell," or "J. Carleton Bicknell," and sometimes they were close-framed, with "Bicknell" stamp or paper labels on the pictures' backing papers. All of these indicate the work of J. Carleton Bicknell. Following the lead of Wallace Nutting, Bicknell photographed a wide variety of Maine's lakes, streams, country roads, mountains, and other rural landscape scenes. He also photographed Maine's southern seacoast, but we don't recall ever seeing a Bicknell colonial interior or foreign scene.

As some point, Bicknell was also marketing some of his pictures under the trade name Pine Cone Prints. We have seen several original unframed pictures still in their original Pine Cone Prints sleeve, which suggests that Bicknell may have been marketing some of his pictures under that name to Maine tourists.

Pine Cone Prints photo sleeve

Several years ago a Gary Bicknell, who described himself as the great-grandnephew of J. C. Bicknell, further confirmed that Bicknell had lost one of his arms. Although he said that he didn't have a whole lot of background information on his great-granduncle, Gary Bicknell did say that family lore recalled that J. C. Bicknell had somehow lost one of his arms. We discussed the difficulties a photographer of that era would have encountered working with only one arm. Imagine driving an old pick-up truck without power steering and simultaneously steering and shifting the truck's manual transmission with only one arm. Imagine traveling miles into the backcountry carrying a bulky box camera and a box of heavy glass-plate negatives and other assorted photographic equipment, while loading and unloading delicate glass plates into an unstable tripod camera, all with only one arm. Talk about a major impediment to an early twentieth century photographic career.

Then quite coincidentally, about one or two weeks later, we received a call from a gentleman from the Portland, Maine, area who said that he was researching early twentieth century Portland photographers and was looking for any information that I might have. I related the story I had just heard about

Paper label,
231 Middle St., Portland, Maine, address

Bicknell having one arm, and he basically said that the story could not be true because he owned a vintage photograph of Bicknell that clearly showed him with two arms. We ended the conversation with me not knowing what to believe. Within 15 minutes, my telephone rang again with the same Portland caller. He stated that he had taken a closer look at his Bicknell photograph and that the photo clearly showed two arms. But upon closer inspection, one arm did indeed appear to be prosthetic.

Also according to Nancy Stone, J. Carleton Bicknell and Edward Alton Bicknell had a falling out at some point and never spoke again. Edward Alton Bicknell then went on to establish the Bicknell Photo Service, while J. Carleton Bicknell continued to run the Bicknell Mfg. Co. Ms. Stone thinks that Edward Alton Bicknell was born with a deformed arm. Although they never spoke again, J. Carleton Bicknell continued to purchase his photographic equipment and supplies from Edward. Apparently, the Bicknell Photo Service closed its doors after the divorce of Edward and his wife, Bertha, who was a successful photographer and artist as well.

"High Twelve Camps,"
found in a Pine Cone Prints sleeve

J. Carleton Bicknell's photographs have become increasingly more collectible in recent years, especially with New England collectors.

REGIONALITY
New England; Portland, Maine

REPRESENTATIVE TITLES & VALUE GUIDE
"Across the Intervale"
"Apple Blossoms"
"Cathedral Ledge"
"College Hall"
"A Country Road"
"Dining Room, Big Island Pond"
"Glen Ellis Falls"
"High Surf"
"The Ledges"
"The Lone Apple Tree"
"Lovejoy Bridge"
"Masonic Temple"
"Meadow Elms"
"The Old Red Home"
"The Old Wooden Bridge"
"Parsacouauay Mountain"
"Phi Kappa Psi"
"Porcupine Island"
"Porcupines from Nupert"
"The Quiet Stream"
"The Salmon Pool"
"Sandy River Cascade"
"Shepherd River"
"Valley Farm"
Typical value range: $50.00 – 200.00

"The Lone Apple Tree"

S. L. BLAIR

BACKGROUND

Little background information on S. L. BLAIR has been found. We have only seen one picture by S. L. Blair, and it was an exterior scene that gave no clue as to its location or origin.

REGIONALITY

Unknown

REPRESENTATIVE TITLES & VALUE GUIDE

Exterior scene
Estimated value range: $10.00 – 50.00+

A Maine Marine Photograph
Copyrighted by Ralph F. Blood
1795 Congress Street Portland, Maine

RALPH BLOOD

BACKGROUND

RALPH BLOOD was a Portland, Maine, photographer whose studio was located at 1795 Congress Street in Portland. Blood specialized in southern Maine marine photography, most likely intended for visiting Maine tourists circa 1920. His picture label read "A Maine Marine Photograph, Copyrighted by Ralph F. Blood, 1795 Congress Street, Portland, Maine." The quality of his work was excellent and on a par with most of the major photographers of his time. "Portland Head Light" was one of his best-selling pictures.

REGIONALITY

New England; Portland, Maine

REPRESENTATIVE TITLES & VALUE GUIDE

"Portland Head Light 1791"
Estimated value range: $50.00 – 100.00+

EVE S. BRADLEY

BACKGROUND
Little background information on EVE S. BRADLEY has been found. We have only seen one Eve Bradley picture, and it was taken at the Pacific Ocean.

REGIONALITY
Western U.S.

REPRESENTATIVE TITLES & VALUE GUIDE
Pacific Ocean seascape
Estimated value range: $25.00 – 50.00+

E. A. BRAGG

BACKGROUND
Little background information on E. A. BRAGG has been found. We have only seen one picture by Bragg, and it was a circa 1910 – 1920 exterior scene that gave no clue as to its location or origin.

REGIONALITY
Unknown

REPRESENTATIVE TITLES & VALUE GUIDE
Exterior scene
Estimated value range: $10.00 – 25.00+

BILL BREHMER

BACKGROUND
Little background information on BILL BREHMER has been found. We have only seen one picture by Brehmer, and that picture suggested he was from Rutland, Vermont. We have seen photographic postcards by "L. F. Brehmer" of Rutland, Vermont, dating circa 1905 – 1910, and we suspect that Bill Brehmer was probably somehow associated with this company.

REGIONALITY
New England; Rutland, Vermont

REPRESENTATIVE TITLES & VALUE GUIDE
Exterior scene
Estimated value range: $25.00 – 50.00

"Road through Yellowstone"

W. BREWER

BACKGROUND

Little background information on W. BREWER has been found. We have only seen one picture by Brewer, and that picture was taken in Yellowstone National Park, which suggests he was working in the western United States circa 1920 – 1930.

REGIONALITY

Western U.S.; Yellowstone National Park, Wyoming

REPRESENTATIVE TITLES & VALUE GUIDE

"Road through Yellowstone"
Estimated value range: $25.00 – 50.00

"Essex Woods"

C. W. BRIGGS

BACKGROUND

Little background information on C. W. BRIGGS has been found. We have only seen one picture by Briggs, and that picture was taken near Lake Tahoe, California, which suggests he was working in the western United States circa 1920 – 1930.

REGIONALITY

Western U.S.; Lake Tahoe, California

REPRESENTATIVE TITLES & VALUE GUIDE

"Essex Woods"
Estimated value range: $25.00 – 50.00+

BROOKS (first name not known)

BACKGROUND
Little background information on BROOKS has been found. We have only seen one picture by Brooks, and that picture suggested it was taken near Weare, New Hampshire, circa 1920 – 1930.

REGIONALITY
New England; Weare, New Hampshire

REPRESENTATIVE TITLES & VALUE GUIDE
Exterior scene
Estimated value range: $25.00 – 50.00+

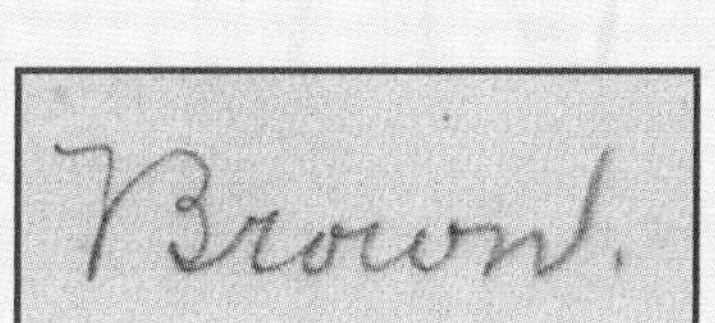

BROWN (first name not known)

BACKGROUND
Little background information on BROWN has been found. Collector Dick Valentinetti reported acquiring a New England exterior scene signed "Brown" but had no further information. We have been unable to confirm any connection between "Brown" and "E. Brown" listed on the next page.

REGIONALITY
New England

REPRESENTATIVE TITLES & VALUE GUIDE
Exterior scene
Estimated value range: $10.00 – 50.00+

E. BROWN

BACKGROUND

Little background information on E. BROWN has been found. We have only seen one picture by E. Brown, and it was an exterior scene and probably New England. We have been unable to confirm any connection between "E. Brown" and "Brown" listed on the preceding page.

REGIONALITY

New England

REPRESENTATIVE TITLES & VALUE GUIDE

Exterior scene
Estimated value range: $10.00 – 50.00+

PUBLISHED & COPYRIGHTED BY
THE C. O. BUCKINGHAM CO
810 - 13th Street, N. W
WASHINGTON, D. C.

Washington DC Cherry Blossoms

C. O. BUCKINGHAM

BACKGROUND

C. O. BUCKINGHAM operated the C. O. Buckingham Co. photographic studio at 810 13th Street NW in Washington DC circa 1915 – 1925. Most Buckingham images we have seen have been Washington DC monument scenes such as the Washington Monument, Lincoln Memorial, Jefferson Memorial, etc. These were marketed as "Buckingham prints of historic Washington." Most Buckingham pictures are marked with either a "C .O. Buckingham" impressed into a lower corner of the image, or with the "C. O. Buckingham" backstamp on the back of the image. Buckingham hand-painted photographs came in the following sizes: 5" x 7", 8" x 10", 11" x 14", 14" x 17", and 16" x 20". All photographs were created from original Buckingham negatives, which each carried a unique Buckingham studio number.

Somewhere between 1918 and 1920, Buckingham hired Royal Carlock (see Royal H. Carlock) as his assistant. It appears that Carlock purchased the C. O. Buckingham Co. at some later date, because many of the Washington

Monument scenes sold by Carlock were exactly the same scenes marked by Buckingham. However, collector Myke Ellis reported that his 1943 Polk address directory for Washington DC listed C. O. Buckingham at 1220 New York Avenue, while in the same edition, Royal Carlock was listed at 913 Pennsylvania Avenue, so this business transfer must have taken place after 1943.

Lincoln Memorial

REGIONALITY
Washington DC

REPRESENTATIVE TITLES & VALUE GUIDE
Jefferson Memorial
Lincoln Memorial
Washington Monument
Assorted non–Washington DC images
Typical value range: $25.00 – 75.00+

EDITHE BUETLER

BACKGROUND

Little background information on EDITHE BUETLER has been found. We have only seen one picture by Edithe Buetler, and it was a hand-colored scene from Hawaii. Our research has also indicated that Buetler also hand painted photographs by other photographers during the early 1940s.

REGIONALITY
Hawaii

REPRESENTATIVE TITLES & VALUE GUIDE
Hawaiian beach scene
Estimated value range: $50.00 – 100.00+

W.H. BURKE

BACKGROUND
Little background information on W. H. BURKE has been found. We have only seen one picture by W. H. Burke, and it was an exterior scene from the White Mountains of New Hampshire.

REGIONALITY
New England; New Hampshire

REPRESENTATIVE TITLES & VALUE GUIDE
"White Mountains, New Hampshire"
Estimated value range: $25.00 – 50.00+

BURNELL STUDIO

BACKGROUND
Little background information on the BURNELL STUDIO has been found. We have only seen one picture by the Burnell Studio, and it was an exterior scene identified as Keuka Lake, New York. We have also seen postcards from the Keuka Lake, New York, area also by a photographer identified as "Burnell." And we have located references to a photograph of Bluff Point on Lake Keuka taken by a "Burnell." We suspect that all three are same photographer.

REGIONALITY
Keuka Lake, New York

REPRESENTATIVE TITLES & VALUE GUIDE
Exterior scene
Estimated value range: $25.00 – 100.00+

BURNHAM (first name not known)

BACKGROUND
Little background information on BURNHAM has been found. We have only seen one picture by Burnham, and it was an exterior scene that, in our opinion, was taken in New England.

REGIONALITY
New England

REPRESENTATIVE TITLES & VALUE GUIDE
Exterior scene
Estimated value range: $10.00 – 50.00+

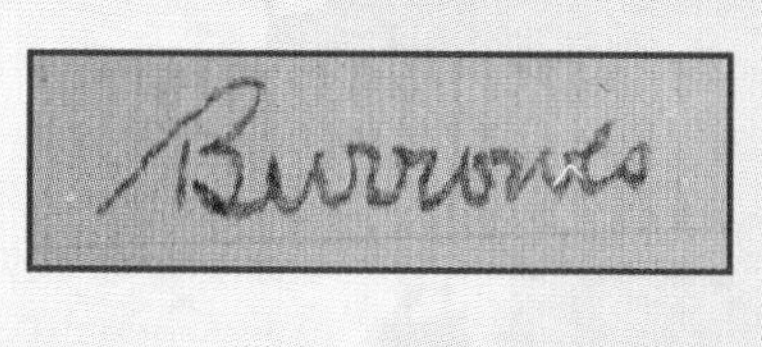

"Natural Bridge of Virginia"

HAROLD JOHN "HAL" BURROWES (1880 – 1926)

BACKGROUND

Researching HAL BURROWES (1880 – 1926) presented one of the most interesting and confusing challenges that we had encountered in our 30-plus years of research into hand-colored photography, because over the years, we had seen identical Lamson and Fred Thompson pictures appearing over the Burrowes signature. And then a series of postcards printed by the "H. J. Burrowes Co." appeared that also featured Fred Thompson and Lamson photographs. Who was Burrowes, and how did he gain access to these Lamson and Thompson pictures?

Thanks to Kirsten Henry, the great-granddaughter of the owner of the H. J. Burrowes Co., we located the final answer to the Lamson-Thompson-Burrowes connection.

Somewhere around 1920, Hal Burrowes (Harold John Burrowes) formed the H. J. Burrowes postcard company on 13 Middle Street in Portland (the same Middle Street where J. Carleton Bicknell operated his photography studio in Portland). This business sold hand-painted photographs done in a style very similar that of to Nutting and the other leading photographers of the time. It also sold a variety of postcards and hand-painted advertising calendars as well.

Hal Burrowes died in 1926, and his business was purchased by his sister (Esther Burrowes Morton) and her husband (Ernest Morton), who then moved to Portland from Johnstown, Pennsylvania. Keeping the H. J. Burrowes name, the company grew under Ernest Morton to the point where it had up to 12 colorists hand tinting pictures on any given day. Sometime shortly after taking control of the business, Morton purchased what remained of the Thompson Art Co., including all remaining supplies, inventory, and most importantly, all glass-plate negatives — which included the Lamson glass-plate negatives that had been purchased by Fred Thompson circa 1905. Morton apparently purchased the inventory of several other local photographers as well. Uncovering this expansion solved the mystery of how the H. J. Burrowes Co. ended up marketing some of the same images that had been sold by both Fred Thompson and the Lamson Studios.

There has even been some speculation that photographs signed "LeBusch" were also Burrowes photographs, because they look so similar in style and coloring, but no one has yet positively confirmed this speculation.

Perhaps the saddest part of this story is what happened to all of the surviving glass-plate negatives. After the death of Ernest Morton in 1952, his son Rutledge Morton was faced with the task of closing up the business and deciding what to do with the thousands of original glass negatives that had been part of the business. Photographic technology had certainly changed over the years, and bulky glass negatives had been replaced by celluloid film. The 1950s was a time well prior to the start of America's collecting phenomenon, and no one really wanted the glass negatives. Rutledge Morton tried to donate the glass-plate negatives to several historical societies, but none had the means or ability to store such a massive inventory. So with no other alternative, Rutledge sold the glass negatives to a florist, who washed the photographic emulsion off the Norwegian plate glass and used the glass as part of a greenhouse. Quite literally, that piece of Lamson, Thompson, and Burrowes photographic history went down the drain.

Fortunately, a few of the glass negatives do remain. Rutledge Morton passed away fairly recently, but his granddaughter, Kirsten Henry, and her family have preserved approximately 25 – 30 of the original negatives and are selling reproductions of these images. Fortunately, these reproductions can be clearly differentiated from the original pictures.

Postcard using Fred Thompson picture

REGIONALITY
New England; Portland, Maine

REPRESENTATIVE TITLES & VALUE GUIDE
"A Country Road"
"The Expected Letter"
"Homeward"
"The Intervale"
"Natural Bridge of Virginia"
"Spring Charms"
"Winter Time"
Typical value range: $50.00 – 100.00+

Postcard marking

"The Expected Letter"

Ernest Winthrop Morton (d. 1952)

Harold John Burrowes (1880 – 1926)

"A Country Road"

Pedro Cacciola

PEDRO CACCIOLA

BACKGROUND

Most of this information about PEDRO CACCIOLA was provided to us by his two daughters, Irene Colonna and Fran Donovan. Pedro Cacciola (pronounced Pee-dro Cassiola) began working for Wallace Nutting in 1921, when he was only 18 years old and spoke practically no English. He started at a salary of $10.50 per week, and within only a few months became one of Nutting's valued printers (darkroom men). At this time, Nutting had five printers working in the darkroom whose primary job was to process enough black and white platinotype pictures to keep Nutting's nearly 200 colorists busy. As the years went on and Nutting's staff was greatly reduced, Cacciola remained a trusted Nutting employee, and he was the individual who developed most of the thousands of black and white glossy pictures used in the production of Nutting's ten States Beautiful and two Furniture Treasury books. Cacciola remained with the Nutting business until after Wallace Nutting's death in 1941 and Mrs. Nutting's death in 1944.

Along the way Cacciola learned the fine art of hand coloring his own photographs, and after the Wallace Nutting business was permanently closed in the mid-1940s, Cacciola opened his own photography studio at 69 Howe Street in Framingham, Massachusetts. We have also seen a label indicating that he worked at 53 Cedar Street in Framingham as well. Most of his pictures were typical New England exterior scenes, including fall trees, spring blossoms, and typical rural New England sights. He also photographed certain areas of Italy when he returned for a visit to his homeland.

The quality of Cacciola's pictures was equal to that of the best of the major photographers. Unfortunately, the mid-1940s start of his business coincided with the public introduction of color film, which caused the art of hand-colored photographs to become generally considered a passé art form.

We have seen several labels from Cacciola's business, including one promoting the fact that he had formerly worked for Wallace Nutting.

Our auction company sold the remaining portion of the Pedro Cacciola estate over two auctions in 2003 and 2004, and prices were quite strong because his pictures were so beautiful. His floral scenes were absolutely gorgeous, and every bit as beautiful as Wallace Nutting's.

New England covered bridge

"Bridge of Flowers"

Italian snow-capped peaks

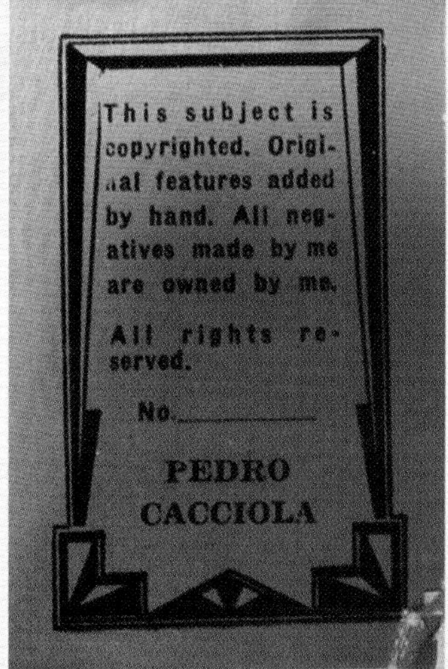
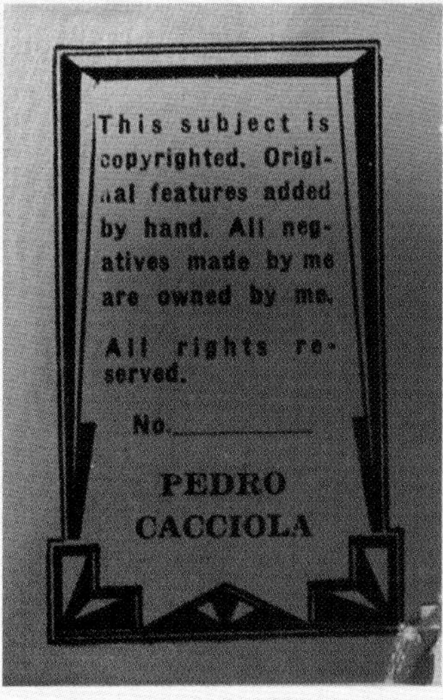

Gold Foil paper label

REGIONALITY

New England; Framingham, Massachusetts; some pictures taken in Italy

REPRESENTATIVE TITLES & VALUE GUIDE

New England scenes: $50.00 – 100.00+

Italian scenes: $75.00 – 150.00+

Floral scenes: $10.000 – 300.00+

Paper label.
Note the similarity to
Nutting's copyright label.

CLASS J pub. No. 37743

COPYRIGHT OFFICE
OF THE UNITED STATES OF AMERICA

THE LIBRARY OF CONGRESS :: WASHINGTON

CERTIFICATE OF COPYRIGHT REGISTRATION

This is to certify, in conformity with section 55 of the Act to Amend and Consolidate the Acts respecting Copyright, approved March 4, 1909, as amended by the Act approved March 2, 1913, that TWO copies of the photograph, named herein have been deposited in this Office under the provisions of the Act of 1909, and that registration of a claim to copyright for the first term of twenty-eight years for said work has been duly made in the name of

Pedro Cacciola,
49 - Cedar St.,
Framingham, Mass.

Title: Baby's Cradle.
Author, of United States.

Date of publication in the United States Dec. 1,1944

Copies received Mar. 19,1945

Sam B. Warner
Register of Copyrights

Original floral U.S. copyright

"A Tunnel of Joy"

COLORED PRINT
ORIGINAL FEATURES
ADDED by HAND
PEDRO CACCIOLA
FORMER PRINTER FOR
WALLACE NUTTING
69 HOWE ST.
FRAMINGHAM, MASS.

"Formerly with Wallace Nutting" label

Close-framed florals

CALL (first name not known)

BACKGROUND
Little background information on CALL has been found. This is the only Call picture we have seen, and it was taken at Mt. Katahdin, Maine, which suggests that Call was probably a Maine photographer.

REGIONALITY
New England; Maine

REPRESENTATIVE TITLES & VALUE GUIDE
"Mt. Katahdin, Maine"
Estimated value range: $25.00 – 50.00+

HAL H. CAMPBELL

BACKGROUND
Little background information on HAL H. CAMPBELL has been found. We have only seen one Hal Campbell picture, and it was taken in Redlands, California. A backstamp read "Campbell Photo, All pictures bearing this stamp are genuine photographs, Hal H. Campbell, Redlands, Calif."

REGIONALITY
Western U.S.; California

REPRESENTATIVE TITLES & VALUE GUIDE
California exterior scene
Estimated value range: $50.00 – 100.00+

CAMPBELL ART CO.

BACKGROUND
Little background information on the CAMPBELL ART CO. has been found. We have only seen one Campbell Art Co. picture and it was taken in Washington DC, which suggests that Campbell Art may have been a Washington DC studio.

REGIONALITY
Washington DC

REPRESENTATIVE TITLES & VALUE GUIDE
Washington Monument
Estimated value range: $10.00 – 50.00+

Washington Monument

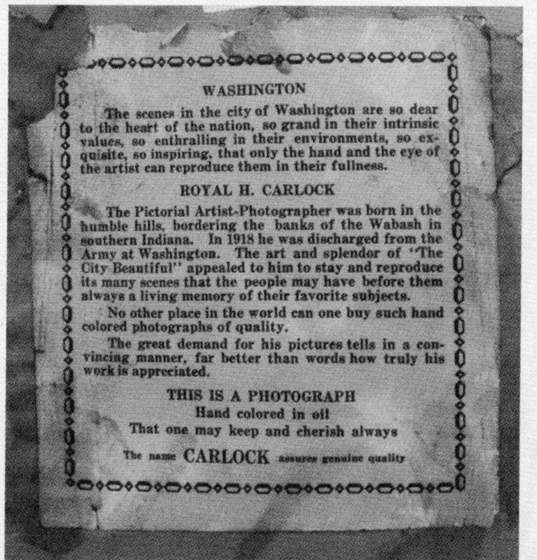

WASHINGTON

The scenes in the city of Washington are so dear to the heart of the nation, so grand in their intrinsic values, so enthralling in their environments, so exquisite, so inspiring, that only the hand and the eye of the artist can reproduce them in their fullness.

ROYAL H. CARLOCK

The Pictorial Artist-Photographer was born in the humble hills, bordering the banks of the Wabash in southern Indiana. In 1918 he was discharged from the Army at Washington. The art and splendor of "The City Beautiful" appealed to him to stay and reproduce its many scenes that the people may have before them always a living memory of their favorite subjects.

No other place in the world can one buy such hand colored photographs of quality.

The great demand for his pictures tells in a convincing manner, far better than words how truly his work is appreciated.

THIS IS A PHOTOGRAPH
Hand colored in oil
That one may keep and cherish always

The name CARLOCK assures genuine quality

Paper label #1

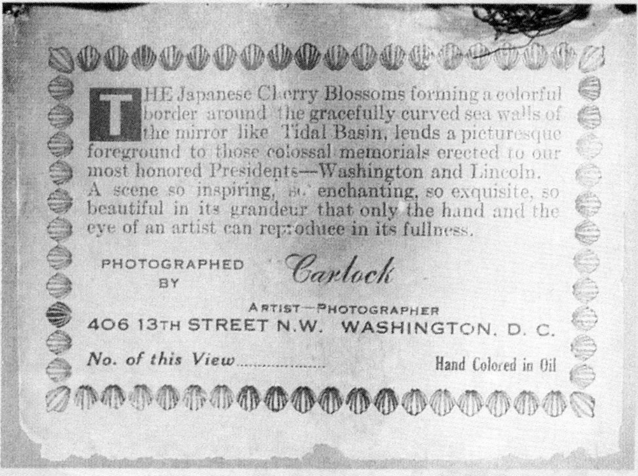

THE Japanese Cherry Blossoms forming a colorful border around the gracefully curved sea walls of the mirror like Tidal Basin, lends a picturesque foreground to those colossal memorials erected to our most honored Presidents—Washington and Lincoln. A scene so inspiring, so enchanting, so exquisite, so beautiful in its grandeur that only the hand and the eye of an artist can reproduce in its fullness.

PHOTOGRAPHED BY *Carlock*

ARTIST—PHOTOGRAPHER
406 13TH STREET N.W. WASHINGTON, D. C.

No. of this View.................... Hand Colored in Oil

Paper label #2

ROYAL H. CARLOCK (1899 – 1970)

BACKGROUND

ROYAL HUBERT CARLOCK was born in Paris Crossing, Indiana. One of six children, he was born to Benjamin and Ellen Carlock. After graduating from Indiana University, Carlock married Ethel Wohrer in 1917. He entered the U.S. Army near the end of World War I, where he specialized in aerial photography as part of the U.S. Army Corps of Engineers, and after the war ended, the couple moved to Washington DC in 1918, where their first daughter was born.

After his discharge from the army, Carlock secured employment with a photography firm named C. O. Buckingham (see C. O. Buckingham), which at the time was producing hand-painted photographs of the chief tourist attractions in Washington DC. This explains the obvious similarity in style between Carlock and Buckingham hand-colored pictures.

Ethel Carlock died in 1920 during an influenza epidemic, leaving Carlock a widower with a 15-month-old baby.

Carlock was fascinated by the architecture and national treasures found in our nation's capital. He focused his photographic and hand-coloring skills on subjects found in and around the Washington DC area. The only photographer in his company, his black and white photographs were hand painted in oils and sold to the multitude of tourists visiting our nation's capital during the post –World War I era.

In 1922, Carlock married his second wife, Emma Clarke. In that same year, he also left the employment of the Buckingham studios and opened his own photography studio at 406 13th Street NW in Washington DC. Carlock's Snappy Snap Shop specialized in quick development of tourists' film and sold his increasingly famous hand-colored photographs of Washington DC landmarks and monuments, including the White House, the Jefferson Memorial, the Lincoln Memorial, the Washington Monument, the U.S. Capital Building, and of course, Washington's colorful cherry blossoms. Working as a team, Carlock took the pictures and Emma, along with other colorists, hand-tinted them.

Known Photographers

Lincoln Memorial

We have seen Carlock pictures identified in three distinct manners:

- ❋ Matted pictures signed "Carlock" on the lower right corner beneath the picture, with or without a title lower left
- ❋ Unmatted, close-framed pictures with "Carlock" embossed on the lower-left corner of the actual picture
- ❋ No marking on the picture or matting, simply a "Carlock" picture label on the backing

Jane Crandall has reported that Royal Carlock was her uncle and that both of her parents worked for him at some point. She also reported that her mother, Julia Carlock, was one of Carlock's colorists and would bring pictures home to color in the evening. Jane Crandall also reported that many of the signatures found on Carlock pictures were actually signed by her mother.

Royal Carlock kept his business running into the 1940s. Collector Myke Ellis has reported that the 1943 *Polk Washington D.C. Address Directory* listed Royal Carlock as working at 913 Pennsylvania Avenue. Even during the Depression years, when so many other photographers either saw their businesses decline or closed their doors, Carlock's business flourished due, primarily, to the consistently high level of tourism and the large and growing number of people who were gainfully employed by the U.S. government.

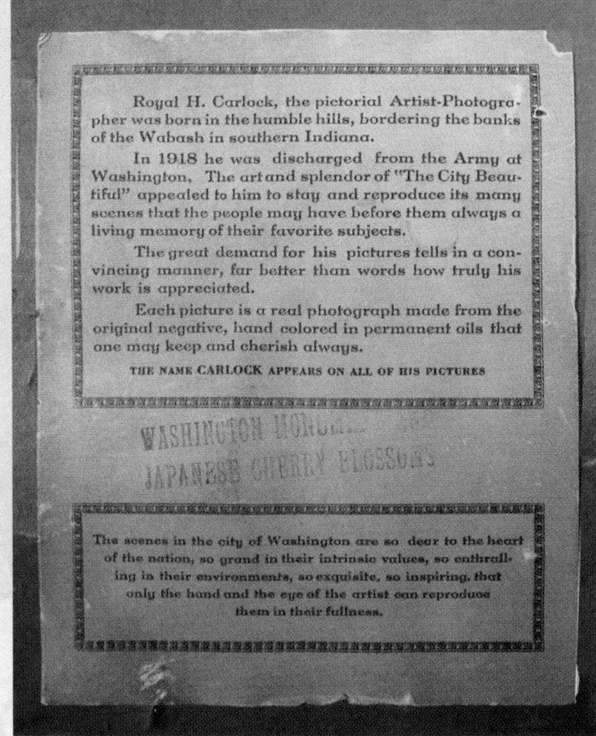

Royal H. Carlock, the pictorial Artist-Photographer was born in the humble hills, bordering the banks of the Wabash in southern Indiana.

In 1918 he was discharged from the Army at Washington. The art and splendor of "The City Beautiful" appealed to him to stay and reproduce its many scenes that the people may have before them always a living memory of their favorite subjects.

The great demand for his pictures tells in a convincing manner, far better than words how truly his work is appreciated.

Each picture is a real photograph made from the original negative, hand colored in permanent oils that one may keep and cherish always.

THE NAME CARLOCK APPEARS ON ALL OF HIS PICTURES

WASHINGTON MONU

JAPANESE CHERRY BLOSSOMS

The scenes in the city of Washington are so dear to the heart of the nation, so grand in their intrinsic values, so enthralling in their environments, so exquisite, so inspiring, that only the hand and the eye of the artist can reproduce them in their fullness.

Paper label #3

Although his photographs usually sold best at cherry blossom time, for several years Carlock also produced a Christmas card that contained a hand-colored photo of Washington DC. These are considered quite rare today.

As it did with the businesses of all other early twentieth century hand-colored picture photographers, the advent of color film led to a decline in sales of Carlock's hand-colored photography. The primary emphasis of his business turned to photo refinishing until 1957, when he retired from the photography business to devote his life to conservation.

In 1962 his 40-year marriage to Emma dissolved, and in 1964 he married Grace Diane Knapp.

Having suffered from cardiac problems during the final years of his life, Royal Carlock died from a heart attack in 1970. His ashes were buried on a small isle in a lagoon at the National Isaac Walton League Conservation Park near Gaithersburg, Maryland.

Carlock pictures are still relatively inexpensive, with most falling within the $25.00 – 75.00 range. Their low price, good quality, and interesting subject matter will probably continue to make them collectible. The only limitation is that there are only approximately 10 – 12 different Washington DC scenes to collect. The next time you see a Washington DC picture in a shop or a show, take a closer look at it. It will probably be a Royal Carlock hand-colored photograph.

REGIONALITY
Washington DC

REPRESENTATIVE TITLES & VALUE GUIDE
Japanese Cherry Blossoms
Jefferson Memorial
Lincoln Memorial
Mount Vernon
Washington Monument
Typical value range: $25.00 – 75.00+

THIS SET CONTAINS
12 OF THE MOST IMPORTANT
SCENES IN
BEAUTIFUL WASHINGTON

1. Capitol
2. White House
3. Washington Monument
4. Lincoln Memorial
5. Mansion at Mount Vernon
6. Scottish Rite Temple
7. Pennsylvania Avenue
8. Union Station
9. Library of Congress
10. United States Treasury
11. State, War and Navy Building
12. Amphitheatre at Arlington

MAIL ORDERS FILLED PROMPTLY

PUBLISHED BY
CARLOCK
406 13TH STREET N. W.
WASHINGTON, D. C.

Listing of 12 popular picture titles

Jefferson Memorial

Royal H. Carlock
(1899 – 1970)

Mount Vernon

RUDOLPH H. CASSENS

BACKGROUND
Collector Jim Graves reported to us that he had located a photograph by RUDOLPH H. CASSENS. It was titled "Mt. Vernon, Maine" and was signed "Rudolph Cassens." A paper label on the back read "Photographic Oil Painting from the Studios of Rudolph Cassens, Belfast, Maine." Cassens also produced a variety of photographs that were issued as postcards, including "Tumbledown Mountain" (Maine) and "The Balsams, Dixville Notch" (New Hampshire). These postcards included the middle initial "H." in the signature.

REGIONALITY
New England; Belfast, Maine

REPRESENTATIVE TITLES & VALUE GUIDE
"Mt. Vernon, Maine"
Estimated value range: $25.00 – 50.00+

Untitled mansion garden

LINDA CATTELL

BACKGROUND
Little background information on LINDA CATTELL has been found. We have only seen one picture by Cattell, and that pictured offered no clues as to its location or origin.

REGIONALITY
Unknown

REPRESENTATIVE TITLES & VALUE GUIDE
Untitled mansion garden
Estimated value range: $10.00 – 50.00+

"Lake Mohonk, NY"

"The Old Sawmill"

A. G. CHANEY

BACKGROUND
Little background information on A. G. CHANEY has been found. We have only seen two pictures by Chaney. One picture was of the Mohonk Lake House at Lake Mohonk, New York, which suggests that Chaney may have been from upstate New York or New England.

REGIONALITY
New York or New England

REPRESENTATIVE TITLES & VALUE GUIDE
"Lake Mohonk, NY"
"The Old Sawmill"
Estimated value range: $10.00 – 50.00+

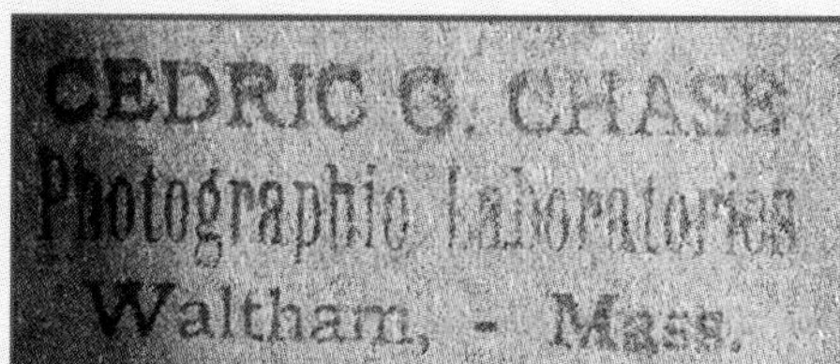

CEDRIC G. CHASE

BACKGROUND
CEDRIC G. CHASE operated a business called the Cedric G. Chase Photographic Laboratories in Waltham, Massachusetts. His label referred to his pictures as "the Chase Series" and the "Standard for New England." We have seen some, but relatively few, Chase pictures over the years, and the overall quality has been very good.

REGIONALITY
Waltham, Mass.

REPRESENTATIVE TITLES & VALUE GUIDE
Close-framed cabins
Close-framed lakeside cottage
Estimated value range: $25.00 – 50.00+

Close-framed cabins

Close-framed lakeside cottage

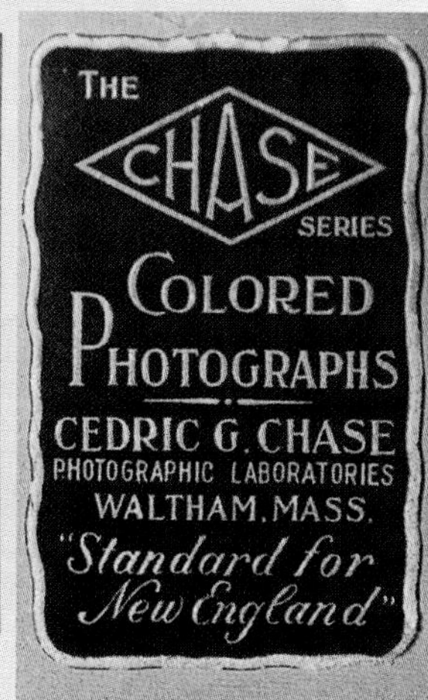

Cedrick G. Chase stamp

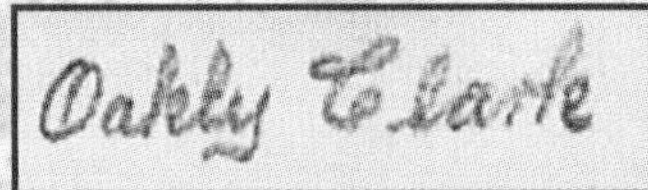

OAKLEY CLARK

BACKGROUND

Little background information on OAKLEY CLARK has been found. We have only seen a limited number of pictures by Oakley Clark, and each was from the Washington DC area, which suggests that Clark was probably from the Washington DC area.

REGIONALITY

Washington DC

REPRESENTATIVE TITLES & VALUE GUIDE

Mount Vernon
Other Washington DC scenes
Estimated value range: $10.00 – 50.00+

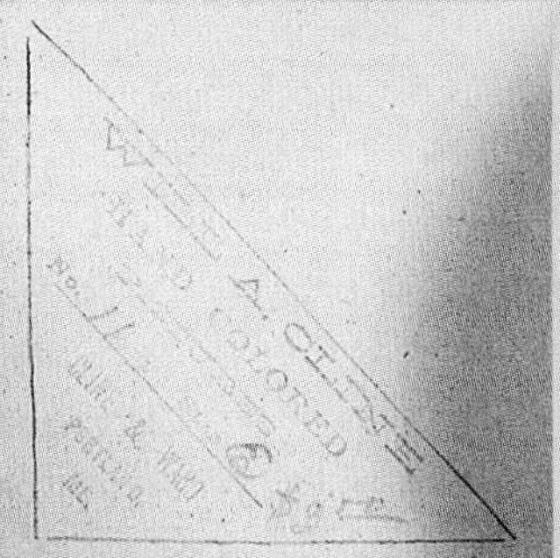

Cline & Ward backstamp

WILL A. CLINE

BACKGROUND

WILL A. CLINE was a partner with Arthur Ward in the Cline & Ward Studio in Portland, Maine. We have seen several "Arthur Ward" hand-colored photos that, when taken apart, reveal one or two paper labels. One label reads "Will A. Cline, Hand-Colored Pictures, Cline & Ward, Portland ME." The other reads "Cline & Ward, Colored Photographs, Portland, Maine." The work seems to date circa 1910 – 1920, and the quality is very good. Most pictures we have seen were from southern Maine and presumably intended for the Maine tourist market.

REGIONALITY

New England; Portland, Maine

REPRESENTATIVE TITLES & VALUE GUIDE

"Flood Tide"
"Portland Head Light"
"Rocky Cliffs"
Estimated value range: $50.00 – 100.00

Arthur Ward, "Rocky Cliffs"

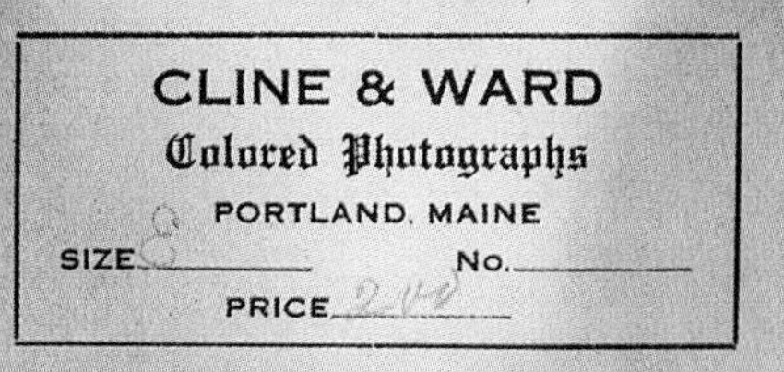

Cline & Ward backstamp

"Straight Wharf, Nantucket"

WILLIAM W. COFFIN

BACKGROUND

We don't know much about WILLIAM W. COFFIN aside from the fact that he created a colorful series of hand-colored photos taken on the island of Nantucket off the coast of Cape Cod, Massachusetts. A Coffin family was one of Nantucket's founding families, and it would probably be a safe assumption that William Coffin was somehow related to that family. Coffin's Nantucket scenes were geared to Nantucket tourists, and most pictures generally seemed to have "Nantucket" in the title. All we have seen are pencil signed, and we would estimate they were taken circa 1905 – 1915. Overall quality is very good, but today many mats frequently show darkened signs of aging. Nantucket hand-painted pictures are highly collectible, and we have seen a limited few Coffin pictures bring in excess of $500.00. The key is to find the right Nantucket collectors, because they are a serious, but limited, group.

"West Cliff, Nantucket"

REGIONALITY

New England; Nantucket, Massachusetts

REPRESENTATIVE TITLES & VALUE GUIDE

"Along the Beach, Nantucket"
"Rounding Brant Point, Nantucket"
"Straight Wharf, Nantucket"
"Surfside, Nantucket"
"West Cliff, Nantucket"
Typical value range: $200.00 – 400.00+

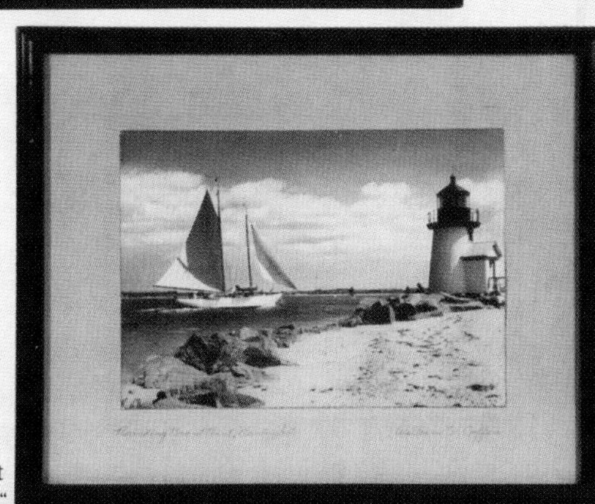

"Rounding Brant Point, Nantucket"

"Along the Beach, Nantucket"

"Surfside, Nantucket"

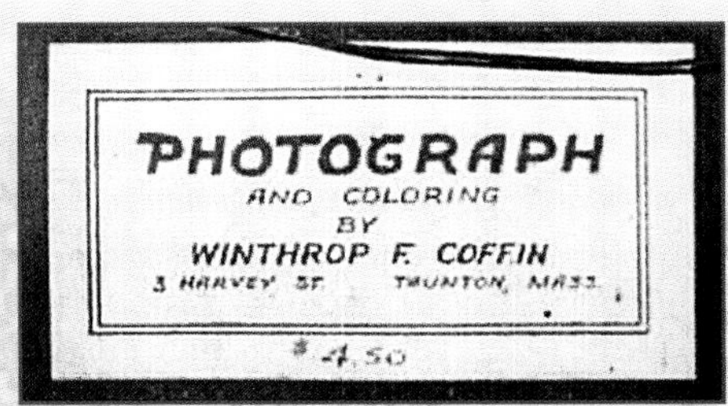

WINTHROP F. COFFIN

BACKGROUND

WINTHROP F. COFFIN worked at 3 Harvey Street in Taunton, Massachusetts, but we have found no other background information on this photographer. We have only seen one picture by Coffin, and it was from the New England area. We have been unable to confirm any relationship to William W. Coffin.

REGIONALITY

Taunton, Massachusetts

REPRESENTATIVE TITLES & VALUE GUIDE

Exterior scene
Estimated value range: $25.00 – 75.00+

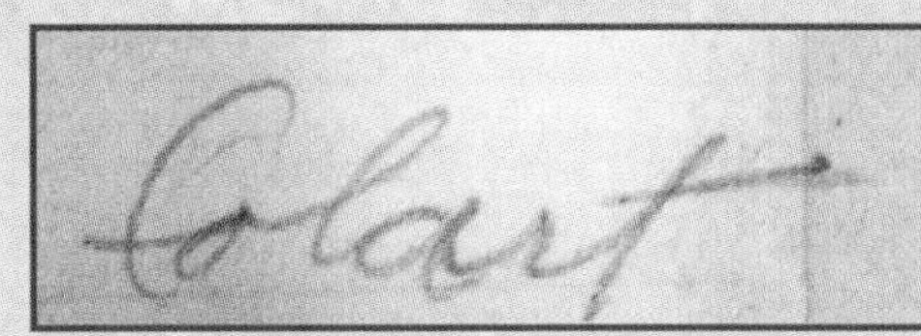

COLART (first name not known)

BACKGROUND

Little background information on COLART has been found. We have only seen a few Colart pictures, and each had the same 1930s look. We have noticed a strong similarity of style, tone, theme, and coloring of "Colart" and "Villar" pictures, and have wondered whether "Colart" may have been a pseudonym for Villar, but have been unable to confirm this suspicion.

REGIONALITY

Unknown

REPRESENTATIVE TITLES & VALUE GUIDE

"Waiting"
Estimated value range: $25.00 – 50.00+

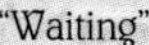
"Waiting"

Backstamp from back of image

PAUL R. COLLIER

BACKGROUND

Little background information on PAUL R. COLLIER has been found. We have only seen only one picture by Collier, and it was a garden scene. The back of the photo was stamped "Paul R. Collier, Photographic Expert, 140 E. 6th St, Plainfield NJ." We would date this image circa 1930 – 1940 based upon Collier's 4-digit telephone number.

REGIONALITY

New Jersey

REPRESENTATIVE TITLES & VALUE GUIDE

Untitled garden scene, probably New Jersey
Estimated value range: $10.00 – 50.00+

Garden scene

JAMES WALTER COLLINGE (1883 – 1964)

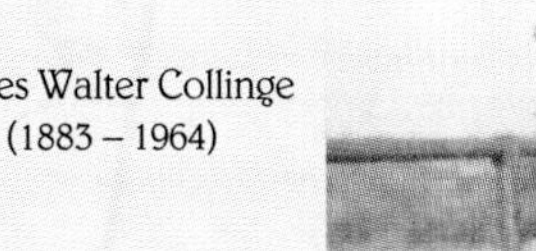

James Walter Collinge (1883 – 1964)

BACKGROUND

J. WALTER COLLINGE was sometimes referred to as "Santa Barbara's master photographer of the early 1900s." Born in Glendive, Montana, in 1883, Collinge grew up to capture the spirit and natural beauty of the Santa Barbara–central California region, photographing his images in black and white, and often hand painting them to accent their natural beauty. He photographed people, landscapes, homes and gardens, the Channel Islands, and even tall ships and automobiles.

Collinge's work was extensively exhibited at both national and international shows and exemplified the romantic images of the Pictorialist movement in America during the era. His photographs have been displayed at the U.S. National Museum, the 1930 Exhibition of American Pictorial Photography, and the 1934 Royal Photographic Society of Great Britain, among others. Probably better known for his black and white rather than his hand-painted images, Collinge also had some of his images distributed as postcards by the California Pictures Co.

REGIONALITY

Western U.S.; Santa Barbara, California

REPRESENTATIVE TITLES & VALUE GUIDE

"Redwoods"
Estimated value range: $50.00 – 150.00+

"Redwoods"

Paper label

CONSOLIDATED ART CO.

BACKGROUND

Little background information on the CONSOLIDATED ART CO. has been found. This is the only Consolidated Art Co. picture that we have seen. The original paper label indicates that the company was based in Boston, Massachusetts, which suggests that at least some of its work was done in New England. The company specialized in platinum prints.

REGIONALITY

New England; Boston, Massachusetts

REPRESENTATIVE TITLES & VALUE GUIDE

Untitled train scene
Estimated value range: $25.00 – 50.00+

Untitled train scene

Exterior scene

L. COOPER

BACKGROUND

Little background information on L. COOPER has been found. This is the only L. Cooper picture that we have seen, and the subject matter suggests that Cooper was based in the western U.S.

REGIONALITY

Western U.S.

REPRESENTATIVE TITLES & VALUE GUIDE

Untitled exterior scene
Estimated value range: $25.00 – 75.00

Exterior scene

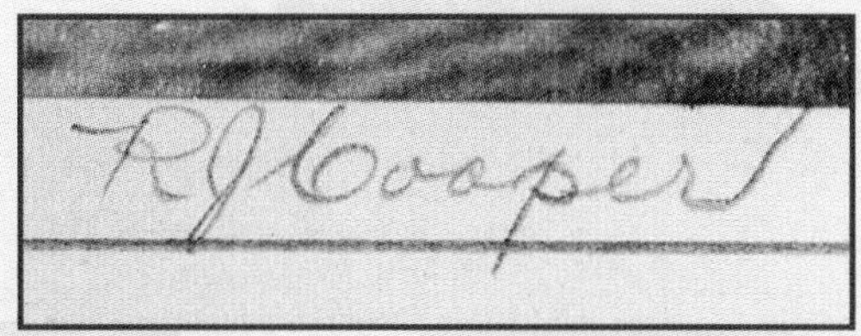

R. J. COOPER

BACKGROUND
Little background information on R. J. COOPER has been found. This is the only R. J. Cooper picture that we have seen, and the picture provided no clue as to its location or origin. We have been unable to confirm any relationship to L. Cooper.

REGIONALITY
Unknown

REPRESENTATIVE TITLES & VALUE GUIDE
Untitled exterior
Estimated value range: $25.00 – 50.00+

MRS. N. CORLIS

BACKGROUND
Little background information on MRS. N. CORLIS has been found. We have only seen one picture by her, an exterior scene taken at Post Mills, Vermont. The setting suggests that she was a Vermont photographer.

REGIONALITY
New England; Vermont

REPRESENTATIVE TITLES & VALUE GUIDE
Post Mills, Vermont, exterior scene
Estimated value range: $10.00 – 50.00+

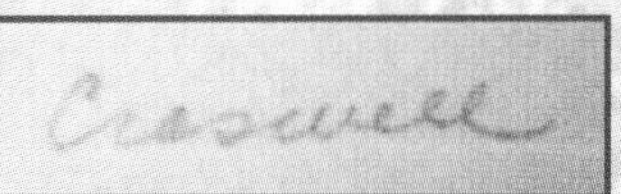

Oliver Cleveland Craswell (1892 – 1966)

OLIVER CLEVELAND CRASWELL (1892 – 1966)

BACKGROUND

OLIVER CLEVELAND "CLEVE" CRASWELL and his wife, Clarina "Babe" MacDonald, operated the Craswell Portrait Studio on Great George Street on Prince Edward Island, Canada, for nearly 40 years. Craswell's photographic career began at age 14, when he began as a photographers apprentice. In 1909, he began working for James Bayer in his Grafton Street photographic studio in Charlottestown, Canada. A short-term career in accounting preceded the opening of his own first photographic studio at 137 Great George Street. The Craswell Portrait Studio took over the Bayer studio in the 1930s and moved to 163 Great George Street.

Like many photographers of this era, Craswell was a commercial portrait, family, and wedding photographer. But he is best known to us for his popular hand-painted landscape scenes of Prince Edward Island and its surrounding area, which he sold to visiting tourists. Craswell was the photographer, and Mrs. Craswell served as the primary colorist.

Craswell Portrait Studio label

Craswell was an award-winning photographer, and was a member of several photographic associations. His work was exhibited at several international exhibitions, and he even photographed royalty, including the Duke of Windsor, King George VI and Queen Elizabeth, and Queen Elizabeth and Prince Phillip, among others. He also sponsored the first place prize in a local photography contest in an attempt to inspire amateur photographers.

REGIONALITY

Canada; Prince Edward Island

REPRESENTATIVE TITLES & VALUE GUIDE

Prince Edward Island

Estimated value range: $25.00 – 100.00+

Prince Edward Island, Canada

BARNETT CROWLEY

BACKGROUND

Little background information on BARNETT CROWLEY has been found. We have only seen one Crowley picture, and it was taken in Lake Charles, Louisiana, which suggests that Crowley may have been a Louisiana photographer.

REGIONALITY

Louisiana

REPRESENTATIVE TITLES & VALUE GUIDE

Untitled exterior
Estimated value range: $25.00 – 50.00+

C. D. CURRIER

BACKGROUND

Little background information on C. D. CURRIER has been found. The only C. D. Currier picture that we have seen was an exterior scene taken in Franklin, New Hampshire, which suggests that he may have been a New Hampshire photographer.

REGIONALITY

New England; New Hampshire

REPRESENTATIVE TITLES & VALUE GUIDE

Franklin, New Hampshire, exterior scene
Estimated value range: $10.00 – 50.00+

ASAHEL CURTIS (1874 – 1941)

Asahel Curtis (1874 – 1941)

BACKGROUND

ASAHEL CURTIS was the younger brother of famous western photographer Edward S. Curtis. He was born in Minnesota in 1874, and moved with his family to the Puget Sound area of Washington in 1888. His brother Edward opened a photographic studio in Seattle in 1892, and Asahel began working there in 1895.

In 1897, Asahel was sent by his brother to Alaska with approximately 3,000 glass-plate negatives to document the Klondike Gold Rush. Although Asahel took all of the photographs, they were credited to Edward Curtis, as was the practice of the time, because Edward was the owner of the business. There apparently was a falling out between the brothers, and Asahel did eventually regain control of the Klondike negatives, but not without causing long-term hard feelings with his brother.

In 1901 Asahel Curtis formed a partnership with William P. Romans, and the two opened the Curtis & Romans Studio. After a short period of time, Curtis went to work in San Francisco, California, and Tacoma, Washington, where he occasionally worked as a photoengraver. He then moved to Seattle, where he briefly worked as a newspaper photographer. From 1907 to 1911 he worked for the Romans Photographic Co., becoming president and manager of that firm. He later formed another partnership, with Walter Miller, and formed the Curtis & Miller Photographic Co. He later returned to the Romans Photographic Co., and sometime around 1920 this business became the Asahel Curtis Photo Co., which he operated until his death in 1941.

Mt. Rainier, Washington

Asahel Curtis was not only well known for the images he took during the Klondike Gold Rush in Alaska, he also took many landscape scenes throughout the Pacific Northwest. He was instrumental in the development of Mt. Rainier National Park and photographed many other outdoor fields, including logging, mining, fishing, and road and railroad construction. He also produced a wide array of other commercial photography.

The University of Washington libraries own a fairly large collection of Asahel Curtis images. Asahel Curtis hand-colored photographs are extremely collectible, and the value of his images is probably beyond the scope of this book.

REGIONALITY

Western U.S.; Washington State

REPRESENTATIVE TITLES & VALUE GUIDE

Mt. Rainier, Washington
Estimated value range: $500.00 – 5,000.00+

EDWARD S. CURTIS (1868 – 1951)

BACKGROUND

EDWARD S. CURTIS is probably one of the early twentieth century's most important and influential western photographers, and his importance and the value of his work is beyond the scope of this book. However, we will give him a quick mention here, and you can find significantly more details about him in other resources.

Edward S. Curtis (1868 – 1951)

Edward Curtis was born in Wisconsin in 1868, to Ellen and Johnson Curtis. He had several brothers and a sister. His most famous sibling was western photographer Asahel Curtis. Edward actually constructed his first camera himself, based upon the specifications found in the *Wilson Photographic Manual.* In 1887, he moved to Washington and settled in the Puget Sound area with his father, the two of them sending for the rest of the family the following spring. In 1892, Curtis married Clara Phillips, and soon thereafter opened a portrait studio in Seattle. In 1897, he dissolved his partnership with Thomas Guptill and renamed his business Edward S. Curtis, Photographer and Photoengraver.

In 1897, Edward sent his brother Asahel to Alaska with approximately 3,000 glass-plate negatives to document the Klondike Gold Rush. Although Asahel took all of the photographs, they were credited to Edward Curtis, as was the practice of the time, because Edward was the owner of the business. There apparently was a falling out between the brothers, and Asahel did eventually regain control of the Klondike negatives, but not without causing long-term hard feelings.

During his life, Curtis met and formed relationships with some very important individuals, including railroad tycoon Edward Harrison, Theodore Roosevelt, and the wealthy J. P. Morgan. While he was involved in numerous photographic activities, his most important activities involved photographing Native Americans. Curtis saw the American Indian as a vanishing race, and set out as his personal goal the task of photographing the culture, lifestyle, and customs of each remaining Indian Tribe before it became absorbed into America's white society and disappeared forever.

We have never had the opportunity to sell an Edward Curtis hand-painted photograph through our auctions, and perhaps we never will. However, you should understand that the works of Edward S. Curtis are extremely valuable and can easily bring in excess of $10,000.00 – 50,000.00-plus for his best work.

REGIONALITY

Western U.S.; Washington State

REPRESENTATIVE TITLES & VALUE GUIDE

Estimated value range: $5,000 – 50,000.00+

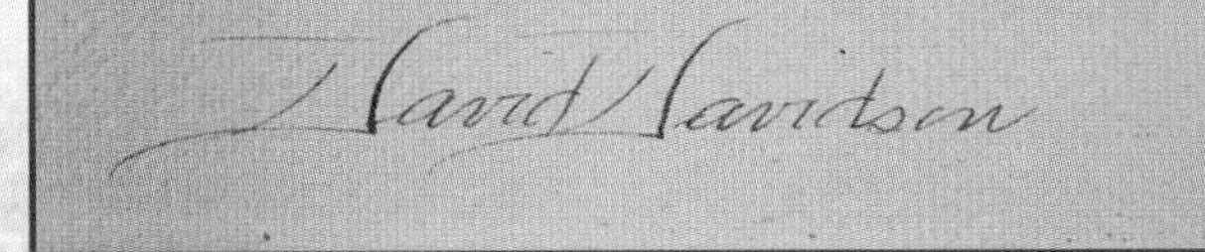

DAVID DAVIDSON (1881 – 1967)

BACKGROUND

DAVID DAVIDSON was born to John H. and Adelaide P. Davidson on February 24, 1881, in Providence, Rhode Island. He grew up in Providence and attended local schools there. In 1901 he entered Brown University, where he majored in civil engineering. Davidson was not born to a family of great means, and he had to work his way through college. While attending Brown, he worked four separate newspaper routes simultaneously to help raise money for tuition and books, living at home to reduce his education expenses.

While a student at Brown, Davidson also attended the Union Congregational Church in Providence. As luck would have it, the pastor at the Union Congregational Church just happened to be Wallace Nutting. Apparently, Rev. Nutting was looking for an assistant to work with him in various aspects of his growing photography hobby/business, and Davidson was only too eager to help. Davidson, then 20, developed a friendship with the 40-year-old Nutting and began working with Nutting on a part-time basis in Nutting's photography studio, which was located in the Edgewood-Cranston area of Rhode Island. Nutting was happy to find a younger man willing to carry his camera equipment, work in his darkroom, handle much of his matting and framing, and do many other related jobs that Nutting didn't really have time to do. And David Davidson was eager to learn the fine art of commercial photography from Wallace Nutting.

David Davidson (1881 – 1967), circa 1940

Although there has been speculation for many years about whether Nutting taught Davidson the art of photography or vice versa, it's quite clear that although Wallace Nutting was still learning and developing his photographic skills at the turn of the century, Nutting was the teacher and Davidson was the student, and they eventually worked together for several years.

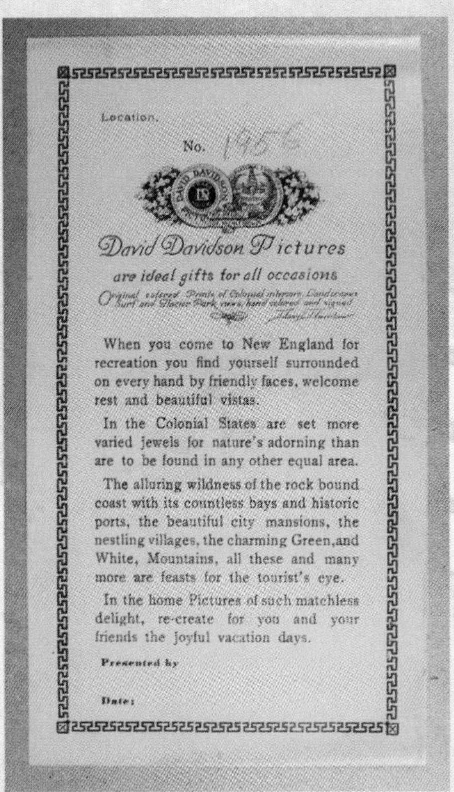

Location.

No. 1956

David Davidson Pictures

are ideal gifts for all occasions

Original colored Prints of Colonial interiors, Landscapes Surf and Glacier Park views, hand colored and signed

When you come to New England for recreation you find yourself surrounded on every hand by friendly faces, welcome rest and beautiful vistas.

In the Colonial States are set more varied jewels for nature's adorning than are to be found in any other equal area.

The alluring wildness of the rock bound coast with its countless bays and historic ports, the beautiful city mansions, the nestling villages, the charming Green, and White, Mountains, all these and many more are feasts for the tourist's eye.

In the home Pictures of such matchless delight, re-create for you and your friends the joyful vacation days.

Presented by

Date:

Paper label, circa 1930 – 1935

They shot many pictures together, trying new techniques and experimenting with different cameras, negatives, lighting, angles, and photographic papers. The most obvious example of their mutual work is a series of sheep pictures that were taken outside of Providence. Nutting's most commercially successful Sheep pictures over the years were "A Warm Spring Day," "On the Slope," and "Not One of the 400." Each of these pictures featured several dozen sheep grazing beside a colorful blue, tree-lined pond.

Davidson's most commercially successful sheep picture was titled "Beside Still Waters." If you look and compare Nutting's

Wallace Nutting, "Life of the Golden Age"

David Davidson, "Beside Still Water"

"A Warm Spring Day" and Davidson's "Beside Still Waters," you'll see the similarity between the two pictures. Based upon the foliage on the trees, the number and location of the sheep, and the time of day, it would seem safe to conclude that both pictures were taken on the same day. Whether both men shared one camera or each used his own equipment, there is no denying the similarity of the two pictures.

In 1904, Wallace Nutting decided to retire from the ministry due to ill health. He left Providence and opened a small photography studio in New York City. Shortly thereafter, he moved to Southbury, Connecticut, where he opened a small studio and continued to develop and refine his photographic process. Over the next 35 years, Wallace Nutting went on to become one of the twentieth century's most famous photographers.

After Nutting left Providence in 1904, Davidson continued his education, graduating from Brown University in 1905. Upon graduation, he took a full-time position with Providence Steel & Iron as a civil engineer, the career he trained for in college. Davidson worked for PS&I for two years while continuing to work with photography as his hobby. Apparently engineering didn't suit him as much as he expected, and he found himself increasingly drawn to photography.

Also in 1905, David Davidson married his college sweetheart, Louise Whitcher, who had graduated from the Pembroke College of Brown University that same year with a degree in English. She worked for several years as a teacher at the Peace Street Grammar School in Providence.

Home & Studio, 57 Whitemarsh St., Providence RI

In 1907, David and Louise Davidson jointly decided to leave their engineering and teaching careers, and together they opened David Davidson Studios at 57 Whitemarsh St. in Providence. The studio was located in a large three-story wood-frame building. The first floor included a picture showroom and was also where the framing, backing, labeling, boxing, packing, and shipping were handled. The second floor included the sales and accounting office and is where pictures were signed and titled. The darkroom was on the third floor, and was where pictures were developed, dried, enlarged, colored, and mounted. The cellar, which could be entered from both inside and outside the building, was used for storing boxes, picture frames, cardboard, glass, and wood shaving packing material. Nearly all aspects of the business were conducted at the Whitemarsh Street studio, and the building remained standing until 1967, when it was demolished to make room for an additional parking lot for a nearby hospital.

Davidson's work, although significantly smaller than Nutting's in both diversity and total volume, was larger in scope and volume than that of all other hand-colored photographers of the early twentieth century except for Wallace Nutting. We believe that David Davidson sold more hand-colored photographs during the early twentieth century than all of his contemporaries except Wallace Nutting.

Known Photographers

Davidson also used a photographic process very similar to that of other photographers. In the early years of his work, a box camera on a tripod stand, glass negatives, platinum paper, proper sizing and coloring, indented matting, and a lower-left title/lower-right signature all paralleled the work of Wallace Nutting. Pencil signatures were used in early years (1907 – 1915) and pen signatures in later years (1915-plus), as volume increased. Louise Davidson applied most of the titles and signatures, and according to Davidson's son Donald, many picture titles originated during meal-time discussions in the Davidson household.

No. 799—BLACKFEET SQUAWS
$2.50 $.50 $.35

Rare American Indian photo, from Davidson's salesmen's catalog

Whereas Nutting traveled throughout much of the country and Europe taking his more than 10,000 different pictures, Davidson remained primarily in New England. He became best known for his pictures of Rhode Island, including those of Roger Williams Park and of colonial Kingston, and his pictures of Vermont and of the White Mountains of New Hampshire. And although Davidson never traveled to Europe, he did take a trip to the western United States and Canada, photographing both the Canadian Rockies and Native Americans. Although Davidson's Canadian Rockies pictures are unusual, they can still be found. Although several are pictured in his 1917 and 1925 salesmen's catalogs, in 25-plus years of searching, we have never had the opportunity to acquire one of his American Indian pictures, which would seem to indicate that they were very poor sellers. Today, almost any Davidson collector would give nearly anything to add such a picture to his or her collection. We have even seen one sell on eBay for more than $1,000.00.

Rare hand-colored lithograph

Over a 40-year period, Davidson produced more than 1,000 picture titles. Some titles sold literally thousands of copies each, while other titles were very poor sellers and resulted in minimal sales. As each new picture title was assigned, it was entered into Davidson's studio number book. Each picture was assigned an individual number; these numbers were used to identify loose pictures within the studio and to facilitate picture orders. Subsequently, Davidson produced various salesmen's picture catalogs, which were given to his salesmen and to department stores, and pictures were ordered by either the title or the studio number. To date, we have seen four separate catalogs (1909, 1911, 1917, and 1925). Each catalog was larger than the one preceding it, indicating that both Davidson's business and picture inventory were growing.

Davidson's business was small in comparison to Nutting's. At its peak, he employed a staff of fewer than 12 people (compared to Nutting's 200+ employees). Hardly a wedding event in the Rhode Island area went by where the bride didn't receive at least one Davidson picture as a wedding or shower gift. When Davidson's son got married, even he received a Davidson picture as a gift, from an acquaintance who didn't realize that David Davidson was his father.

Close-framed interior scene

Davidson pictures were generally sold in department stores and gift shops. The Shepperd Company in Providence had an entire David Davidson room in which Davidson pictures were displayed, framed, and sold. Davidson employed two traveling salesmen who sold his pictures to stores throughout New England and New York, and it was not uncommon for Davidson himself to call on a new prospective client and walk out with a picture order in hand.

Davidson produced colonial interior scenes, with Mrs. Davidson posing in many of them. Although his interiors were very well done and quite colorful and charming, they generally did not equal Nutting's interiors in terms of quality and variety of antique furniture and accessories used, or in the manner the room was decorated. Nutting possessed a knowledge of antiques that was unparalleled by any other photographer of his day, and this, along with Nutting's extensive personal collection of antiques and his knowledge of where to borrow those pieces that he didn't already own, enabled Nutting to put together colonial settings that were unsurpassed by any other photographer.

As his business grew, Davidson began to expand beyond basic framed pictures into calendars, greeting cards, and other, more unusual items. These helped him increase sales, and they are quite desirable to collectors today. As a businessman, Davidson learned to change with the times. Early pictures were more subtly colored than the brightly colored pictures of the 1930s. Although most of Davidson's pictures were mounted on indented matboards, he also produced close-framed pictures and even pictures mounted on gold foil mattings. Davidson also resorted to machine-produced four-color process prints (which he called facsimile prints) as expenses increased and sales declined.

During World War I, David Davidson made the change to motion pictures, producing *The Rhode Island Weekly,* a motion picture newsreel that brought actual World War I film footage to the home front. His weekly war newsreels became a regular feature at local movie theaters during the war. Also during World War I, David Davidson worked as an instructor for enlisted men, teaching them the fine art of photography.

Matted exterior scene

In 1918, Davidson was appointed to the Rhode Island War Photographs Committee by then-governor Beeckman. His objective was to collect and preserve a photographic history of Rhode Island's activities during World War I. This not only included actual war footage from the front, but also home activities such as mobilization, parades, demonstrations of support, industrial contributions, and the like. He completed this assignment with much praise for his precision and accuracy.

But as far as collectors of hand-colored photography are concerned, Davidson's work is well recognized because of the high quality of his pictures. And unlike Nutting, who won no awards for his photography, Davidson once won a bronze medal in the category of hand-colored photography, when he entered the 1915 Panama-Pacific Exposition competition.

After more than 30 years of rising picture sales, the public began to lose interest in hand-colored photographs, including those of David Davidson. His orders began to decline. Davidson continued selling hand-colored photographs into the early 1950s, but on a significantly smaller scale than in the 1910 – 1940 peak period. America's constantly changing tastes and the invention of color photography led to a gradual decline in business, with sales of his hand-colored photographs slowing to a trickle after the Great Depression. Much of Davidson's later business included color photography, for commercial and private commissions and assignments.

Davidson retired in 1955, after spending more than 50 years in the photography business. He died on February 3, 1967, at the age of 85, at the Gray Rock Rest Home in Cumberland, Rhode Island.

Interest in David Davidson hand-colored photographs is on the rise today. As the price of Wallace Nutting pictures has increased over the past 10 years, an increasing number of collectors have been drawn to David Davidson pictures. Their high quality and relatively low price has caused the number of Davidson collectors to grow. Collections of over 100 Davidson pictures are not uncommon today. The largest Davidson collection we know of had more than 300 pictures at last count, and most likely there are many other large collections that we are not even aware of.

Miscellaneous thoughts:

* Other hand-colored items: Davidson also produced a series of calendars and greeting cards, most of which contained a smaller hand-colored picture.

* Facsimile prints: A very limited number of David Davidson titles are machine-produced facsimile prints. If you see the word *facsimile* on the picture label, it means that the picture was machine-produced and has minimal value. Collectors generally prize the hand-colored pictures and have extremely little interest in the machine-produced pictures. If in doubt, inspect the picture with a 15x magnifying glass. If you see a series of small symmetrical dots, it is a machine-produced print.

* Pencil vs. pen signatures: Davidson's earliest pictures were signed in pencil (1907 – 1915). His later pictures (1915-plus) were signed in pen. Many Davidson pen signatures have severely faded. Beware that a faded signature will significantly reduce the value of a picture, perhaps by 50% or more.

Christmas Card, which includes a matted, hand-painted picture inside

1939 calendar

Exterior scene

* Close-framed pictures: Pictures framed without a matting are called "close-framed" pictures and typically date the picture as 1925 or later.

* Backing labels: Over the years, Davidson affixed different advertising labels on the picture backing, and the type of label on the backing paper can help date the picture. Although many backings have become extremely brittle or have fallen off over the years, many still remain intact. A label promoting Davidson's award-winning medal at the 1915 San Francisco Panama-Pacific Exposition will typically date a picture circa 1915 – 1925. A larger yellow label would date the picture circa 1925 – 1940. Knowledgeable collectors frequently look for pictures with these original labels and sometimes pay a premium price for them. An original label on the picture backing can help you to date the picture and can add 10 – 15% to the value of a picture.

Original box

REGIONALITY

New England; Rhode Island; Massachusetts; western U.S.; western Canada

REPRESENTATIVE TITLES & VALUE GUIDE

"The Barefoot Boy"
"Beside Still Water"
"Bridal Aisle"
"Diadem Aisle"
"Her House in Order"
"Old Ironsides"
"Sunset Point"
"Wisteria"
Typical value range: $50.00 – 250.00+

RECOMMENDED READING

See the David Davidson chapter in *Collector's Value Guide to Early 20th Century American Prints* (Collector Books, by Michael Ivankovich), which includes a listing of all known 1,000+ Davidson titles. Also see our Exploring Early 20th C. Prints column on our website:
www.michaelivankovich.com

Unusual Davidson triptych

Clustering birches

WILLIS A. DEANE

BACKGROUND

Little background information on WILLIS A. DEANE has been found. Each of the Willis Deane pictures we have seen was an exterior scene. Although each was pencil signed "Willis A. Deane" in the lower right beneath the image, each was also marked "Copyright 1906 by Taber-Prang Art Co.," which suggests that Dean's hand-colored photographs were distributed by the Taber-Prang Art Co. (See Taber-Prang Art Co.)

REGIONALITY

New England; Vermont

REPRESENTATIVE TITLES & VALUE GUIDE

Franklin, Vermont, exterior scene
Estimated value range: $10.00 – 50.00+

Stately pines

DEGROOT (first name not known)

BACKGROUND

Little background information on DEGROOT has been found. It has been reported to us that a DeGroot hand-painted photo of the Wesley Oak on St. Simon's Island, Georgia, was found. This image contained a "(c) 1931 DeGroot" on the image. A paper label stated that "this picture is copyrighted and sold by Stanton and DeGroot." However, the "Stanton" portion of the label had been crossed out as if the two had parted company and DeGroot was now the sole owner of the business.

REGIONALITY

Georgia

REPRESENTATIVE TITLES & VALUE GUIDE

Wesley Oak
Estimated value range: $10.00 – 50.00+

MACK DEREK

Classic Vermont Scenics

BACKGROUND

MACK M. DEREK was a well-known photographer in the Orleans, Vermont, area for over 60 years. Married for 65 years, he had two daughters. Derek received considerable recognition for his work during his many years as photographer for Vermont Publicity Services, supplying photographs to *Vermont Life* magazine and to assorted Vermont advertising calendars. Two of his most famous pictures were "Dawn of a New Day" (taken on Lake Willoughby) and "Autumn Dryad," which was used as an early 1946 *Vermont Life* cover photo.

Prior to turning to commercial and scenic photography, Derek received wide acclaim as a portrait photographer and was listed in the *Who's Who in American Portrait Photographers*. He was the founder of the Vermont Association of Professional Photographers, served as its first president, and was active in the organization for nearly 50 years.

Over the years, we have seen only a few Derek hand-painted photographs, suggesting that he sold relatively few of this type of image over the years. In more recent years, a company called Creative Image Studio announced that it had purchased the complete collection of "Mr. Mack Derek's Classic Vermont Scenics" and was reissuing them as decorator prints both in framed and unframed format.

REGIONALITY

New England; Orleans, Vermont

REPRESENTATIVE TITLES & VALUE GUIDE

Vermont exterior scenes
Estimated value range: $25.00 – 100.00+

VAN DERK

BACKGROUND

VAN DERK operated the Derk Studios in Orleans, Vermont. We have only seen one Van Derk picture, an exterior scene, and we suspect that it was a later image circa 1960.

REGIONALITY

New England; Orleans, Vermont

REPRESENTATIVE TITLES & VALUE GUIDE

Exterior scene
Estimated value range: $10.00 – 50.00+

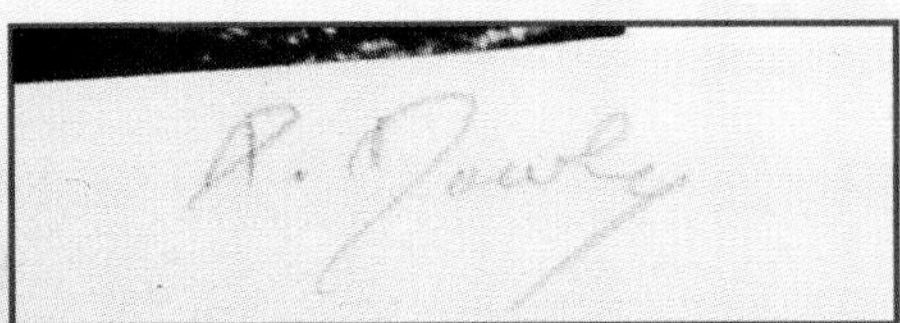

"Lone Palm, Bermuda"

R. DOWLY

BACKGROUND
We have seen several R. DOWLY pictures, and each was taken in Bermuda. Generally the quality has been comparable to that of the major photographers.

REGIONALITY
Bermuda

REPRESENTATIVE TITLES & VALUE GUIDE
"Lone Palm, Bermuda"
"Reid Hall"
Estimated value range: $50.00 – 100.00+

DEPUE BROS.

"The Straggler"

BACKGROUND
Little background information on DEPUE BROTHERS has been found. We have only seen one Depue Bros. picture, a seascape. In our opinion, it was taken in New England, which suggests that Depue Bros. may have been a New England photography company.

REGIONALITY
New England

REPRESENTATIVE TITLES & VALUE GUIDE
"The Straggler"
Estimated value range: $50.00 – 75.00+

EDDY (first name not known)

BACKGROUND
Little background information on EDDY has been found. We have only seen two Eddy pictures, both of which came into the marketplace together, from the same house. Both depicted southern cotton fields, and one depicted African Americans picking cotton. We had never before and have never since seen this particular subject matter. We suspect that Eddy was a southern photographer, probably from Alabama or Mississippi, who sold such pictures as part of the tourist trade.

REGIONALITY
Southern U.S.

REPRESENTATIVE TITLES & VALUE GUIDE
"Cotton Picking Time"
"Southern Pines"
Estimated value range: $50.00 – 150.00+

"A Shady Path," matted, signed, titled

NORMAN S. EDSON (1876 – 1968)

BACKGROUND

Somewhat of a Renaissance man, Norman Edson not only studied photography but was a student of painting in Paris, a poet, and a violinist as well. Edson was born in Montreal, Canada, in May 1876 and was the son of Allan Edson, a noted painter. After following his wife's family to Everett, Washington, he served a photographic apprenticeship under Bert J. Brush, even living with the Brush family for a while. In around 1905, he opened his own studio at 1708 Hewitt St. in Everett. After a move to Chicago, he returned to Everett in 1918, where he continued to work as a photographer for another four years prior to moving to Burton, Washington, on Vashon Island in 1921 (which was a short ferry ride to Seattle). There Edson continued with his photography, painting, poetry, and music, and he did some writing as well. Best known for his colorful hand-painted images of Mt. Rainier and other beautiful northwestern U.S. landscape scenes, he also took a number of Native American images at the Tulalip Reservation around 1905.

One of Edson's specialties was goldtones. A goldtone (or orotone) begins as a black and white photographic image printed on glass. The back of the glass is then painted with a gold and oil mixture or a bronze powder mixed in resin, the same technique one would use to paint a hand-painted mirror. This process creates a brilliant three-dimensional effect that changes as light reflects off the gold backing.

Norman Edson died on January 20, 1968. Some of his work has been acquired by the University of Washington, as part of its photographic collection, and by the Everett Public Library, as part of its collection.

Mt. Rainier, close-framed

REGIONALITY

Northwestern U. S.; Vashon Island, Washington

REPRESENTATIVE TITLES & VALUE GUIDE

The Knoll, Bolton Pass
"Mt. Rainier"
"A Shady Path"
Typical value range: $100.00 – 300.00+

close-framed view of Mt. Rainier

White ink signature on image

"Norman Edson (c)," lower right on image

J. BOYD ELLIS

BACKGROUND

Little background information on J. BOYD ELLIS has been found. We have only seen one Ellis image, and it was a Washington State scene of Mt. Baker, which suggests that Ellis was a Washington State photographer. We have also seen reference to Washington State postcards being issued by a J. Boyd Ellis.

REGIONALITY

Northwestern U.S.; Washington State

REPRESENTATIVE TITLES & VALUE GUIDE

Mt. Baker
Estimated value range: $50.00 – 100.00+

P. ERIKSON

BACKGROUND

Little background information on P. ERICKSON has been found. We have only seen one Erikson picture, an exterior scene, and in our opinion it was taken in New England, which suggests that Erikson may have been a New England photographer.

REGIONALITY

New England

REPRESENTATIVE TITLES & VALUE GUIDE

Untitled exterior scene
Estimated value range: $10.00 – 50.00+

MAY FARINI

BACKGROUND

May Farini was primarily a postcard artist, not a photographer, but we have included her in this book because her work is so often confused with hand-colored photographs. Like Bessie Pease Gutmann and the Guttman & Gutmann Co., May Farini introduced a series of colonial scenes in an attempt to compete with Wallace Nutting's Colonial Revival interior scenes. Although they look like, and are often confused with, hand-painted photographs, Farini's pictures are actually color lithographs. They are typically pencil signed "Farini" in the lower right and range in size from 5" x 7" to 11" x 14".

REGIONALITY

Unknown

REPRESENTATIVE TITLES & VALUE GUIDE

"Au Revoir"
"Days of Old"
"In the Garden"
"An Old Sweet Song"
Typical value range: $25.00 – 75.00+

LESTER FARNUM (1880 – 1970)

BACKGROUND

According to collectors Lee and Joan Owens, Lester Farnum was born in 1880 in Manchester, Vermont, and was an only child. His father was a builder, a carpenter, and a house painter. In 1904, Lester Farnum began work for the MD&G Railroad. He was also a sign painter, and a clarinetist in the Manchester band. In 1917 he married Hilda Barrett, and they had two children (Mary and Allen). In 1926 Farnum moved to Boston to find work, but he later returned to Manchester to begin work for David Bulkley as a photographer's assistant. During the 1950s Farnum's health failed, at which time he sold his house in Manchester and went to live with his daughter in Oregon. Lester Farnum died in 1970.

We have seen relatively few Lester Farnum hand-painted pictures over the years, but those that we have seen were comparable in quality and theme to those of the other major photographers.

"Mt. Equinox, Manchester, Vermont"

REGIONALITY

New England; Manchester, Vermont

REPRESENTATIVE TITLES & VALUE GUIDE

"Mt. Equinox, Manchester, Vermont"
Estimated value range: $50.00 – 100.00+
Typical value range: $25.00 – 75.00+

E. L. FOOTE

BACKGROUND
Little background information on E. L. FOOTE has been found. We have only seen one Foote picture, an exterior scene. In our opinion, it was taken in New England, which suggests that Foote may have been a New England photographer.

REGIONALITY
New England

REPRESENTATIVE TITLES & VALUE GUIDE
Untitled exterior scene
Estimated value range: $10.00 – 50.00+

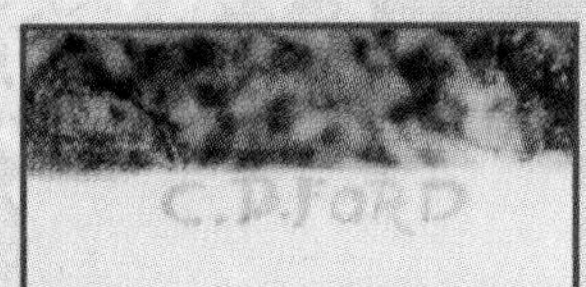

C. D. FORD

BACKGROUND
Little background information on C. D. FORD has been found. We have only seen one Ford picture, an exterior scene taken in the western U.S. and possibly in the Red Rocks or Garden of the Gods region of Colorado. This suggests to us that Ford was probably a western U.S. photographer.

REGIONALITY
Western U.S.; Colorado

REPRESENTATIVE TITLES & VALUE GUIDE
Untitled western U.S. scene
Estimated value range: $50.00 – 75.00+

Western U.S. scene

GEORGE FOREST

BACKGROUND

Little background information on GEORGE FOREST has been found. We have only seen one Forest picture, an exterior scene. In our opinion, it was taken in New England, which suggests that he was a New England photographer.

REGIONALITY

New England

REPRESENTATIVE TITLES & VALUE GUIDE

"The New Divinity"
Estimated value range: $10.00 – 50.00+

Emma B. Freeman (1880 – 1928)

EMMA B. FREEMAN (1880 – 1928)

BACKGROUND

EMMA BELLE FREEMAN was born in Nebraska in 1880. She apparently studied painting in San Francisco and operated a small store there. She left San Francisco in 1906, due to the earthquake and fire, and relocated with her husband in Eureka, California, where she was a commercial photographer circa 1906 – 1919. Between 1910 and 1920, Freeman produced a series of portraits of Native Amerians. In 1919 she relocated to San Francisco, where she died in 1928. Best known for her images of American Indians, she also took hand-painted photographs of California landscape scenes and even some U.S. military images, including American submarines circa 1916. Many of her photographs are marked "Freeman Art Co."

Though sometimes shunned for her bohemian early twentieth century feminist lifestyle, Freeman did much to enhance public awareness for northern California Native Americans. An album of Freeman's photographs can be found at the California State Library in Sacramento, California, and other photographs may be seen at the Newberry Library in Chicago, Illinois.

REGIONALITY

Eureka, California

REPRESENTATIVE TITLES & VALUE GUIDE

Close-framed California redwoods scene
Estimated value range: $50.00 – 150.00+

California redwoods

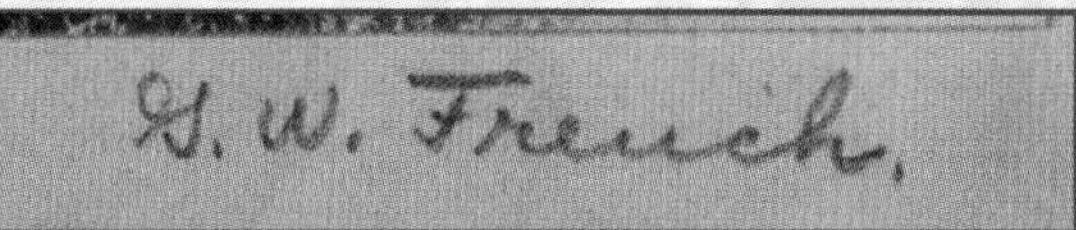

"Monson, Mass."

G. W. FRENCH

BACKGROUND

Little background information on G. W. FRENCH has been found. We have only seen one French picture, which was taken in Monson, Massachusetts. This suggests that French may have been a Massachusetts photographer.

REGIONALITY

New England; Massachusetts

REPRESENTATIVE TITLES & VALUE GUIDE

"Monson, Mass."
Estimated value range: $25.00 – 50.00+

City skyline

LEO FURBACK

BACKGROUND

Little background information on LEO FURBACK has been found. We have only seen one Furback picture, an exterior scene with a 1918 copyright on the image. The large mountain rising in the distance behind a large metropolitan city suggests it was taken in the Pacific Northwest.

REGIONALITY

Western U.S.; possibly Pacific Northwest

REPRESENTATIVE TITLES & VALUE GUIDE

Close-framed western U.S. city
Estimated value range: $50.00 – 100.00+

"Misty Harbor, Nova Scotia"

GALLOWAY

BACKGROUND

Little background information on GALLOWAY has been found. We have only seen one Galloway picture, a seascape harbor scene taken in Nova Scotia, Canada which suggests that he was a Canadian photographer.

REGIONALITY

Canada; Nova Scotia

REPRESENTATIVE TITLES & VALUE GUIDE

"Misty Harbor, Nova Scotia"
Estimated value range: $50.00 – 75.00+

GANDARA (first name not known)

BACKGROUND

Little background information on GANDARA has been found. We have only seen one Gandara picture, an exterior scene. In our opinion, it was taken in New England, which suggests that he was a New England photographer.

REGIONALITY

New England

REPRESENTATIVE TITLES & VALUE GUIDE

Exterior scene
Estimated value range: $10.00 – 50.00+

H Marshall Gardiner

H. MARSHALL GARDINER (1884 – 1942)

H. Marshall Gardiner (1884 – 1942)

BACKGROUND

H. MARSHALL GARDINER was born on September 18, 1884, into a photographic family led by his father, W. H. Gardiner. Some sources list his first name as *Harry*; other sources list it as *Henry*. He was born in Windsor, Ontario, Canada, but his family immigrated to the United States circa 1890. Once the family was settled, W. H. Gardiner opened two photographic studios, one in Detroit, Michigan, to operate during the winter months, and a second at Mackinac Island, Michigan, to operate during the more tourist-oriented summer months. Recognizing the potential of Florida's rapidly growing tourist trade, around 1894 or 1895 H. Marshall Gardiner moved with his family from Detroit to Daytona, Florida, which proved much more accommodating to the family's photography business during the colder winter months.

H. Marshall Gardiner learned many of his photographic techniques from his father prior to going out on his own at a relatively early age. Whereas his father generally used wet collodian negatives, technology had advanced enough that H. Marshall Gardiner was able to use gelatin dry plates in his earlier years. And in later years, he was able to utilize the less expensive and much more convenient roll film.

Another very important lesson Gardiner learned from his father was that one of the keys to operating a successful photography business was to set up shop in a tourist resort. Early in his career, Gardiner traveled to Bermuda. There he shot a series of beautiful Bermuda scenes that he hand-colored and sold as part of the Bermuda tourist trade. Sold there over a considerable period of time, these Bermuda scenes provided a nice revenue stream as the years went on. They proved so popular that we have even seen some with pre-printed (vs. hand-signed) signatures, suggesting a significant enough sales volume to justify the considerable expense of pre-printing mats.

Art Shops paper label

Around 1910, Gardiner first traveled to the island of Nantucket, just off the coastline of Massachusetts's Cape Cod. He was around 26 at the time, and the year-round population of Nantucket was just over 2,500, not nearly enough to sustain a photography business for the entire year. On Nantucket, Gardiner opened a joint photography and art supplies store. Working as Nantucket's exclusive agent for Eastman Kodak, his business expanded to include the island's only photofinishing service. However, with such a small year-round population, even the addition of a gift shop to compliment the hand-painted photographs, general portrait and photographic services, and art supplies couldn't sustain him on Nantucket year-round.

So during the winter months he helped with the family's photography businesses in Daytona and on Mackinac Island. And upon his father's death in 1935, Gardiner took over the family business in Daytona on a full-time basis.

H. Marshall Gardiner was married twice. His first marriage was to a Nantucket Macy, who was a descendent of one of the founding families of Nantucket. She died after eight years of marriage. He then married Bertha Coffin Chase, a descendent of another Nantucket founding family.

"The Rainbow Fleet, Homeward Bound"

H. Marshall Gardiner's hand-painted photographs are very similar to those by Wallace Nutting and the other leading New England photographers. That is, most are matted, usually on white matboard, have platemark indentations around the images, are signed "H. Marshall Gardiner" lower right beneath the images, and are titled lower left beneath the images. And most are framed in thinner frames, also in the style of Wallace Nutting.

It seems that H. Marshall Gardiner produced works in three primary locations, Nantucket, Florida, and Bermuda. And the desirability of Gardiner's work with collectors generally ranks in that order.

"Main Street, Nantucket"

H. Marshall Gardiner's Nantucket hand-painted photographs are undoubtedly his most desirable works. Money generally lives on Nantucket, and both full-time and part-time residents, as well as visitors and tourists, love to collect Gardiner's hand-painted Nantucket photographs. Scenes with buildings and people are often the most desirable. Seascapes and location-specific exterior scenes are also highly collectible. His more generic exterior scenes are probably the least collectible of his various Nantucket views. Although for a short period of time around 2000 – 2002 prices were topping $1,000.00 for the rarest Nantucket scenes in the best condition, the high-end market has softened somewhat, and today the better Gardiner Nantucket scenes will more commonly sell in the $250.00 – 500.00 range. Apparently the Gardiner Nantucket market on eBay was driven by only a small handful of collectors, and once they either acquired a desired title or dropped out of the market, top prices started to fall back into line. More common Nantucket titles and those pictures in damaged condition can bring considerably less.

Gardiner's Florida hand-painted photographs are becoming increasinly collectible to both hand-painted photography collectors and general-line Florida collectors. Most of Gardiner's Florida scenes are more generic (palms, coastlines, hanging moss, streams, sand, etc.). Location-specific pictures will generally bring stronger prices than will the more generic Florida scenes, and you can typically expect Gardiner's Florida hand-colored photos to sell in the $100.00 – $250.00 range.

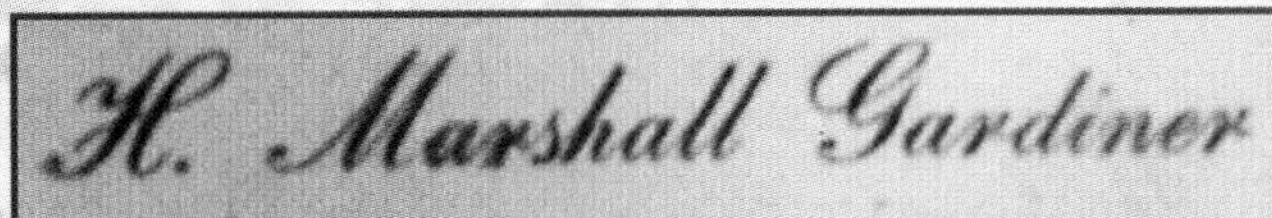

Pre-printed signature

And his Bermuda scenes, although the least collectible of the three primary Gardiner categories, are still highly prized by collectors. However, since we have seen fewer Bermuda collectors than Florida or Nantucket collectors, prices for Bermuda scenes will generally run between $75.00 and $150.00 at our auctions.

Gardiner's postcards are also widely collected. Unlike his hand-painted photographs, which can command a premium price today, his Nantucket postcards are much easier to locate and are much more affordable. And if you like the photography of H. Marshall Gardiner, you will be able to find considerably more views in postcards than in hand-colored photographs. Most of Gardiner's postcards were produced by the Detroit Publishing Company using its Phostint patented printing process. Although some black and white postcards may be found, his most popular and numerous postcards are in color. Generally, H. Marshall Gardiner postcards will bring $2.50 – 10.00 each, although certain ones may bring somewhat higher prices.

Book about H. Marshall Gardiner

H. Marshall Gardiner died on December 4, 1942, and is buried on his beloved Nantucket.

REGIONALITY

New England; Nantucket, Massachusetts; Daytona, Florida; Bermuda

REPRESENTATIVE TITLES & VALUE GUIDE

"The Barney House, Nantucket"
"Bermuda"
"Main Street, Nantucket"
"Morning Duties"
"The Rainbow Fleet, Nantucket"
"Sconset By-Paths"
Bermuda: $75.00 – 150.00+
Florida: $150.00 – 25.00+
Nantucket: $25.00 – 50.00+

"Bermuda"

RECOMMENDED READING

For further information on H. Marshall Gardiner we refer you to a book by his daughter, Geraldine Gardiner Salisbury, titled *H. Marshall Gardiner's Nantucket Postcards: 1910 – 1940.*

W. H. GARDINER (1861 – 1935)

"Arch Rock, Mackinac"

BACKGROUND

WILLIAM HENRY GARDINER was born in Canada on December 10, 1861, and was best known for his hand-colored photographs of Mackinac Island, Michigan, and Daytona, Florida. Gardiner's photographic career began in around 1881 in Toronto, Canada, when he was approximately 20 years old. In 1883 Gardiner married Louise East, and in 1884 they had their first son, H. Marshall Gardiner.

At this time, W. H. Gardiner had the opportunity to work with several highly regarded photographers who helped him expand his photographic knowledge. He also opened his own business, specializing in studio portraits, cabinet cards, and commercial photography. But by 1890 he found it increasing difficult to make a fair living as a photographer in Canada, so W. H. Gardner picked up his family and business and moved to the United States, settling in Detroit, Michigan.

While starting his new business venture in Detroit, Gardiner heard about the beauty of Mackinac Island. Located in northern Michigan, where Lake Michigan and Lake Huron meet between Michigan's upper and lower peninsulas, its natural beauty made it a favorite gathering place for the rich and famous. Gardiner saw some significant business opportunities here and moved his family and business from Detroit to Mackinac Island.

Here is an interesting tidbit of information. The first federally declared national park in the United States was Yellowstone National Park in Wyoming. The beauty of Yellowstone attracted such famous hand-colored picture photographers as F. Jay Haynes, and it was Haynes's beautiful hand-colored photographs that helped to popularize and promote Yellowstone with the American public.

What was the second federally declared national park in the United States? Mackinac Island, of course. Somewhere around 1895, Gardiner established a summer photography studio at Mackinac Island, first publishing postcards and tourist photo packs with his original Mackinac photographs. A few years later, around 1900 – 1905, Gardiner expanded his photography business to include hand-colored photographs. And just as Haynes's photographs helped popularize and promote Yellowstone with the American public, Gardiner's photographs helped to popularize and promote Mackinac Island with America's growing tourist trade. At the same time, Gardiner's Mackinac Island photography probably brought him more national attention than anything else that he did.

It was right around this time, in 1905, that America's hand-colored photography craze was beginning to take off. Wallace Nutting was just getting started in Southbury, Connecticut, David Davidson was an amateur photographer in Providence, Rhode Island, Fred Thompson's studio was up and running in Portland, Maine, Charles

Sawyer was just beginning in Farmington, Maine, and W. H. Gardiner's studio was rapidly growing in Mackinac Island, Michigan.

As tourists frequented Mackinac Island in sufficient numbers only during the summer months, W. H. Gardiner made a very intelligent business move. Around 1895, he moved his family and business to the warmer climate of Daytona during the colder winter months. Gardiner used the same formula in Daytona as he did on Mackinac Island: studio portraits, cabinet cards, and commercial photography for the local trade, and postcards, photo packs, and hand-painted photographs for the tourist trade.

W. H. Gardiner's Mackinac and Florida hand-colored photographs were typical of the period. A hand-tinted photo was mounted upon a white mat, had a platemark indentation around the picture, was signed "W. H. Gardiner" or, occasionally, "Gardiner" on the lower right below the image, was usually pencil signed, and was titled on the lower left below the image. Gardiner sold primarily exterior scenes — lakes, streams, and local foliage in Michigan, and palm trees, warm-weather lakes, hanging moss, and other stereotypical southern outdoor scenes in Florida. Some of Gardiner's most desirable works were taken of the historic fortifications at Ft. Mackinac, and location-specific titles (e.g., Arch Rock, Mackinac) will generally bring higher prices than generic scenes taken in unknown locations. We have never seen a colonial interior scene by W. H. Gardiner.

Near Daytona, Florida

"Fort Mackinac"

Gardiner's Mackinac pictures will generally be more desirable to Michigan collectors, and Florida pictures are typically valued higher by Florida collectors. Hand-colored photographs by W. H. Gardiner can bring anywhere from $75.00 to 200.00-plus, with final value depending upon size, rarity, and condition.

W. H. Gardiner died of a heart attack on October 22, 1935, in Georgia, while enroute to another winter season in Daytona. He was buried in Canada.

Fortunately, nearly 3,000 of Gardiner's original glass-plate negatives have been preserved. After his death, they were donated to the Mackinac State Historical Parks (MSHP). Today they are stored in a climate controlled storage vault at the Mackinac State Historic Parks Heritage Center at Mackinac Island.

REGIONALITY
Mackinac Island, Michigan; Daytona, Florida

REPRESENTATIVE TITLES & VALUE GUIDE
"Arch Rock, Mackinac"
"Fort Mackinac"
"Giant Staircase, Mackinac"
"Tomoka River, Florida"
Mackinac Island: $100.00 – 300.00
Florida: $100.00 – 250.00

RECOMMENDED READING

For further details on W. H. Gardiner, we refer you to an in-depth article published by Lisa Calache in *Photographic Canadiana*, volume 24 number 2, September-October 1998, pages 8 – 14.

Backstamp

GARLAND (first name not known)

BACKGROUND

GARLAND was a Massachusetts photographer who worked out of Rockland, Massachusetts. We have only seen two exterior scenes by Garland, with each featuring typical New England subject matter such as covered bridges, foliage, blossoms, etc. A backstamp on several of his images read "Photo by Garland, Rockland Mass."

REGIONALITY

New England; Rockland, Massachusetts

REPRESENTATIVE TITLES & VALUE GUIDE

Miniature covered bridge
Miniature fall-colored trees
Estimated value range: $25.00 – 50.00

Close-framed covered bridge

F. E. GARRETT

BACKGROUND

We have only seen one F .E. GARRETT hand-painted photograph, and we believe he was from Darling's Island, New Brunswick, Canada.

REGIONALITY

Canada; Darling's Island, New Brunswick Province

REPRESENTATIVE TITLES & VALUE GUIDE

Exterior scene
Estimated value range: $25.00 – 50.00+

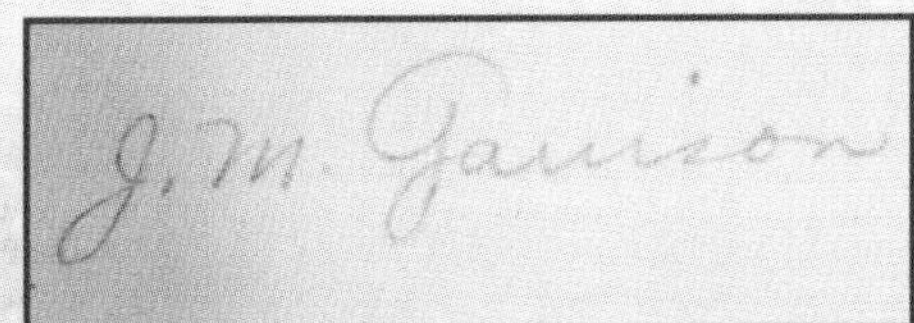

J. M. GARRISON

BACKGROUND

Researching J. M. GARRISON has probably been the oddest part of writing this book about hand-painted photography, because although we have seen more than 25 Garrison pictures and titles, we have found absolutely no information about the photographer. It would appear that Garrison worked primarily in the American Southwest, most likely California, because most images we have seen are desert or Spanish mission scenes. His work is beautiful, its quality is excellent, there is a fair amount of it available, yet to date we have learned little about J. M. Garrison.

REGIONALITY

Western U.S.

"Yucca Blossoms"

REPRESENTATIVE TITLES & VALUE GUIDE

Desert verbanas and primroses
Typical value range: $50.00 – 150.00

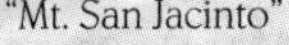
"Mt. San Jacinto"

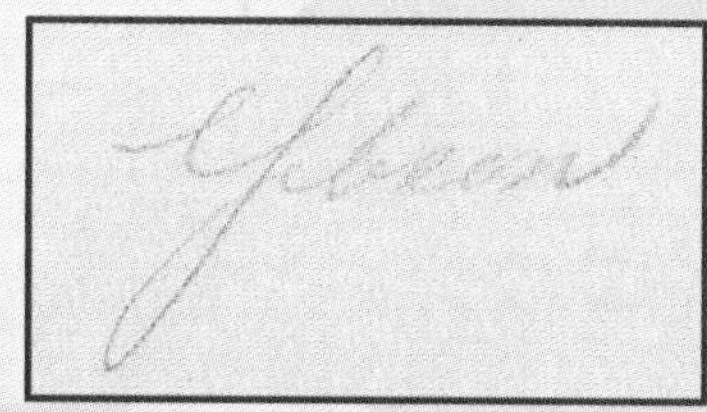

Pre-printed signature

GIBSON (first name not known)

BACKGROUND

Gibson presents a major quandary for us, because although we have seen and sold a significant number of Gibson hand-painted photographs over the years, we have never been able to locate a shred of documentation about this individual. We seem to see more Gibson pictures in Pennsylvania than anywhere else, which would suggest that he was from Pennsylvania. But we have never seen a label, stamp, biography, piece of sales literature, or anything else that would provide any background information at all. All Gibson pictures we have seen have been exterior scenes, and we have never seen a Gibson interior or foreign scene. Titles and signatures are mostly seen in pencil, yet we have also seen pre-printed Gibson titles and signatures, which would suggest fairly large production runs on certain individual titles. Most pictures have fairly light coloring, and we have never seen a brightly colored Gibson. If you have any information on Gibson, please share it with us.

"A Shady Path"

REGIONALITY

Northeastern U.S.

REPRESENTATIVE TITLES & VALUE GUIDE

"The Afterglow"
"Beacon Light"
"The Bending Tree"
"Country Road"
"Lover's Road"
"Peaceful Brook"
"The Two Birches"
"Waterfall in Autumn"
"Weeping Willow"
Typical value range: $50.00 – 100.00

GIDEON (first name not known)

BACKGROUND

Little background information on Gideon has been found. We have only seen one Gideon picture, and it was an exterior scene. In our opinion, it was taken in New England, which suggests that he was a New England photographer.

REGIONALITY

New England

REPRESENTATIVE TITLES & VALUE GUIDE

Exterior scene
Estimated value range: $10.00 – 50.00

BENJAMIN A. GIFFORD (1859 – 1936)

Benjamin A. Gifford (1859 – 1936)

BACKGROUND

BENJAMIN A. GIFFORD was a photographer from the Pacific Northwest and was part of a relatively famous photographic family. He was born in Dupage County, Illinois. He attended the Kansas Normal College and served a two-year apprenticeship in a photographic gallery in Fort Scott, Kansas. He later completed his photographic apprenticeship in Sedalia, Missouri, under William LaTour, and became a partner in that studio upon his return to Ft. Scott.

Gifford married Mary Peck in 1884. They moved to Portland Oregon, in 1888, and opened their photography studio in Portland in 1891. Gifford also opened a studio in The Dalles in 1895, and he ran it for several years. He returned to Portland in 1910. His first wife died in 1919, and he later married Rachel Morgan. Gifford was recognized as the first Portland photographer to use electric lights for making photographic enlargements.

Gifford worked primarily in Oregon circa 1890 – 1920, around such photographic areas as the Columbia River, the Columbia River Highway, the Cascade Mountains, The Dalles, the Deschutes River, and other regions in eastern and central Oregon. He was also well-known for his photographs of Native Americans. Many of his pictures were hand-painted by Wilma Roberts of the Dalles (see Wilma Roberts in this chapter).

Benjamin A. Gifford died on March 5, 1936.

REGIONALITY

Northwest U.S; Oregon

REPRESENTATIVE TITLES & VALUE GUIDE

Estimated value range: $50.00 – 100.00+

C. M. GILBERT

BACKGROUND

Little background information on C. M. Gilbert has been found. We have only seen one Gilbert hand-painted picture, which had a label indicating that the Gilbert Studio was located at 926 Chestnut St., Philadelphia PA. We have seen very few Gilbert pictures over the years.

REGIONALITY

Pennsylvania

REPRESENTATIVE TITLES & VALUE GUIDE

Untitled exterior scene
Estimated value range: $10.00 – 50.00+

GOULD (first name not known)

BACKGROUND
Little background information on GOULD has been found. We have only seen one Gould hand-painted picture, and it provided a 1933 date. We have seen very few Gould pictures over the years and none have provided a clue as to location or origin.

REGIONALITY
Unknown

REPRESENTATIVE TITLES & VALUE GUIDE
Untitled exterior scene
Estimated value range: $10.00 – 50.00+

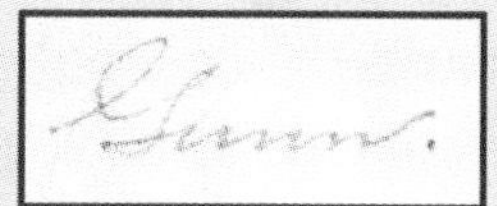

GUNN (first name not known)

BACKGROUND
Little background information on GUNN has been found. We have only seen one Gunn hand-painted picture, a Florida scene taken in Lake Worth, Florida, which suggests that he may have been a Florida photographer.

REGIONALITY
Florida

REPRESENTATIVE TITLES & VALUE GUIDE
"Lake Worth, Florida"
Estimated value range: $25.00 – 50.00+

"Lake Worth, Florida"

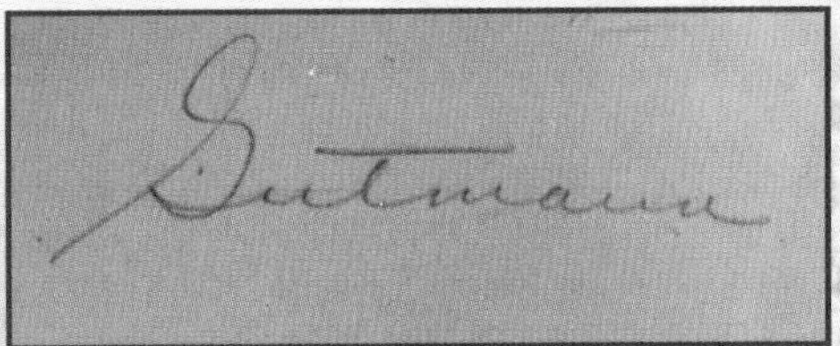

BESSIE PEASE GUTMANN (1876 – 1960)
GUTMANN & GUTMANN

BACKGROUND

Technically, BESSIE PEASE GUTMANN colonial prints are hand-colored lithographs and not actually hand-painted photographs, but we will mention them here because they are so often confused with hand-painted photos. Bessie Pease Gutmann, best known for her adorable infant and children prints, also produced a series of lesser-known colonial interior scenes. Beginning around 1916, Gutmann & Gutmann released the first of its Colonial Series prints in an attempt to compete with Wallace Nutting in the colonial interiors market. Unlike Nutting interiors, Gutmann colonials were not photographs, but machine-produced prints of original drawings by either Bessie Pease Gutmann or two of her employees, Eda Doench and Meta Grimball. Each of these pictures featured a colonial theme, typically a woman or a mother and daughter, in a parlor or bedroom, or near a fireplace.

Unlike the infant and children prints that generally included the full "Bessie Pease Gutmann" signature within the picture, Gutmann colonials more directly copied the style that Wallace Nutting had used for more than 15 years. These pictures are typically found:
1) on a light-colored matting
2) with a plate mark indentation surrounding the picture
3) titled lower left beneath the picture
4) signed "Gutmann" lower right beneath the picture
5) glued to the matting on the top of the picture only
6) framed in a frame-style typical of a Wallace Nutting interior.

Bessie Pease Gutmann (1876 – 1960)

Just as in Wallace Nutting's business, where Wallace Nutting rarely signed a picture himself, it was typically a Gutmann & Gutmann employee who signed the title and signature; the signatures are clearly not always signed by the same hand. Colonial sizes vary, but the most common mat sizes are 7" x 9", 11" x 14", and 14" x 17". Smaller sizes are generally more common than larger sizes.

Prices vary widely. You can sometimes find them in the $25.00 – $45.00 range, offered by dealers who don't realize that Gutmann is actually the more famous Bessie Pease Gutmann. Other times you will see Gutmann colonials priced within the $100.00 – $250.00 range, usually being offered by dealers who known that Gutmann is Bessie Pease Gutmann, but who overvalue the Gutmann name. The more appropriate value for Gutmann Colonials generally seems to be in the $50.00 – 100.00 range, with higher

"Hush-a-bye!" colonial scene

values for larger pictures. Rarer colonials in excellent condition can sometimes sell higher than this range.

Gutmann colonials are generally not highly prized by collectors. Bessie Pease Gutmann collectors usually prefer the baby and infant prints, and collectors of hand-painted photography typically prefer photographic interiors to Gutmann's machine-produced colonial interiors. Yet prices on good-quality Gutmann colonials have been rising. The pictures are relatively easy to locate, quite affordable, and from a dealer's perspective, fairly easy to sell if appropriately priced.

REGIONALITY

Mt. Holly, New Jersey

REPRESENTATIVE TITLES & VALUE GUIDE

"An Afternoon Call"
"Afternoon Tea"
"At Tea"
"Bed Time"
"A Bit of Old China"
"The Breakfast Hour"
"Candle Making"
"A Chilly Day"
"Dancing Lesson"
"The Dancing Lesson"
"The Family Album"
"First Breakfast"
"Her Wedding Day"
"Hush-a-Bye"
"In the Library"
"Mending"
"Mending Day"
"The New Bonnet"
"The New Home"
"The Patchwork Quilt"
"Tea for Two"
"Yes or No"
Typical value range: $50.00 – 125.00+

Note the print vs. the photographic look.

EDWARD GUY

BACKGROUND

After Wallace Nutting purchased the Saugus Iron Works in 1916 (the Saugus Iron Works was actually the first working ironworks in the American colonies during the early 1700s), Nutting decided to reproduce Early American ironwork using the same approach he later used to produce his famous furniture. EDWARD GUY was Nutting's ironmaster and actually worked Nutting's forge for many years and oversaw the production of the ironworks. Nutting and Guy had a falling out around 1921, and apparently Guy took a stab at selling hand-colored photography, perhaps in an attempt to compete with his ex-employer. It would seem that Guy's attempt at commercially selling hand-painted photographs was short-lived and not very successful, because we have seen very few Edward Guy hand-painted photographs over the years.

REGIONALITY

New England; Massachusetts

REPRESENTATIVE TITLES & VALUE GUIDE

Untitled stone church
Estimated value range: $25.00 – 50.00+

H. S. HANNUM

BACKGROUND

Little background information on H. S. HANNUM has been found. We have only seen one Hannum hand-painted exterior scene, and it provided no clue as to its location or origin.

REGIONALITY

Unknown

REPRESENTATIVE TITLES & VALUE GUIDE

Untitled stream
Estimated value range: $10.00 – 50.00+

Byron Harmon (1876 – 1942)

HARMON's

BYRON HARMON (1876 – 1942)

BACKGROUND

BYRON HARMON was a professional mountain climber, photographer, filmmaker, and businessman who lived in Banff, Alberta, Canada, and who worked primarily in the Canadian Rockies. Born near Tacoma, Washington, Harmon briefly operated a portrait studio there. While traveling as an itinerant photographer in the United States and Canada, Harmon decided to move to Banff around 1903. He opened a studio there circa 1906, and by 1907 he had produced a large enough volume of pictures to introduce a line of Banff-area postcards. Other Harmon business interests there included a curio shop, soda fountain, and movie theater.

Harmon was an avid mountain climber and was a charter member of the Alpine Club of Canada, and he served as its official photographer from 1906 to 1913. Traveling by foot, snowshoe, pack horse, and dog sled, and often living in teepees or canvas tents, he traveled to areas that few had ever visited before him. His breathtaking photography was used on postcards, for hand-painted photographs, in travel portfolios, or resold for commercial use. In later years, Harmon took motion pictures that were shown to large numbers of theater audiences.

"Lake Louise"

Between 1906 and 1913, Harmon, as the official photographer for the Alpine Club of Canada, made numerous photographic trips into the high mountain regions of Banff. On later trips, he produced both still photographs and motion pictures, which he used for commercial purposes.

Byron Harmon: Mountain Photographer (1992)

Series of 12 hand-tinted postcards

Most Harmon photographs were taken with a 5" x 7" view camera and on cellulose-nitrate negatives, as the much heavier glass-plate negatives would have been much too cumbersome when traveling. Although most of Harmon's motion picture footage has been lost, the Byron Harmon Negative Collection is now archived with the Whyte Museum of the Canadian Rockies, and its 6,000-plus pictures are an enduring legacy of Byron Harmon.

REGIONALITY

Canada; Banff, Alberta

Canadian Rockies portfolio of 18 hand-colored photos

REPRESENTATIVE TITLES & VALUE GUIDE

"Bow Valley"
"Lake Louise"
"Mt. Eisenhower"
Typical value range: $50.00 – 100.00+

Canadian Rockies postcard package

RECOMMENDED READING

Byron Harmon: Mountain Photographer, by Carole Harmon (Harman's daughter) and Bart Robinson, 112 pages, published by Altitude Publishing, 1992.

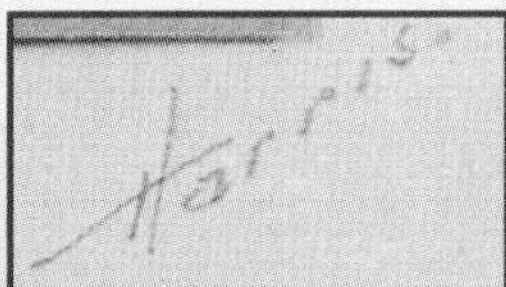

WILLIAM JAMES HARRIS (1868 – 1940)

BACKGROUND

WILLIAM JAMES HARRIS was born on October 12, 1868, in Herefordshire, England. His family immigrated to America in 1870, settling in the Wilkes Barre, Pennsylvania, area. Known in his youth as both Will and Willie, by age 20 he apprenticed under a local photographer. Within one year, he was able to start his first photography business while living with his parents, setting up a studio in their house.

William James Harris (1868 – 1940)

In 1890, the 22-year-old Harris moved with his family to West Pittston, Pennsylvania, where, although he continued operating a studio in his parents home, he also began his career as a traveling photographer. During the early 1890s, he spent considerable time photographing coal miners and mining operations in eastern Pennsylvania's coal regions. Soon thereafter he began utilizing the railroads to transport him, and his photography equipment, to the mountains, lakes, cities, and wherever else he decided to take his camera. Cabinet photographs sold by Harris around this time listed his address as West Pittston, Pennsylvainia; Tunkhannock, Pennsylvania; Pittston, Pennsylvania; Penn Yan, New York; Binghamton, New York; and Keuka, New York.

In 1893 Harris traveled to the World's Columbia Exposition in Chicago. While there his began the first of many subsequent promotional feats. One of the focal points of the 1893 Columbia Exposition was the first-ever introduction of George Ferris's great Ferris Wheel. And it was Harris who was the first to photograph it. He envisioned that by climbing upon a roof approximately the same height as the Ferris Wheel's center shaft, he would be able to produce a view whereby the curves of the wheel were not distorted vertically by perspective. This photograph was so impressive that Harris donated 2,000 copies of it to the Ferris Wheel Company, each of which included his name and address, which helped to make an early name for the young photographer.

In 1895 he married Maude Dunn, but the marriage was short-lived because she died unexpectedly in 1897. Shortly after Maude's death, Harris and some friends opened a tourist business in Pennsylvania's Pocono Mountains, selling pictures of Buck Hill Falls, the Delaware Water Gap, and other local attractions to tourists and local residents. While he operated from the Harris Gallery, his services also included cabinet cards and tin-type photographs,. This portable studio once again served as an excellent promotional feat, because it enabled him to both advertise his business, and process his photographic work, wherever he went.

"Ft. Marion, St. Augustine, Florida"

Around 1901, Harris married a second time, making Marion E. Briant the second Mrs. Harris. Together they had two children, a daughter (Ruth) and a son (Carver). This marriage lasted until about 1920. After the divorce, Marion Harris returned to her Dover, New Jersey, home with Ruth, leaving Carver with his father.

Soon thereafter, Harris married Ella Anderson, his third and final wife.

It was in 1898 that Harris moved to a location that would play a vital role in his life — Lake Hopatcong, New Jersey. Located in northern New Jersey, its nine miles of coastline and coves make it New Jersey's largest lake, and by the turn of the century, Lake Hopatcong had become a summer mecca for the rich and famous. Conveniently located to nearby New York City, Lake Hopatcong offered an easy summer getaway from the city heat, and many summer "cottages," which in many instances were more like mansions, began springing up around the lake. Harris quickly recognized the need for his photographic services here during the summer months.

Beautiful sunsets became the Harris trademark while he worked on Lake Hopatcong, and he was farsighted enough to set himself up on a part of the lake that was recognized as having the best sunsets. Being the great promoter that he was, Harris began advertising his studio as offering the finest sunset photographs on the lake. Soon tourists began flocking to his studio for their personal and family photographs on Lake Hopatcong.

"Charlotte St., St. Augustine, Fla.," close-framed

In another move of public relations genius, Harris created his own personal floating studio in the summer of 1899. Replacing his land-based portable studio, this floating studio was actually a houseboat specially outfitted as a photographic studio. Called the Harris Photo Float, this 16' x 50' floating studio was capable of traveling around the lake and even had a special porch for Harris's famous sunset photos. Although other photographers were also working around the lake, Harris's floating studio and his gift for promotion gave him a competitive edge over the other photographers, and he controlled a sizeable portion of the lake's photography business. Unfortunately, in 1903 Harris's floating studio sprang a knothole leak and sank, taking with it much of Harris's photographic equipment.

But he quickly recovered from this disaster and went on to continue a nearly 40-year relationship with Lake Hopatcong. Harris continued his summer visits to the lake until as late as 1939, when he was in his 60s and his photographic career began winding down.

In 1898 Harris moved to St. Augustine, Florida, where he opened the Acme View Company. Harris's Florida photographic services included the sale of cameras and equipment, free photographic instructions to amateur photographers, and the use of his darkroom, as well as professional photographic services to local residents or visiting tourists. He also lost no time in photographing the beautiful sights in St. Augustine and the surrounding Florida countryside.

Harris quickly fell in love with St. Augustine and, to a larger extent, nearly all of Florida. Between 1898 and 1940, Harris had a photographic career that many of us would love to have today, spending summers along the shorelines of beautiful Lake Hopatcong, New Jersey, and winters in warm and sunny St. Augustine, Florida.

"Florida Wilds"

St. Augustine offered a variety of photographic subjects that appealed to Florida's growing tourist trade, including the Fountain of Youth, the Oldest House in America, Ft. Marion, the city gates, and the Old Slave Market, among others.

In 1912 Harris began a long, and sometimes controversial, relationship with the St. Augustine Historical Society. Serving as its business manager and head curator, Harris was instrumental both in recruiting new members to the Historical Society as well as promoting both the history and heritage of St. Augustine. While on his watch, certain members began to dispute some of the Historical Society's unsubstantiated claims. Was the Oldest House in America actually as old as claimed? Had the "Old Slave Market" truly been a slave market, or simply a public produce market? The "well, they could have been" responses by certain area businesspeople met resistance from other historical purists, and some changes in St. Augustine's historical claims resulted.

Regardless of the controversy, Harris's association with the St. Augustine Historical Society lasted until his death in 1940, and all the while, Harris continued to promote his St. Augustine postcard and photography business.

It was in 1893, while visiting the Columbia Exposition, that Harris saw a glimpse of the next coming trend — postcards. By 1898, Congress had passed a law authorizing the manufacture and use of "private mailing cards," and what started as a trickle soon exploded into a huge business. And Harris was in a perfect position to earn his share of the business. The telephone was not yet commonplace, and postcards soon became a primary means of casual communication. In 1901, Harris was selling a grouping of 30 Lake Hopatcong views that were capable of being inserted into a letter, so converting them into postcards was a relatively simple task. Quickly converting much of his existing stock into postcards, and adding new views each year, Harris soon had literally hundreds of Lake Hopatcong postcard views, and became known around Lake Hopatcong as "Harris the Postcard Man." Anyone wishing to send a personal message about their special trip or vacation on

THIS IS A

Harris Picture

Hand-Painted Water Color

IMPRISONED sunshine, tropical warmth of color, the glow of the sunset skies, the beauty of wind-swept beaches and shifting sand dunes, the shimmer of water on a silver shore—all these are found in HARRIS PICTURES.

Depending first for their success upon the most advanced development of the photographic art, then colored true to nature by skilled artists.

The furnishings of a home show forth the character of the occupants, and nowhere is this more clearly noted than in the pictures. They are an evidence of the appreciation of the finer things, and indicate a love of beauty that finds expression in a charming way.

Those who choose HARRIS PICTURES are safe, for they show distinction and good taste.

Pictures paper label

Pictures gold-foil label

Lake Hopatcong usually did it using a Harris postcard. In 1909 alone Harris claimed to have sold over 200,000 Lake Hopatcong postcards, and he projected even more sales for 1910.

As his postcard business grew, he expanded into the souvenir and novelty field, selling paperweights, cups, fancy holders, and other assorted wooden and birch bark novelties, all with "Lake Hopatcong" on them. Although such a souvenir business was common in St. Augustine and other places, Harris was one of the first to start such a business at Lake Hopatcong.

As the postcard craze began to wind down around 1915, Harris, who had been watching from a distance the success of Wallace Nutting in Massachusetts, soon decided to enter the field of hand-colored photography himself. With his background, it was natural.

Harris's earliest attempt with hand-colored photographs came when he first hand-tinted his Lake Hopatcong postcards. After working in black and white for many years, starting around 1905 Harris assumed that the added color could lead to increased sales. But he also soon learned that the added expense of hand-painting his postcards led to a higher unit price and eventually to lower sales. Ultimately Harris went the route of so many other postcard photographers, having his postcards produced in color on large-run color printing presses.

As part of his New Jersey summer–Florida winter cycles, Harris began taking new photographs with the intention of hand-coloring them for resale. His best-selling pictures soon came to be from the New York Adirondack region (especially Ausable Chasm) and Florida (especially The Singing Tower), although his northeastern pictures came from throughout a four-state region and his Florida pictures came from throughout the entire Miami–St. Augustine stretch.

Before long, pictures began to replace postcards as his primary source of income. According to his son Carver, "what money he had, he made from colored pictures." And apparently he made enough money to buy houses in Florida and New Jersey, an imposing automobile, a houseboat, and several launches and speedboats (which enabled him to get around Lake Hopatcong faster than ever).

Like Wallace Nutting pictures, Harris pictures were usually hand-painted photographs, tipped onto a linen-type matboard, signed in the lower right, titled in the lower left, and usually signed in pencil. Most Harris pictures were matted, although a fair number were close-framed and signed directly on the picture without any matting. And quite often, you will still find an original Harris label either on the matboard back or on the backing paper.

Yet Harris pictures carry several subtle differences from those of Nutting and some of the major Nutting-like photographers:

* Most Harris pictures were oblong views, with the length usually being more than twice the width (or vice versa).
* Harris only sold exterior (outdoor) views. He never sold colonial interior scenes.
* You will only see "Harris" signed on the picture, never "W. J." or any other variation of his first or middle names. There is also never any mention of Harris's first or middle name on any of his picture labels.
* Although the name is usually written parallel to the picture, occasionally you will see the name written at a 45-degree angle.
* While more unusual, it is not uncommon for the Harris name to be lower left and the title to be lower right.
* Most Harris signatures are signed in pencil.

And perhaps most different from Nutting, many Harris pictures are hand-colored *photogravures* rather than hand-colored photographs. Although his earliest scenes were produced on photographic paper, some of his later and best-selling views were reproduced in larger black and white quantities using the photogravure printing method, and then individually hand-colored. Whereas Nutting had nearly 100 colorists at his peak, Harris never had more than five people coloring his pictures at any given time.

Watkins Glen NY

One interesting story about Harris pictures relates to several of his pictures that feature an egret standing in the Florida water. Apparently for the sake of simplicity, Harris carried a stuffed egret as part of his photographic equipment, presumably because it was easier to shoot a still bird for effect rather than a live, uncontrollable bird. He was also known to carry a stuffed alligator for effect as well.

Harris Hand Colored Picture-

Number.......1.......

Dealers
Detach this and order

Number.......1.......
W. J. Harris Co., Artists
St. Augustine, Fla.
Lake Hopatcong, N. J.

Price..................

Pictures dealer order tag

Not surprisingly, Harris was usually his own best salesman, and his photographic expeditions became sales trips as well. Whenever he went into the countryside to shoot new pictures, he usually stopped at various art and gift shops along the way to obtain new wholesale and retail orders for his picture business. It was estimated that more than 70 shops on both coasts of Florida alone carried Harris's hand-colored pictures. Many hotels used Harris pictures on their walls to promote the beauties of early twentieth century Florida, and it is estimated that Harris would typically need more than 25,000 pictures per season just to satisfy the demand of his Florida sales outlets. And as the Florida season would end, Harris would pack his car, head back north, and start the cycle all over again at New Jersey's Lake Hopatcong.

William James Harris died on August 2, 1940, after suffering through a long illness, and was buried in his adopted city of St. Augustine. Although not as well known as Wallace Nutting or some of Nutting's other contemporaries, Harris did achieve a considerable level of fame and he enjoyed a reasonable financial success in his chosen photographic field. He enjoyed the travel and work between the northeast in the summer months and Florida in the winter months, he had a diverse family life, he developed a strong bond with his adopted city of St. Augustine, Florida, and his photographic works certainly helped to popularize Florida more than did those of any other photographer of his time.

RECOMMENDED READING

* St. Augustine Historical Society *El Escribano* article: "North and South with W. J. Harris, Photographer" (volume 28, 1991).
* *Florida's Golden Age of Souvenirs: 1890 – 1930* (2001, by Larry Roberts). This book includes a chapter on Barnhill and Harris Florida hand-colored photographs.

REGIONALITY

New England: St. Augustine, Florida; Lake Hopatcong, New Jersey; New York

REPRESENTATIVE TITLES & VALUE GUIDE

"The Falls, Clifton, NJ"
"Fountain of Youth, St. Augustine"
"From Black Bear Mt. Inley NY"
"Garden, Oldest School House"
"Mt. Whiteface — Lake Placid"
"Old City Gates"
"Oldest School House, St. Augustine"
"Patio, Oldest House, St. Augustine"
"Peace River, Florida"
"River Palms, Florida"
"Royal Arch Oak, Fla"
Typical value range: $50.00 – 200.00+

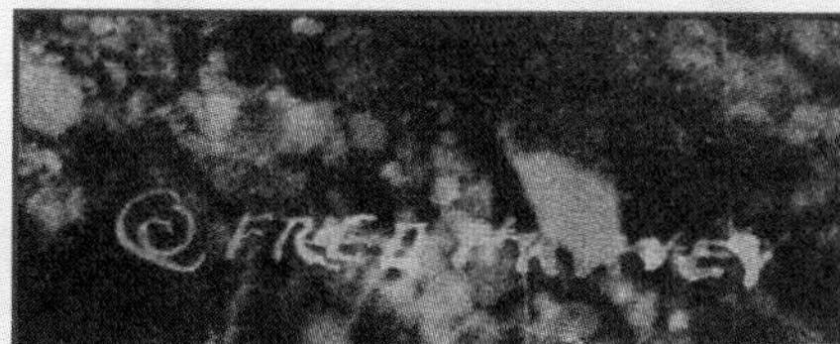

FRED HARVEY
FRED HARVEY COMPANY

BACKGROUND

The FRED HARVEY COMPANY was a large chain of large restaurants, hotels, and gift shops that extended far throughout the southwestern U.S. (an early Howard Johnson's, if you will). Its businesses were located from as far east as Kansas City and Missouri to as far west as Arizona, New Mexico, and California, often following the route of the Atchison, Topeka, and Santa Fe railroads. The Fred Harvey Company later formed a partnership with the Santa Fe Railroad in order to glamorize and promote tourism in the southwestern U.S.

Fred Harvey was born in 1835 in England, and immigrated to the United States with his family circa 1850. Early in his life, Fred Harvey opened a café in St. Louis, Missouri, which provided him with his first experience in food management. Later he obtained employment as a railroad clerk, and while employed at the railroad, Harvey became appalled by railroad food and service. He decided that somebody needed to do it right — and that someone was Fred Harvey.

"Northwest from Mojave Point"

Fred Harvey's concept was fairly simple: if you provided railroad customers with good quality food and lodging, they would be more likely to use your railroad and facilities again. The logic is fairly simple by today's standards, but in the early years of transcontinental rail travel, no one else paid much attention to such details until Fred Harvey came along.

One of the first things that Harvey did in his series of restaurants was replace all-male wait staffs with his all new "Harvey Girls." These girls were pretty, clean cut, and fairly well paid.

By 1905, the Grand Canyon had become a premier tourist destination, and Fred Harvey played a big roll in all that, building the still-standing El Tovar Hotel on the South Rim of the Grand Canyon. Up to this point, there were no formal concessions at the South Rim, but Fred Harvey changed that. The grand opening of the El Tovar served to attract more tourists to the Grand Canyon than ever before. Its gift shops sold numerous items, including books, toys, knick-knacks, Grand Canyon and other tourist destination memorabilia, anything pertaining to Native Americans, and of course, hand-painted photographs.

Carl Moon (see Carl Everton Moon) was the art director for the Fred Harvey Company from 1907 to 1914 and took numerous photographs for Fred Harvey. And more often than not, these pictures are stamped "Fred Harvey" rather than "Carl Moon," because Fred Harvey (the employer) owned the rights to any pictures taken by Carl Moon (the employee) during this time. Carl Moon left the employ of Fred Harvey in 1914 and went on to a successful photographic career of his own.

"Tourist Party on Bright Angel Trail"

REGIONALITY
Western U.S.; Grand Canyon, Arizona

REPRESENTATIVE TITLES & VALUE GUIDE
American Indian scenes
Grand Canyon scenes
Typical value range: $75.00 – 250.00+

HARVEY STUDIO (not Fred Harvey)

BACKGROUND
Little background information on the HARVEY STUDIO has been found. We have only seen one Harvey Studio hand-painted picture, which was an exterior scene and which indicated it was taken in Frederickton, Campbellton, Woodstock, Sussex, which we assumed to be England based upon the subject matter.

REGIONALITY
England

REPRESENTATIVE TITLES & VALUE GUIDE
Exterior scene
Estimated value range: $10.00 – 50.00+

Interior scene

Thomas C. Hawks

THOMAS C. HAWKS

BACKGROUND

Little background information on THOMAS C. HAWKS has been found. We have only seen one Hawks hand-painted picture, an interior scene. It was pencil signed, untitled, and had absolutely beautiful color, comparable to Wallace Nutting and the other major photographers' finest hand-painted pictures. In our opinion, it was taken in New England, which suggests that he was a New England photographer.

REGIONALITY

New England

REPRESENTATIVE TITLES & VALUE GUIDE

Untitled interior scene
Estimated value range: $25.00 – 75.00+

F. JAY HAYNES (1853 – 1921)

BACKGROUND

While Wallace Nutting was busy photographing the relatively tame back roads of New England, F. JAY HAYNES was just as busy photographing the considerably less-tamed western American frontier. He began his photographic career in the mid-1870s, and the Haynes photographic tradition was eventually passed along to his son, Jack Ellis Haynes, who continued the Haynes family photography business until the 1950s. Both father and son probably contributed more to popularizing Yellowstone National Park than anyone else, and their work is being actively collected today by a growing number of collectors.

Born in Saline, Michigan, Frank Jay Haynes began his photographic career around 1874 in Michigan and Wisconsin. In 1876 he opened his own studio in Moorhead, Minnesota and in 1879, when it became obvious that Fargo, North Dakota was becoming a major city, the 26-year-old Haynes shifted his main studio there. His earliest photographic commissions were primarily portrait views. This portion of his business proved to be an immediate success and at the height of his early career he had two employees in his Fargo establishment whose sole job was making portraits.

F. Jay Haynes (1853 – 1921)

Known Photographers

Up to the 1870s, the railroads usually employed skilled artists who painted or sketched spectacular western views in order to glamorize the scenery offered by their respective railway routes. Wet plate photography was the standard photographic process at this time. This typically involved a bulky camera, heavy glass plate negatives, and portable darkrooms necessary for developing sensitized negatives almost immediately upon their initial photographic exposure and the difficulty of utilizing this process in the harsh western U.S. environments should be apparent.

Pencil-signed Yellowstone Falls

Haynes's career took a major turn in the late 1870s, when the Northern Pacific Railroad hired him to become its official photographer. In addition to a fair salary, Haynes was given a rebuilt Pullman railroad car that became his personal rolling photographic studio. His job was to thoroughly photograph the railroad's facilities such as stations, bridges, rail yards, rolling cars and stock, and company buildings. Haynes also photographed the beautiful countryside wherever the railroad's tracks went...horses, wild animals, stagecoaches, military forts, trading posts, Indians, tepees, river boats, etc. The Northern Pacific then used Haynes' photographs in their advertising and travel brochures, hoping to attract more commercial and passenger business for the railroad.

Haynes also promoted his personal photography business while traveling on railroad business. Recognizing the need for a professional photographer among the increasing volume of settlers moving west, Haynes would advertise in local papers along the Northern Pacific route that the Haynes Palace Studio Car would be in town on a particular day and that his photographic services would be available in towns having no permanent professional photographer. This advanced notice enabled families to travel to town in the family wagon, dressed in their Sunday best, for the annual family photogravure. Businesses, merchants, and anyone needing photographic services could take advantage of his availability. Haynes would then perform his developing and processing right there in his rolling studio car, thereby earning both private commissions and railroad pay. Haynes traveled through the Dakotas, Wyoming, Montana, Idaho, Oregon, and Washington for the Northern Pacific, and to Yellowstone in the 1882/1883 season, taking a large number of pictures wherever he went.

Early Yellowstone Park hand-painted albumen photos

He continued to operate the Haynes Studio railroad car gallery from 1885 to 1905. He moved his studio to St. Paul, Minnesota, in 1889 and traveled throughout the West and Alaska earning the reputation as one of the West's finest early photographers.

F. Jay Haynes also covered many special events during his career. For example, in 1883 President Chester A. Arthur, along with a party that included a Lt. General, the Secretary of War, and a U.S. senator, traveled by horseback touring Ft. Washakie, the Tetons, and Yellowstone Park. With fresh horses positioned every 20 miles to provide the traveling party with communication with the outside world, F. Jay Haynes traveled along with that party as its official photographer.

Because of his familiarity with the photographic requirements needed to popularize a railroad Haynes was also hired by the Canadian Pacific Railroad in 1881 as its first official photographer as well. While working for the Canadian Pacific Haynes utilized a stereo camera and sold stereo cards glamorizing the Canadian Pacific route and was rewarded with a free unlimited-use railway pass in honor of his services.

Views of Yellowstone Park, the Holy Grail of F. Jay Haynes collectors

But is was the beauty of Yellowstone Park that would capture most of Haynes' life. Haynes work at Yellowstone began in the early 1880s, and in 1884 he became Yellowstone's first official photographer. Yellowstone was the first national park designated as such by the federal government, and F. Jay Haynes obtained the first federally-issued license to operate a photographic concession in Yellowstone at Mammoth Hot Springs. Haynes opened the Log Cabin Studio, which served Yellowstone for many years selling photos to visiting tourists.

Photography wasn't Haynes only business venture at Yellowstone. The Northern Pacific used Haynes photography to lure tourists to visit Yellowstone and the Western U.S. but, once they arrived, someone had to transport them from the railroad station to their lodgings and throughout Yellowstone Park. Again enter F. Jay Haynes. His short-lived Yellowstone National Park Transportation Company was later replaced by the Monida and Yellowstone Stage Line which became the principal carrier of passengers entering through Yellowstone's western park entrance. At its peak Haynes's stage line had 18 stagecoaches and surreys and was responsible for transporting nearly 40% of all of Yellowstone's annual visitors. However in 1916 control of the newly founded national park was turned over to the National Park Service which terminated Haynes transportation contract and replaced it with a motorized transportation company under their direct control.

HAYNES
HAND-PAINTED PHOTOGRAPHS
of
YELLOWSTONE NATIONAL PARK

Size of Picture.........2" x 5½"
Size of Mount (approx.) 5" x 8½"

SUBJECTS

TITLE	NEG. No.
Cleopatra Terrace	17352
Crested Pool and Castle Cone	10101
Eagle Nest Rock	35M1713*
Elk and Jupiter Terrace	35M0304
Golden Gate Canyon	34067*
Great Falls from Red Rock	16253*
Index Peak from Highway	35394*
Mt. Washburn from Highway.	35991*
Mule Deer Fawn	24272*
Old Faithful Geyser	10378*
Old Faithful Geyser	35921*
Sylvan Lake and Top Notch Peak	17296
Sylvan Lake and Top Notch Peak	35377
Upper Falls of the Yellowstone	14053*
Yellowstone Lake, Mt. Sheridan	10116
Yellowstone Lake, Steamboat Point	35373

*Vertical Subjects.

Please specify when ordering: Hand-painted 2" x 5½" and state Neg. No. of subjects desired, and whether framed or unframed.

HAYNES PICTURE SHOPS, INC.
Established 1884 In
Yellowstone National Park

Selby, Corner Virginia Aves.
ST. PAUL, MINNESOTA, U. S. A.
YELLOWSTONE PARK
WYOMING, U.S.A.

Assorted Yellowstone Park titles

Partly due to the closing of his transportation business, and partly due to his age, Haynes retired in 1916, turning control of the photography business to his son, Jack Ellis Haynes.

The volume of Haynes's work was tremendous. In addition to 2,400 stereoviews, Haynes produced thousands of cabinet cards, thousands of individual and family portraits, and tens of thousands of hand-colored photographs. Today more than 24,000 glass and film negatives from the Haynes Collection reside at the Montana Historical Society. These include Haynes pictures from Minnesota, North Dakota, South Dakota, Montana, Washington, Idaho, Alaska, many of his Northern Pacific Railroad pictures, and of course, his Yellowstone Park images.

Probably the Holy Grail of F. Jay Haynes collecting is a presentation portfolio of early Yellowstone pictures titled Views of Yellowstone Park. Henry Vihlein (1844 – 1922), a nephew of Joseph Schlitz (founder and owner of Milwaukee's Schlitz Brewery) commissioned Haynes to take a series of 12 Yellowstone pictures, which were then bound in a high-quality leather-bound book and given to a very limited number of his friends and associates. We have only personally seen one of these complete books, and they are considered extremely rare and desirable among Haynes collectors. Value can run from $2,500.00 to 5,000.00+.

Haynes cabinet cards, carte-de-vistes, portraits, and stereo cards are highly sought-after by photography collectors. Subject matter and condition will generally determine value.

But from the perspective of this book, Haynes hand-colored photographs are his most highly sought-after collectibles by collectors of early 20th c. hand-colored photography. The most desirable are Haynes earliest hand-colored albumen prints which are often unsigned or unmarked in any way.

Far and away the most common hand-colored Haynes views that you will find are from Yellowstone Park and usually include Old Faithful, other Geysers, Animals, Great Falls, Lower Falls, and other magnificent views throughout the park. These pictures were hand colored in oils in the Haynes Studio and typically sold to Yellowstone visitors and tourists, with some being much rarer than others. Those earlier hand-colored pictures issued by F. Jay Haynes himself are generally more desirable than those later pictures issued by his son.

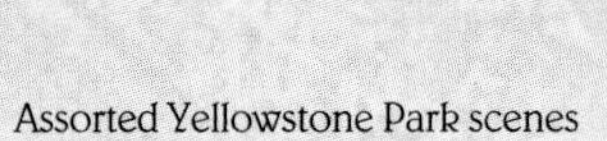

Assorted Yellowstone Park scenes

More often than not, Haynes pictures were impressed with "Haynes" rather than signed in pencil or pen. Usually "Haynes, Yellowstone Park" or "Haynes Studio, St Paul" will be impressed in small letters, either into the image itself or into the matting. Usually no more than about thirty commercial Yellowstone titles were sold, yet these came in a multitude of sizes (2½" x 5" to 24" x 36") and in several different formats (matted and close-framed, rectangular and round frames, etc.). Round frames and larger sizes are fairly unusual.

F. Jay Haynes died in 1921.

REGIONALITY
Western U.S.; Yellowstone National Park, Wyoming

REPRESENTATIVE TITLES & VALUE GUIDE
"Emerald Pool"
"Great Falls"
"Great Falls from Red Rock"
"Mule Deer Fawn"
"Old Faithful"
"Sylvan Lake and Top Notch Peak"
Typical value range: $50.00 – 175.00+

Two books about F. Jay Haynes

RECOMMENDED READING

Several books have been written about F. Jay Haynes, including *Following the Frontier* (Freeman Tilden) and *F. Jay Haynes, Photographer* (Montana Historical Society). Each of these books includes significant Haynes biographical information and reproductions of many of his photographs.

Yellowstone Park hand-painted bear scene

JACK ELLIS HAYNES (d. 1964)

BACKGROUND

The F. Jay Haynes photographic tradition was passed along to his son, JACK ELLIS HAYNES, who continued the Haynes family photography business until the 1950s. Both father and son probably contributed more to popularizing Yellowstone National Park than any others, and their work is being actively collected today by a growing number of collectors.

Although Jack Ellis Haynes created new photographic subjects by himself, he also continued to sell hand-painted photographs made from his father's negatives. His pictures can usually be distinguished from his father's by the light but still visible "Jack E. Haynes" impressed lower right into the image.

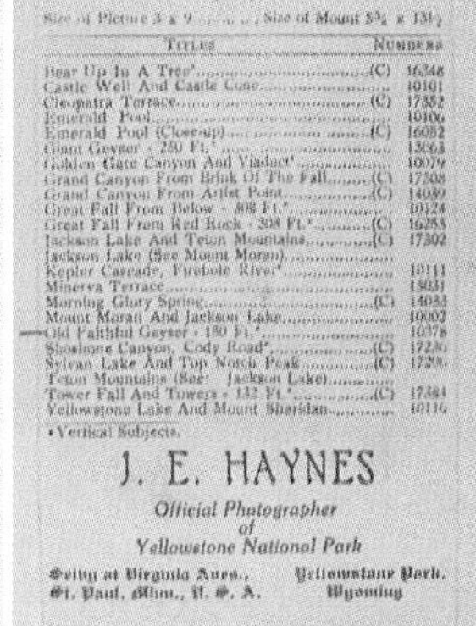

YELLOWSTONE NATIONAL PARK
HAND PAINTED PICTURES
by Haynes

Size of Picture 3 x 9 .... Size of Mount 8½ x 13½

TITLES		NUMBERS
Bear Up In A Tree*	(C)	16348
Castle Well And Castle Cone		10101
Cleopatra Terrace	(C)	17352
Emerald Pool		10106
Emerald Pool (Close-up)	(C)	16082
Giant Geyser - 250 Ft.*		13063
Golden Gate Canyon And Viaduct*		10079
Grand Canyon From Brink Of The Fall	(C)	17308
Grand Canyon From Artist Point	(C)	14089
Great Fall From Below - 308 Ft.*		10124
Great Fall From Red Rock - 308 Ft.*	(C)	16283
Jackson Lake And Teton Mountains	(C)	17302
Jackson Lake (See Mount Moran)		
Kepler Cascade, Firehole River*		10111
Minerva Terrace		13031
Morning Glory Spring	(C)	14033
Mount Moran And Jackson Lake		10002
Old Faithful Geyser - 150 Ft.*		10378
Shoshone Canyon, Cody Road*	(C)	[illegible]
Sylvan Lake And Top Notch Peak	(C)	[illegible]
Teton Mountains (See: Jackson Lake)		
Tower Fall And Towers - 132 Ft.*	(C)	17384
Yellowstone Lake And Mount Sheridan		10116

*Vertical Subjects.

J. E. HAYNES

Official Photographer of Yellowstone National Park

Selby at Virginia Aves., St. Paul, Minn., U. S. A. — Yellowstone Park, Wyoming

Listing of hand-painted picture titles

Haynes hand-painted photographs are highly sought after by collectors of early twentieth century hand-colored photography. Pretty much the only hand-colored Haynes views that you will find are from Yellowstone Park and usually include Old Faithful, other geysers, animals, the Great Falls, the Lower Falls, and other magnificent views throughout the park. These pictures were hand colored in oils in the Haynes Studio and typically sold to Yellowstone visitors and tourists, with some scenes being much rarer than others.

Most of Jack's work consisted of machined-produced prints reprinted from his father's works, including postcards, travel brochures, Yellowstone travel books, etc. The pictures of Jack Ellis Haynes are generally not as collectible as those by his father. Jack ran the family business until the 1950s. He had hoped that his daughter would become the third generation to carry on the family's Yellowstone Park business, but his only child, Lida Haynes, died in an automobile accident in 1952 at the age of 20. Jack Ellis Haynes died in 1964.

The *Haynes Guide*, Yellowstone's #1 tourist guide

The *Haynes Guide* was published and updated nearly every year between 1890 and 1966. These books were widely regarded as the best Yellowstone guidebooks in print and included facts and trivia about Yellowstone Park, along with, of course, many Haynes Yellowstone pictures.

Machine-produced triptych

As time and technology progressed, Haynes's hand-colored pictures were replaced by less expensive machine-produced color litho prints. These prints were sold both individually and in packaged portfolios. Machine-produced prints are from the later Jack Ellis Haynes years and are not nearly as collectible as Haynes's hand-colored pictures. Haynes's Yellowstone pictures were widely sold as various individual postcards, in souvenir postcard folders, and as smaller photo packs. These were sold both by

Haynes and through other Yellowstone vendors. Most were from the later Jack Ellis Haynes years and have estimated values of $10.00 – 35.00 each.

Over the years, the Haynes Studio either issued its own souvenir photo albums or had some of its Haynes Yellowstone pictures appear in Yellowstone photo albums and booklets issued by others. We have seen at least six such albums, and most likely there are many others. Most of these were from the later Jack Ellis Haynes years and have estimated values of $25.00 – 75.00 each.

Machine-produced Yellowstone postcard pack

We have also seen other non-Haynes items sold with the "Haynes" name attached. For example we have seen an "Old Faithful" etching that carried both the original artist's name alongside the "Haynes" name. We have seen an R. Atkinson Fox Yellowstone print that carried both the "Fox" name on the print and the "Haynes" name impressed into the matting. We have seen governmental Yellowstone publications which featured Haynes pictures. And we have even seen a hand-colored framed window glass designed to attract sunlight through Old Faithful.

REGIONALITY
Western U.S; Yellowstone National Park, Wyoming

REPRESENTATIVE TITLES & VALUE GUIDE
Hot Springs
Jupiter Terrace, Monmouth Springs
Hand-painted pictures: $50.00 – 100.00+
Machine-produced prints: $10.00 – 50.00+

STUART HAYWARD

BACKGROUND
Little background information on STUART HAYWARD has been found. We have only seen a few Stuart Hayward hand-painted pictures, and each was a Bermuda scene. We have found no connection between Stuart Hayward and A. H. Hayward.

REGIONALITY
Bermuda

REPRESENTATIVE TITLES & VALUE GUIDE
Assorted Bermuda titles
Estimated value range: $50.00 – 75.00

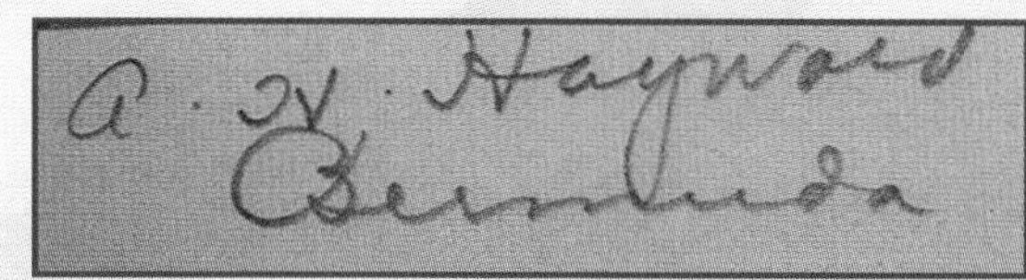

A. H. HAYWARD

BACKGROUND

Little background information on A. H. HAYWARD has been found. We have only seen several A. H. Hayward hand-painted pictures and each was a Bermuda scene. We have found no connection between A. H. Hayward and Stuart Hayward.

REGIONALITY

Bermuda

REPRESENTATIVE TITLES & VALUE GUIDE

"Poet Moore's House, Bermuda"
Estimated value range: $25.00 – 75.00+

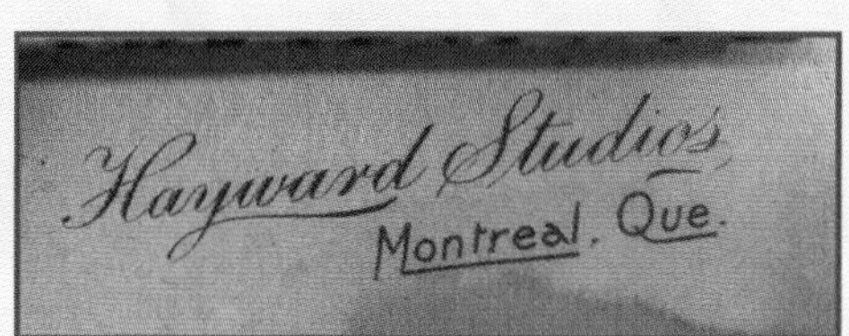

HAYWARD STUDIOS

BACKGROUND

Little background information on HAYWARD STUDIOS has been found. We have only seen one Hayward Studios hand-painted picture, and it indicated that the studio was located in Montreal, Quebec, Canada.

REGIONALITY

Canada; Montreal, Quebec

REPRESENTATIVE TITLES & VALUE GUIDE

Untitled seascape
Estimated value range: $25.00 – 50.00+

Seascape

C. HAZEN

BACKGROUND

Little background information on C. HAZEN has been found. We have only seen one C. Hazen hand-painted picture, and it provided no clues as to where it was taken.

REGIONALITY

Unknown

REPRESENTATIVE TITLES & VALUE GUIDE

Untitled exterior scene
Estimated value range: $10.00 – 50.00+

A. S. HEMENWAY

BACKGROUND

Little background information on A. S. HEMENWAY has been found. Dealer Carol Franzosa reported seeing an A. S. Hemenway hand-painted photo in her antiques shop. This picture was signed "A. S. Hemenway" lower right, titled "Snowbound" lower left, and had an "A.S.H." lower right on the image.

REGIONALITY

Unknown

REPRESENTATIVE TITLES & VALUE GUIDE

"Snowbound"
Estimated value range: $10.00 – 50.00

Untitled exterior scene

HENDRICKSON (first name not known)

BACKGROUND
Little background information on HENDRICKSON has been found. We have only seen one Hendrickson hand-painted picture, which was signed "Hendrickson" in red ink on the lower right of the image and was otherwise unsigned and untitled. It was an exterior scene that, in our opinion, was taken in New England.

REGIONALITY
New England

REPRESENTATIVE TITLES & VALUE GUIDE
Untitled exterior scene
Estimated value range: $10.00 – 50.00+

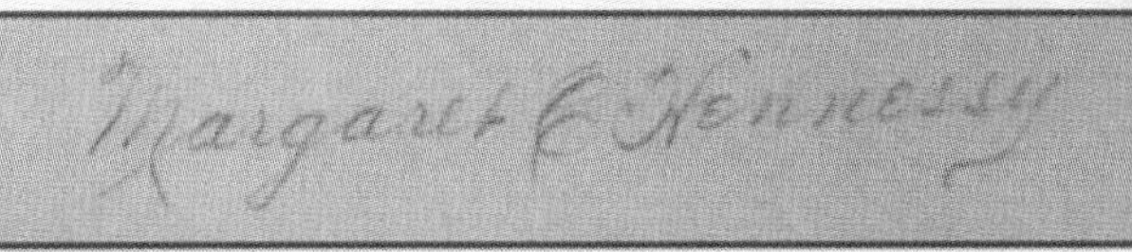

MARGARET HENNESSEY

BACKGROUND
Little background information on MARGARET HENNESSY has been found. We do know that she worked in Massachusetts and that at some point she was employed by Wallace Nutting. The few Margaret Hennessy pictures we have seen have been exterior scenes.

REGIONALITY
New England; Massachusetts

REPRESENTATIVE TITLES & VALUE GUIDE
"Chain Bridge"
Untitled exterior scenes
Estimated value range: $10.00 – 50.00+

"Chain Bridge"

CHARLES R. HIGGINS

Allen's Lane, Bath ME label

BACKGROUND

CHARLES R. HIGGINS is another New England photographer who did some very nice work. He was born in 1867 in Dedham, Massachusetts, and his father, John C. Higgins, was also a well-known professional Maine photographer, whose early photographs of ship launchings have hung in the Maine Maritime Museum in Bath, Maine.

Not surprisingly, Charles Higgins received much of his early photographic training from his father. While living in Bath, Higgins studied many photographic techniques as a child and eventually joined his father in his photography business. After his father passed away, Higgins continued operating the business on his own. Initially working in his father's studio, he later moved to 138 Front St. and eventually to Allen's Lane, both in Bath.

The photographic process used by Charles Higgins was also comparable to that used by Wallace Nutting. Traveling around with his box camera and tripod, Higgins would photograph scenes that caught his attention throughout Maine, blossoms, birches, mountains, and winter scenes. He also photographed interior scenes with and without people, exterior views of houses, seascapes, children, and the like. Glass negatives were used to develop black and white pictures onto the much-preferred platinum paper. In later years, the platinum paper was replaced with a substitute paper when platinum became unobtainable.

"The Old Chaise"

Although Charles Higgins took all photographs, most were colored by Carrie Doherty, Higgins's primary colorist. She used the same Windsor and Newton moist watercolors that were used by Wallace Nutting and would highlight those portions of the pictures that she wanted to accentuate.

The scope of Charles Higgins's business was considerably smaller than that of Nutting's, even at its peak. Whereas Wallace Nutting employed nearly 200 people as colorists, framers, salesmen, and administrative office personnel, Higgins's staff numbered less than 10 at its peak in the 1920s. Some of Higgin's staff performed several duties. For example, Carrie Doherty, the colorist, was also the primary model used in the interior scenes. When a second model was needed, Higgins used his bookkeeper, Mary Spear.

As was true of the settings used by most other photographers selling hand-colored pictures of colonial interior scenes at that time, none of Higgins's interior settings appeared as

"A Call from Sally"

authentic or detailed as those in Wallace Nutting's interior pictures. The furniture used by Charles Higgins was not of the finest form or design, the rooms were not as precisely decorated as the finest rooms of the day would have been, and the models were not always dressed in the correct attire. Carrie Doherty and Mary Spear frequently had to make their own costumes, as those provided by Higgins did not always fit.

Most pictures were mounted upon an indented, linen-type mat. Titles were signed in the lower left corner under the picture, and Higgins's name was placed under the lower right side of the picture. In many Higgins pictures, "Chas R. Higgins" appears within the mat indentation and the title appears considerably below the indentation line. Most titles and signatures were applied by Carrie Doherty.

Higgins framed pictures came in a variety of sizes, with mats ranging from 5" x 7" to 15" x 22", the largest we have seen. Many seem to be approximately 10" x 16". Frames were generally a thin gold or brown wood frame, again very similar to the style used by Wallace Nutting.

Wallace Nutting's influence is evident throughout Higgins's work, from the types of exterior and colonial interior scenes sold, to the title and signature placement, framing, and type of matting used. In addition to colonial interior and exterior pastoral pictures, Higgins also sold scenes with children, Indians, boats, seascapes, and even a stagecoach scene. An authentic Higgins label may add 10 – 15% to the value of a picture

Charles Higgins also offered a line of what he called novelties. These were hand-colored pictures that were small enough to decorate the tops of cork stoppers, match boxes, or wrapping paper for bars of soap. Few of these items seem to have survived today.

Higgins's pictures were marketed in several ways. Generally, they were sold through several larger Maine department stores or through summer resorts throughout the Bath area. Other pictures were also sold to customers who stopped by the studio or who ordered through the mail. There is no doubt that Charles Higgins hand-colored platinotype pictures provided many fond memories of family vacations to far-away Maine in the early twentieth century.

Paper label

A 1919 advertisement in a Bath, Maine, business directory summed up the work of the Charles Higgins Studios this way:

> The most appreciated gift for any occasion is one of
> HIGGIN'S HAND COLORED PLATINUMS
> These pictures are from artistic bits of nature's
> best scenery, and colonial studies.
> Write for illustrated catalog and prices.
> The Higgins Pictures Studios
> Allen's Lane, Bath Maine

Charles Higgins also built and operated the Greenmoors Inn in Kittery, Maine. This establishment quickly became a popular shore dining resort. Its initial success as a restaurant led Higgins to broaden its services to include lodging as well.

Higgins was extremely active in local community affairs, both in Bath and from his winter home in later years, in Frostproof, Florida. He was a member of the Poplar Star Lodge; the Masons; Montgomery and St. Bernard, R.A.C.; Dunlap Commandry; K. T. and the Council in Brunswick; Kora Temple; Mystic Shrine of Lewiston; and the Bath Elks Lodge.

Charles Higgins died of a heart attack in 1930 at the age of 67.

REGIONALITY
New England; Bath, Maine

REPRESENTATIVE TITLES & VALUE GUIDE
"Birches on the Bank"
"By the Fireside"
Close-framed horse and carriage
Close-framed interior scene
"A Colonial Stairway"
"Fireside Reflections"
"Going Shopping"
"Grandfather's Clock"
"Highway and Byway"
"In Colonial Days"
"The Lane"
"Near Sugar Mill"
"A November Sunset"
"The Old Chaise"
"Road by the River"
"A Rocky Shore"
"A Slow Fire"
"Spring on the Old Farm"
"Tower Surf"
"Twin Birch"
"A Winding Stair"
"A Winter Sunset"
Typical value range: $50.00 – 300.00+

"Trudging Homeward"

"Sentinels, Estes Park Colo."

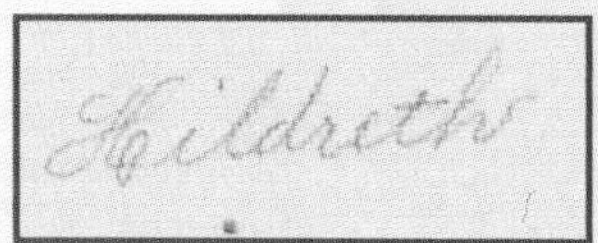

CARL F. HILDRETH

BACKGROUND

Little background information on CARL F. HILDRETH has been found. We do know that he worked in Colorado and took certain pictures at Estes Park, Colorado. It appears that Hildreth died in 1935.

REGIONALITY

Western U.S.; Colorado

REPRESENTATIVE TITLES & VALUE GUIDE

"Sentinels, Estes Park, Colorado"
Estimated value range: $25.00 – 75.00+

T. J. HILEMAN (1882 – 1945)

BACKGROUND

TOMAR JACOB HILEMAN was born on November 6, 1882, in Marienville, Pennsylvania, and eventually graduated from the Effingham School of Photography in Chicago. In 1911 he moved to Kalispell, Montana, and opened a portrait studio there. In 1913 he married Alice Georgeson, exchanging vows near Bridal Falls, supposedly making them the first couple to have ever been married in Glacier National Park. T. J. Hileman then went on to become more closely associated with Glacier National Park than any other photographer. Over the years, his beautiful landscape photography was used on travel portfolios, postcards, brochures, magazines, and books. And over the years he sold thousands of his hand-colored photographs that captured the natural beauties of Glacier Park.

Scenes in Glacier National Park travel portfolio

Hileman became associated with the Great Northern Railroad early in his career. He would move his bulky camera equipment and supplies by mule and horseback up the trails and over the mountains throughout the park. Hileman was an exceptional mountain climber and became known in some circles as

"Mountain Goat Hileman" because of his ability to climb to seemingly unascendable locations and wait for the precise moment to take the perfect picture. By 1925, Hileman became the official photographer for the Great Northern, signing a contract that paid him $125 per month.

Hileman was also an astute businessman. Although on the payroll of the Great Northern, he retained the copyright of all of his picture negatives, and the Great Northern was allowed to purchase as many copies as it wanted of any picture that it wanted — at 35 cents per copy. The Great Northern sent Hileman on various promotional tours, where he met with publishers and newspaper editors, and with copies of his images being distributed throughout the country, Hileman became somewhat of a national celebrity.

"Josephine Lake and Grinnell Glacier"

In 1926, Hileman opened a photofinishing lab within Glacier Park that enabled visiting tourists to drop off their film in the evening and pick up finished pictures the next morning. Over the years, he sold enough hand-colored photographs to enable him to build a home on Flathead Lake in 1931.

The Great Depression of the 1930s and the advent of World War II both negatively impacted Glacier Park tourism and picture sales. With his wife's health declining, Hileman sold his Glacier Park studio and began to work out of his home. He suffered a stroke in 1943, and died in his home at Flathead Lake on March 13, 1945.

In 1985, the Glacier Park Natural History Association acquired more than 100 of Hileman's negatives, and today it also has more than 2,000 T. J. Hileman pictures in its photographic archives.

REGIONALITY
Western U.S.; Glacier National Park, Montana

REPRESENTATIVE TITLES & VALUE GUIDE
"Josephine Lake and Grinnell Glacier"
Estimated value range: $25.00 – 75.00+

FREDERICK ATHERTON "ADIRONDACK" HODGES (1888 – 1959)

BACKGROUND

Much of the information on FREDERICK A. HODGES was supplied by Michael and Brenda Gridley. Frederick Atherton Hodges, the son of famous New York photographer Frederick B. Hodges, went on to a successful photographic career of his own, earning the nickname "Adirondack" from his peers. Between the years 1910 and 1950, Adirondack Hodges roamed throughout the Adirondack Mountains region of New York, producing more than 8,000 negatives throughout each photographic season of the year. With these pictures and 23 reels of black and white and colored movie film shot in the later years, Adirondack Hodges probably did as much as anyone else to record the beauties of New York State's Adirondack Mountains.

Born in Rome, New York, at the foothills of the Adirondacks, Hodges became infatuated with the region at an early age. As early as age nine Hodges would travel to the Adirondacks on family vacations and travel the backroads with his father and his camera. Attending school in the Rome area, Hodges decided early on to become a professional photographer. Like most photographers of the era, The sale of hand-colored photographs usually didn't pay all the bills, so like most photographers who sold hand-painted photographs, he had to take on indoor photography commissions such as portrait and commercial photography.

Each summer he would use Blue Mountain Lake Camp as his outdoor photography headquarters. He would hand paint his most recent pictures, taken during the preceding season, and display them in various camps and hotels within the region. Sometimes sales were brisk; sometimes they were slow. Oftentimes he would lecture on the current Adirondack season and use his lectures to increase picture sales. But if nothing else, Hodges hand-painted photographs did two things: 1) they helped preserve the unspoiled beauty of the Adirondacks for future generations, and 2) they provided a wonderful souvenir of a family's spring, summer, fall, or winter vacation to the Adirondack Mountains.

Frederick Atherton Hodges (1888 – 1959)

Frederick A. Hodges died at Blue Mountain Lake on August 15, 1959, only four years after the death of his father, Frederick B. Hodges, in 1955.

REGIONALITY

New York State; Adirondack Mountains

REPRESENTATIVE TITLES & VALUE GUIDE

Assorted Adirondack mountain scenes
Estimated value range: $50.00 – 100.00+

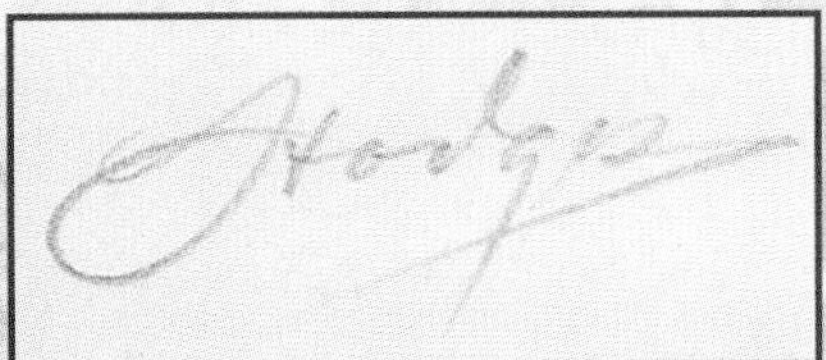

FREDERICK B. HODGES (1868 – 1955)

Frederick B. Hodges (1868 – 1955)

BACKGROUND

FREDERICK B. HODGES was a native of Rome, New York, and is considered by some to be the premier early twentieth century photographer of central New York. Born on September 13, 1868, in Rome, Hodges formed a duel career both in photography and botany. His first wife, Esther M. Hall, whom he married in 1886, died in 1918. Hodges had two sons, Breck W. Hodges and Frederick A. "Adirondack" Hodges, who also went on to a successful New York State photography career.

Together with his second wife, Alzuma Whittemore, whom he married in 1919, Hodges went on to identify 376 different species of wildflowers in Oneida County, New York, alone. Perhaps Hodges crowning botanical achievement came in 1922, when he discovered a colony of Ram's Head Lady Slippers just outside of Rome.

Beginning with the acquisition of his first camera in 1886, Hodges gained considerable recognition for his photographic achievements throughout New York State. His specialty was landscape scenes taken in such areas as the Mohawk River, the Erie Canal, the Black River Canal, and the Sand Plains. Hodges would often return to the same location again and again, photographing something new each time he went. He also extensively photographed such subject matter as covered bridges, wagon roads, footpaths, and the central New York canal system, including its canals, tow paths, locks, boats, and people. His hand-painted "gum prints" were widely exhibited in Boston, Pittsburgh, and Buffalo, and 30 of his pictures were placed on exhibition in 1945, at the Rome Women's Club.

"Canal Gossip"

From 1938 until his death in 1955, Hodges wrote a weekly column entitled "Nature Speaking" in the *Rome Daily Sentinel.* This column combined his love and knowledge of the outdoors and botany with his photographic skills, which he used to illustrate his column.

Five Hodges pictures have been reproduced as a limited editition set , the Heritage Keepsake Prints, by the Rome Historical Society. The five titles included "Black River Canal" (1915), "Wood Creek" (1900), "Boonville Gorge" (1915), "Canal Gossip" (1900), and "Pastoral Beauty" (1900).

"The Old Covered Bridge Near Poland N.Y."

REGIONALITY
New York State; Rome, New York

REPRESENTATIVE TITLES & VALUE GUIDE
"Black River Canal"
"Boonville Gorge"
"Canal Gossip"
"Pastoral Beauty"
"Raquette Lake"
"Raquette Lake Birches"
"Wannamaker Falls"
"Wood Creek"
Typical value range: $50.00 – 200.00+

HOMER (first name not known)

BACKGROUND
Little background information on HOMER has been found. We have only seen one picture signed "Homer," and it was an exterior scene that gave no clue as to its location or origin.

REGIONALITY
Unknown

REPRESENTATIVE TITLES & VALUE GUIDE
Untitled exterior scene
Estimated value range: $10.00 – 50.00

HOMES (first name not known)

BACKGROUND
Little background information on HOMES has been found. We have only seen one picture signed "Homes," and it was an exterior scene that indicated it was taken in Chocorua, New Hampshire, which suggests that Homes may have been a New Hampshire photographer.

REGIONALITY
New England; New Hampshire

REPRESENTATIVE TITLES & VALUE GUIDE
Untitled exterior scene
Estimated value range: $10.00 – 50.00

THEODOR HORYDCZAK (1890 – 1971)

BACKGROUND

THEODOR HORYDCZAK was a professional photographer whose work spanned nearly 40 years. Little is known about his early life. It is thought that he was born in Eastern Europe and that he took up photography shortly after World War I, where he served in the U.S. Army Signal Corps. He worked and resided in Washington from the early 1920s until his retirement, and then death, in 1971.

Lincoln Memorial, circa 1930

Working primarily in Washington DC, Horydczak documented much of the people and events, machines and industrial subjects, and buildings and urban development, as well as most of the historical buildings and monuments in and around Washington. Important events such as the 1932 bonus army encampment, the 1933 World Series, and the World War II preparedness campaigns were all recorded by Horydczak.

Horydczak typically used a large-format Gold Ansco camera that was well suited to photographing views and buildings. His preferred negative format was 8" x 10". Virtually identical views of certain subjects abound in Horydczak's negatives as the result of his use of a technique called "bracketing" whereby he made multiple exposures at different camera aperture settings.

Lincoln Memorial, different angle, circa 1930

Many of Horydczak's pictures were stamped "Copyright Published, Theo. Horydczak, Photographer, 1223-12th Street NW, Washington DC." His best-selling pictures were the typical Washington DC tourist scenes such as the Washington Monument, Jefferson Memorial, Lincoln Memorial, White House, Capitol Building, Arlington Cemetery, Mt. Vernon, and other such locations. Horydczak's pictures were typically close-framed and carried a "Horydczak" impressed marking somewhere in the lower portion of the image. His pictures look so similar to those Washington DC pictures by Carlock and Buckingham that we thought that there might have been some connection between the three, but we have found no firm evidence of this.

The Library of Congress currently maintains the Theodor Horydczak Collection, which includes 32,000+ items including nearly 15,000 black and white photographs, 14,000 negatives, and 1,500 color transparencies. More than 14,000 digital images are also included with the

Backstamp on image

Horydczak Collection. Many of these can be viewed at the Library of Congress's website.

REGIONALITY
Washington DC

REPRESENTATIVE TITLES & VALUE GUIDE
Arlington Cemetery
Capital Building
Jefferson Memorial
Lincoln Memorial
Mt. Vernon
Washington Monument
White House
Typical value range: $25.00 – 75.00

K. P. HOWARTH

BACKGROUND
Little background information on K. P. HOWARTH has been found. We have only seen one Howarth image, and it was a Minnesota lake scene, which suggests that Howarth may have been a Minnesota photographer, or at least from the northcentral portion of the U.S..

REGIONALITY
Northcentral U.S.; Minnesota

REPRESENTATIVE TITLES & VALUE GUIDE
Exterior lake scene
Estimated value range: $25.00 – 50.00+

JOSEPH H. HUDSON

The Wissahickon in Autumn Arrayed

BACKGROUND

We have seen a fair number of HUDSON pictures over the years, and all were taken in or around Philadelphia, Pennsylvania. We have seen Hudson images from Fairmont Park, Mount Airy, Chestnut Hill, Valley Forge, and the Wissahickon Creek. We have been told by Hudson's grand daughter Harriet Hudson Mullen that his name was Joseph H. Hudson and that his studio was located in the Germantown section of Philadelphia. There have been an increasing number of collectors grabbing up Philadelphia-area hand-painted photographs, and the price of Hudson pictures has been on the rise over the past several years.

REGIONALITY

Pennsylvania

REPRESENTATIVE TITLES & VALUE GUIDE

"Autumn Arrayed"
"Fairmont Park Byroads"
"Mt. Airy Blossoms"
"The Wissahickson in Autumn Arrayed"
"Wissahickon Waters"
Typical value range: $50.00 – 100.00+

WOODBURY E. HUNT

BACKGROUND

Little background information on WOODBURY E. HUNT has been found. We have only seen one Hunt image, and it was an exterior scene that included a block "Copyright 1904 by Woodbury E. Hunt" on the image. The clapboard house in the picture appeared to be of New England origin and, in our opinion, Hunt was a New England photographer.

Untitled house scene

REGIONALITY

New England

REPRESENTATIVE TITLES & VALUE GUIDE

Untitled house scene
Estimated value range: $25.00 – 50.00+

NICK HUTCHINSON

BACKGROUND

Little background information on NICK HUTCHINSON has been found. We have only seen one Hutchinson image and it was an Exterior scene. The picture appeared to be of New England origin and, in our opinion, Hutchinson was a New England photographer.

REGIONALITY

New England

REPRESENTATIVE TITLES & VALUE GUIDE

Untitled exterior scene
Estimated value range: $10.00 – $50.00+

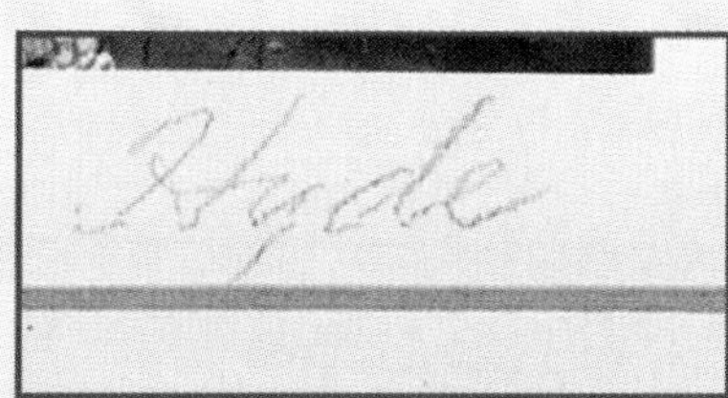

"Mt. Stream"

HYDE (first name not known)

BACKGROUND

Little background information on HYDE has been found. We have only seen one Hyde image, and it was an exterior scene. The picture appeared to be of New England origin and, in our opinion, Hyde was a New England photographer.

REGIONALITY

New England

REPRESENTATIVE TITLES & VALUE GUIDE

"Mt. Stream"
Estimated value range: $10.00 – 50.00+

Alaskan glacier scene

HEATH ARLO IVES

BACKGROUND
HEATH ARLO IVES was a photographer who worked out of Hyder, Alaska. We have only seen a few Ives images and each were Alaska scenes. We have seen various photographs shot by Ives for the Copper River and North Western Railway dating from the 1920s. We have also seen an Ives pictures marked "(c) H.A. Ives, Hyder Alaska" on the image. Good quality hand-colored photographs from Alaska are fairly unusual and Ives pictures are among the best hand-painted Alaska scenes that we have seen.

REGIONALITY
Alaska

REPRESENTATIVE TITLES & VALUE GUIDE
Men and horses on Alaskan glacier
Estimated value range: $100.00 – 250.00

WESLEY JACKSON

BACKGROUND
Little background information on WESLEY JACKSON has been found. We have only seen one Jackson image, and it was a Florida scene, which suggests that Jackson may have been a Florida photographer.

REGIONALITY
Florida

REPRESENTATIVE TITLES & VALUE GUIDE
Florida palm trees
Estimated value range: $25.00 – 50.00+

W. F. JACKSON

BACKGROUND
Little background information on W. F. JACKSON has been found. Don Wiesenberg reported adding a W. F. Jackson picture, titled "Prier Lake at Sunset — Olivet," to his collection.

REGIONALITY
Unknown

REPRESENTATIVE TITLES & VALUE GUIDE
Exterior lake scene
Estimated value range: $10.00 – 50.00+

"A Shallow Spot"

KABEL

BACKGROUND
Little background information on KABEL has been found. We have seen a fair number of Kabel pictures over the years, but none have included a first name or initial, or any labels with additional background information. We have noticed the similarity in color and style between Gibson and Kabel, but have found no evidence linking the two. All that we have seen suggests Kabel was from New England or the mid-Atlantic states.

REGIONALITY
New England

REPRESENTATIVE TITLES & VALUE GUIDE
"A Shallow Spot"
Typical value range: $25.00 – 75.00+

J. B. KAHILL

BACKGROUND
Little background information on J. B. Kahill has been found. We have only seen one Kahill over the years, and this one had an interesting twist. The untitled exterior salesman's sample scene included "Copyright 1907 by JB Kahill" on the image, yet the matting was unsigned and untitled, and the backing paper carried a Bicknell Mfg. Co. paper label on the back. This suggested to us that perhaps, for a brief period of time, the Bicknell Manufacturing Co. was publishing images by photographers other than J. Carleton Bicknell.

REGIONALITY
New England; Portland, Maine

REPRESENTATIVE TITLES & VALUE GUIDE
Untitled exterior salesman's sample
Estimated value range: $25.00 – 75.00+

Exterior scene

Paper label on back of Kahill exterior scene

Untitled girl by house scene

VICTOR KAHILL

BACKGROUND

Little background information on VICTOR KAHILL has been found. We have seen only one Kahill over the years. We have noticed the similarities of colors and styles between Fred Thompson, David Davidson and Victor Kahill but have found no evidence linking the three. Kahill, in our opinion, appears to have been a New England photographer.

REGIONALITY

New England

REPRESENTATIVE TITLES & VALUE GUIDE

Untitled girl by house
Estimated value range: $25.00 – 50.00+

KAMERA ART STUDIOS INC.

BACKGROUND

Little background information on the KAMERA ART STUDIOS has been found. We have only seen one Kamera Art image, and it was a California palm tree scene that retained a paper label that indicated the studio was located in Los Angeles, California.

REGIONALITY

Western U.S.; Los Angeles, California

REPRESENTATIVE TITLES & VALUE GUIDE

California palm trees
Estimated value range: $25.00 – 50.00+

KATTLEMAN (first name not known)

BACKGROUND
Little background information on KATTLEMAN has been found. We have seen only one Kattleman over the years, and that exterior scene provided no clue as to its location or origin.

REGIONALITY
Unknown

REPRESENTATIVE TITLES & VALUE GUIDE
Untitled exterior scene
Estimated value range: $10.00 – 50.00+

GEORGE C. KEEP

BACKGROUND
Little background information on GEORGE C. KEEP has been found other than that he was another Portland, Maine, photographer. We have seen relatively few Keep pictures over the years, and most have been Portland Head Lighthouse pictures (which was perhaps the highest-selling southern Maine tourist location). One Keep paper label reads "Portland Head Light, Geo. C. Keep, Artist, Portland, Maine." Another Keep backstamp is amazingly similar to Fred Thompson's triangular backstamp label. Barbara and John Snyder have even reported taking apart a Keep picture that had a Keep label pasted over an original Fred Thompson triangular backstamp.

So, who was George C. Keep? A private photographer, an employee of Fred Thompson, one of the companies bought out by Fred Thompson circa 1900 – 1905, or someone who purchased some Thompson inventory after the Thompson Art Co. closed its doors, only to sell it as his own?

All good questions. And if you know the answers, please let us know.

REGIONALITY
New England; Portland, Maine

REPRESENTATIVE TITLES & VALUE GUIDE
"Portland Head Light"
Typical value range: $50.00 – 100.00+

"Portland Head Light"

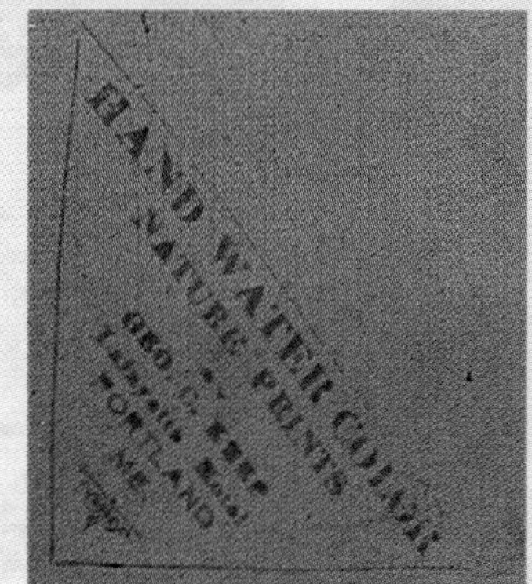

Note the Fred Thompson–style backstamp.

KELLY STUDIO

BACKGROUND

Little background information on the KELLY STUDIO has been found. We have seen only one Kelly Studio picture over the years, and that exterior scene had "Kelly Studio" impressed into the mat and indicated that the studio was located in Miami, Arizona.

REGIONALITY

Western U.S.; Arizona

REPRESENTATIVE TITLES & VALUE GUIDE

Untitled western U.S. scene
Estimated value range: $25.00 – 50.00+

RALPH KIMBALL (1886-1952)

BACKGROUND

RALPH KIMBALL was born in 1886 in Maine. He was a minister in Berlin, New Hampshire, and took pictures both in Berlin and in Woodbury, Connecticut, where he subsequently lived. We have only seen a Kimball exterior scene, and it was done in the style of the major photographers. Ralph Kimball died in 1952.

REGIONALITY

New England

REPRESENTATIVE TITLES & VALUE GUIDE

Exterior scene, birches
Exterior scene, blossoms
Estimated value range: $25.00 – 50.00+

Santa Ines Spanish mission

By Jean Woolman Kirkbride, Camden N. J.
Original water color photograph.

JEAN WOODMAN KIRKBRIDE

BACKGROUND

JEAN WOODMAN KIRKBRIDE worked out of Camden, New Jersey, circa 1915 – 1920. She produced a series of hand-painted watercolor photographs for the 1915 Panama-Pacific Exhibition. She also produced a centennial anniversary piece for the Santa Ines Mission (Santa Barbara, California) that included a hand-painted photograph of the mission.

REGIONALITY

New Jersey; California

REPRESENTATIVE TITLES & VALUE GUIDE

California mission scene
Estimated value range: $25.00 – 50.00+

KIRWAN (first name not known)

BACKGROUND

Little background information on KIRWAN has been found. We have seen only one Kirwan picture over the years, and that exterior scene was a snow-capped Rocky Mountain scene. The matting was pre-printed lower right with "Kirwan, Glenwood Springs, Colo."

REGIONALITY

Western U.S.; Colorado

REPRESENTATIVE TITLES & VALUE GUIDE

Rocky Mountains, Colorado
Estimated value range: $50.00 – 100.00+

Rocky Mountains, Colorado

FRED H. KISER (1878 – 1955)

BACKGROUND

FRED H. KISER is probably the best-known photographer from the Crater Lake region of Oregon. Born in Grand Island, Nebraska, Kiser moved with his family to Portland, Oregon where his family ran a Hotel and Nursery. Fred became interested in photography at an early age and in conjunction with his brother Oscar established his first photographic studio, Kiser Brothers. Much of his earliest work was done at Crater Lake, and a 1903 exhibition of his Crater Lake images brought him local and regional acclaim.

In 1905, Kiser was honored by being named as the official photographer for the Lewis and Clark Centennial Exhibition in Portland. Shortly thereafter, Kiser was hired by the Great Northern Railroad to become its official photographer. He spent much of the next six years photographing the Glacier Park region and many of his pictures were used to popularize the region, in various postcards, books, magazines, brochures, and sales literature. After his business relationship with the Great Northern ended, Kiser returned to Crater Lake. In 1921 he built a studio there and became its official photographer.

Unlike the majority of photographers who colored their pictures in watercolors, Kiser hand painted his images in oils. The depression of the 1930s severely impacted tourism to the region, which negatively impacted his business. Fred Kiser eventually moved to California, where he died in Newport Beach in 1955.

REGIONALITY

Western U.S.; Crater Lake, Oregon

REPRESENTATIVE TITLES & VALUE GUIDE

Crater Lake, Oregon
Estimated value range: $75.00 – 200.00

KISER'S STUDIO
773 Milwaukee Street
Corner Bismark (Sellwood Car)
Phone, Sellwood 1842, Portland, Ore.

Backstamp

Crater Lake, Oregon

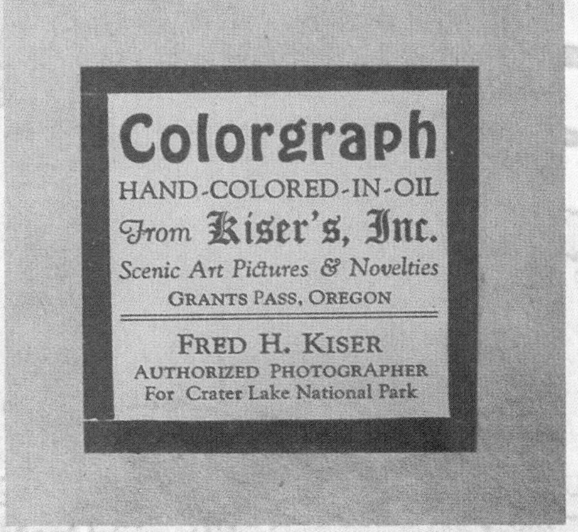

Paper label

KNAFFLE & CO.

BACKGROUND
Little background information on KNAFFLE & CO. has been found. We have seen only one Knaffle & Co. picture over the years, and that picture provided no clue as to its location or origin,

REGIONALITY
Unknown

REPRESENTATIVE TITLES & VALUE GUIDE
Untitled exterior scene
Estimated value range: $10.00 – 50.00+

KNOFFE (first name not known)

BACKGROUND
Little background information on KNOFFE has been found. We have seen only one Knoffe picture over the years, and it was an exterior scene that, in our opinion, was taken in New England.

REGIONALITY
New England

REPRESENTATIVE TITLES & VALUE GUIDE
Exterior scene
Estimated value range: $25.00 – 50.00+

Exterior scene

Ellsworth (l) and Emery (r) Kolb

KOLB BROTHERS

BACKGROUND

EMERY and ELLSWORTH KOLB first came to the Grand Canyon in 1902, and for the next 70 years they explored, photographed, and catered to the Grand Canyon tourist trade. Operating a photography studio on the South Rim, they offered a wide variety of photographic services. Shortly after the turn of the century, the Grand Canyon saw a significant increase in tourism, after its natural beautifies were shared with much of early twentieth century America through the photographs of the Kolb Brothers, Fred Harvey, and other Grand Canyon photographers. Rail transportation to the Grand Canyon greatly improved around this time, and the 1905 opening of the South Rim's El Tovar Hotel further served to increase Grand Canyon tourism.

The Kolb brothers' photographic equipment included heavy Seneca view camera, including 5" x 7" and 8" x 10" sizes. These cameras included a Goerz shutter mounted upon a changeable lens board. Their equipment also included a Weno-Hawkeye stereo camera and a small Kodak camera as well. Burros and mules were often used in the Kolb brothers' Grand Canyon photographic expeditions. During the first several years the brothers were forced to use a vacant mine shaft as a darkroom, prior to their building a darkroom studio in 1906.

Grand Canyon, Arizona

One major part of their business was the sale of hand-painted views of the Grand Canyon to visiting tourists. Nearly every who visited the Grand Canyon needed to take home a memory of their trip and a Kolb brothers hand-painted photograph was the choice of many. Usually their Grand Canyon pictures were sold individually, but often they were included in a portfolio format. In addition to their scenic landscape views, the Kolb brothers were also there to photograph most of the daily mule parties that descended into the canyon. Nearly everyone who experienced these once-in-a-lifetime descents wanted a memory of that trip and the Kolb Brothers were there to provide it. Theodore Roosevelt, William Howard Taft, William Jennings Bryant, and Frederick Remington were just a few of the more famous Americans to be photographed on such a trip.

Perhaps their most noteworthy experience came in 1911, when they ran the Colorado River with their motion picture camera. The result was the first motion picture footage ever shot within the Grand Canyon and seen by the outside world.

Kolb Brothers

In re-ordering trail pictures, the date and number will be found on the face of the pictures. Duplicates may be had at any time post paid 55¢.

KOLB BROTHERS

GRAND CANYON ARIZONA

HISTORICAL INFORMATION OF INTEREST

Major J. W. Powell's famous trip of 1869 through the Colorado River Canyons, was duplicated and modernized in a realistic manner by Kolb Brothers who were established as the Grand Canyon photographers before El Tovar Hotel was built.

Their journey began at Green River City, Wyoming, September 8th, 1911. In two open row boats they ran 365 bad rapids, descending 6000 feet, touching six states and after 101 days they landed at Needles, California. Afterwards continuing to the Gulf of California. Then again in 1921 to 1923, the Kolb Bros. piloted the U.S. Geological Survey through these same canyons and rapids from Green River, Utah to Needles Calif. Hundreds of photographic studies were secured together with the first Motion Pictures ever made recording the dangers and hardships involved on this trip.

The story, in connection with both still and moving pictures, has been given before the leading societies and clubs of our large cities. Canyon visitors can see the pictures and hear the lecture at KOLB BROTHERS' Studio. Here reliable information may be obtained, unusual and exclusive pictures may be seen and you may talk with the makers of the views who have been over the ground. This thrilling account in book form with 344 pages, 100 pictures and an interesting foreword by Owen Wister, autographed and post paid, $ 4.75.

This studio is independent of all Hotels, and stores: located at the head of Bright Angel trail, 200 feet past the company's rock lookout. Our telescope is worth while.

ADDRESS ALL MAIL TO KOLB BROS., GRAND CANYON, ARIZONA.

Paper label

These movies were seen nationwide and even caught the eye of Thomas Edison, which served to further publicize the Kolb brothers' works.

The Kolb Brothers studio finally closed in 1976.

REGIONALITY
Western U.S.; Grand Canyon, Arizona

REPRESENTATIVE TITLES & VALUE GUIDE
Untitled Grand Canyon scene
Typical value range: $50.00 – 100.00+

KRABEL (first name not known)

BACKGROUND
Little background information on KRABEL has been found. We have seen only one Krabel picture over the years, and it was an exterior scene. It didn't include a first name, a paper label, or anything else that could provide any additional background information. Nor did it give any clues as to its location or origin. It is also possible that "Krabel" may be "Kabel."

REGIONALITY
Unknown

REPRESENTATIVE TITLES & VALUE GUIDE
Exterior scene
Estimated value range: $10.00 – 50.00+

LaBELLE STUDIOS

BACKGROUND
Little background information on LaBELLE STUDIOS has been found. We have seen only one LaBelle Studios picture over the years, and it was an exterior scene that included a paper label indicating that the LaBelle Studio was located in Marlboro, Massachusetts.

REGIONALITY
New England; Marlboro, Massachusetts

REPRESENTATIVE TITLES & VALUE GUIDE
Exterior scene
Estimated value range: $10.00 – 50.00+

LAKE (first name not known)

BACKGROUND
Little background information on LAKE has been found. We have seen only one Lake picture over the years, and it was an exterior scene that provided no clue as to its location or origin.

REGIONALITY
Unknown

REPRESENTATIVE TITLES & VALUE GUIDE
Untitled exterior scene
Estimated value range: $10.00 – 50.00+

Greeting card cover

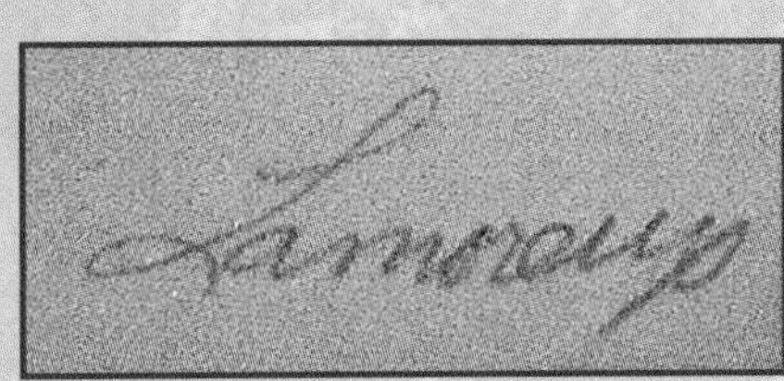

LAMOREAUX (first name not known)

BACKGROUND
Little background information on LAMOREAUX has been found. We have seen only one Lamoreaux picture over the years, and it was a Florida Singing Tower scene mounted upon a folding greeting card, most likely intended for the Singing Tower tourist trade. It failed to include a first name, a paper label, or anything else that could provide any additional background information.

REGIONALITY
Florida

REPRESENTATIVE TITLES & VALUE GUIDE
"Bok Singing Tower" greeting card
Estimated value range: $25.00 – 50.00+

Greeting card

J. H. LAMSON
LAMSON STUDIO

Cabinet card marking

BACKGROUND

The LAMSON STUDIO was one of the larger Portland studios selling hand-painted photographs around 1900. We say this not based upon any hard evidence or documented facts, but simply because of the number of Lamson pictures that have come through our auctions, and that we see in our travels through antique shows, group shops, and other auctions throughout New England and the mid-Atlantic states.

For years we were unable to locate much biographical information on Lamson, and then collector Bob Frishman sent us a cabinet card photo that was taken by "J. H. Lamson, Photographer, 244 Middle Street, Portland, Maine. "Everything suggests that this J. H. Lamson and Lamson Studios are one and the same — Portland, Maine, 244 Middle Street, the time period for the cabinet card, all suggest the same individual.

Paper label

The Lamson Studios, like most other early twentieth century hand-painted photographers, followed the lead of Wallace Nutting. It sold primarily exterior landscape scenes, including mountains, lakes, streams, rivers, birches, blossoms, and other assorted outdoor scenes. Summer scenes are the most common, but winter scenes and seascapes taken along the southern Maine coastline are also sometimes found. Most Lamson pictures were taken in Maine or northern New England. They are typically characterized by a lighter shade of coloring, with the image mounted upon an indented matting, signed "Lamson" lower right, titled lower left, and framed within a darker ½" frame.

Lamson also photographed a series of larger schooners sailing off the Maine coastline. Tourists were always looking for souvenirs to take back with them as mementos of their Maine vacations and Lamson apparently felt that vintage ship photographs might be a good seller for them. Based upon the number of Lamson schooner pictures that are found today, we would guess that not very many such pictures were ever sold by his studio.

Machine-produced print

Lamson pictures are always signed "Lamson," with no first name, and we assume that Lamson was a man. Lamson Studios was large enough to have several different styles of a pre-printed "Lamson Studios" label, and was seemingly large enough to have some of its pictures reproduced and sold as four-color process prints. Four-color process printing is a type of printing that usually implies a press run of 1,000 or more copies of the same picture.

It would be our guess that Lamson Studios was in business for only a few years, based upon the relatively small volume of Lamson pictures that remain in circulation today; it operated perhaps from 1900 to 1905. The Lamson Studios closed its doors circa 1905 after being bought out by the Fred Thompson Art Co., also of Portland, Maine, which, for a brief period of time, continued to market "Lamson Nature Prints" over its own Fred Thompson Art Company paper label and backstamp.

Photogravure paper label

What is even more interesting is that after the Fred Thompson Art Co. went out of business in the mid-1920s, all of Thompson's glass negatives, including those Lamson Studios negatives which were acquired by Fred Thompson circa 1905, were purchased by the Hal Burrowes Co. of Portland, Maine. Therefore, you may see certain Lamson pictures being sold over the Lamson, Thompson, and Burrowes names (see Hal Burrowes and Fred Thompson in this chapter).

"Lamson Nature Prints Thompson Art Co." paper label

REGIONALITY
New England; Portland, Maine

REPRESENTATIVE TITLES & VALUE GUIDE
"Full Sail"
"Grasp of Winter"
"Grazing Sheep"
"Lakeside Mansions"
"Noon Time Rest"
"Placid Waters"
"Sailing Ship by Rock"
"Tea Time"
"The Cliff"
Untitled snow scene
"Woodland Road"
Typical value range: $50.00 – 175.00

"Grasp of Winter"

"The Old Fishing Hole"

Deck Lane

DECK LANE

BACKGROUND
Little background information on DECK LANE has been found. We have seen only one Deck Lane picture over the years, and it was a little boy fishing scene giving no clue as to the picture's location or origin.

REGIONALITY
Unknown

REPRESENTATIVE TITLES & VALUE GUIDE
"The Old Fishing Hole"
Estimated value range: $10.00 – 50.00+

LANE'S STUDIO

BACKGROUND
LANE'S STUDIO was based out of Calgary, Alberta, Canada, and specialized in hand-painted photographs taken in the Canadian Rockies primarily for the visiting tourist trade.

REGIONALITY
Canada; Calgary, Alberta

REPRESENTATIVE TITLES & VALUE GUIDE
Canadian Rockies scenes
Estimated value range: $25.00 – 75.00

LANG (first name not known)

BACKGROUND
Little background information on LANG has been found. Collector Austin Minor reported having a Lang picture in his collection, an exterior scene that included a signature very similar in style to the Fred Thompson signature.

REGIONALITY
Unknown

REPRESENTATIVE TITLES & VALUE GUIDE
Exterior scene
Estimated value range: $10.00 – 50.00+

Close-framed seascape

LAWRENCE (first name not known)

BACKGROUND
Little background information on LAWRENCE has been found. We have seen only one Lawrence picture over the years, and it was a sandy shoreline scene that gave no clues as to the picture's location and origin. This picture also closely resembled the work of P. Winslow, who did work on Cape Cod, Massachusetts.

REGIONALITY
Unknown

REPRESENTATIVE TITLES & VALUE GUIDE
Close-framed seascape scene
Estimated value range: $25.00 – 50.00+

"Baby's Welcome"

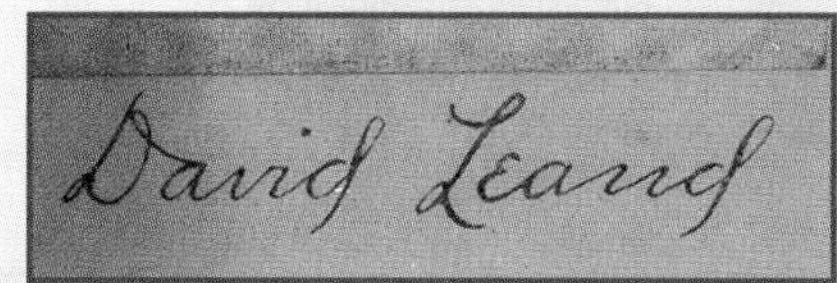

DAVID LEAND

BACKGROUND

Little background information on DAVID LEAND has been found. We have seen only two Leand pictures over the years, and actually, they were the same colonial New England architectural scene.

REGIONALITY

New England

REPRESENTATIVE TITLES & VALUE GUIDE

"Baby's Welcome"
Estimated value range: $25.00 – 75.00+

LEBUSCH (first name not known)

BACKGROUND

Although we have seen quite a few LEBUSCH pictures over the years, we have been unable to locate any information whatsoever about this photographer. LeBusch pictures are usually very lightly colored and are never brightly colored. As a matter of fact, LeBusch's work looks so much like "Burrowes's" work that we suspect that they may have come from the same studio but have been unable to confirm that suspicion. We believe that LeBusch was probably based in Portland, Maine.

REGIONALITY

New England; Portland, Maine

REPRESENTATIVE TITLES & VALUE GUIDE

"Across the Vail"
"A Birch Boundary"
"Birch Highway"
"Bridal Veil Falls"
"A Country Road"
"Homeward Bound"
"In the Pasture"
"Orchard Brook"
"Pine Ledge"
"Rocky Shore"
"A Shady Nook"
Typical value range: $25.00 – 75.00+

"Homeward Bound"

EDGAR BURDETT LEET

BACKGROUND
Little background information on EDGAR BURDETT LEET has been found. We have seen only two Leet pictures over the years, both suggesting that Leet was from Keene, New Hampshire

REGIONALITY
New England; Keene, New Hampshire

REPRESENTATIVE TITLES & VALUE GUIDE
Exterior birch scene
Estimated value range: $10.00 – 50.00+

M. LIGHTSTRUM

BACKGROUND
Little background information on LIGHTSTRUM has been found. We have seen only one Lightstrum picture over the years, and it was an exterior scene that provided no clue as to the picture's location or origin.

REGIONALITY
Unknown

REPRESENTATIVE TITLES & VALUE GUIDE
Untitled exterior scene
Estimated value range: $10.00 – 50.00+

Wallace R. MacAskill (1890 – 1956)

F.P.S.A. pre-printed signature

WALLACE R. MACASKILL (1890 – 1956)

BACKGROUND

WALLACE ROBINSON MACASKILL was one of Nova Scotia's most famous marine photographers. (We have seen conflicting birth years ranging from 1887 to 1890.) He is best known today for his Nova Scotia seascapes and sailing vessel scenes, and his works are becoming increasing collectible both in Canada and the United States.

Born in St. Peters, Cape Breton County in Nova Scotia, MacAskill graduated from the Wade School of Photography in New York in 1907. He opened his first photographic studio in St. Peters, and then in Glace Bay, before moving to Halifax in 1915. In Halifax, MacAskill worked for military photographer W. G. MacLaughlan, and between 1916 and 1919, he worked as a printer at the Elite Studios in Halifax. Between 1920 and 1929, MacAskill worked as a photographic printer for the Commercial Photo Service.

"Sunset, Nova Scotia Coast"

In 1926 MacAskill married Elva Abriel, another professional photographer, and he opened another studio in Halifax around this time. His pictures were used extensively by the Nova Scotia government, and many MacAskill pictures also appeared in two books that he published, *Out of Halifax* (1937) and *Lure of the Sea* (1951). Probably MacAskill's most famous picture was the famous schooner *Bluenose*. The picture appeared as a postage stamp in 1929, apperared in various books, and proved to be one of his best-selling art photographs.

Wallace R. MacAskill died in Halifax on January 25, 1956. In 1964 Mrs. MacAskill sold the contents of MacAskill's studio, including his negatives, to Maurice Crosby, another Halifax photographer. In 1970, Crosby sold them to the Maritime Supplies & Exchange Ltd. And in 1984, National Art Ltd. was given exclusive rights to produce new hand-colored pictures using MacAskill's original negatives. These pictures were still hand colored in oils, but are not as highly prized by collectors as MacAskill's earliest and original works. This agreement expired in 1986, and in 1987 MacAskill's negatives were donated to

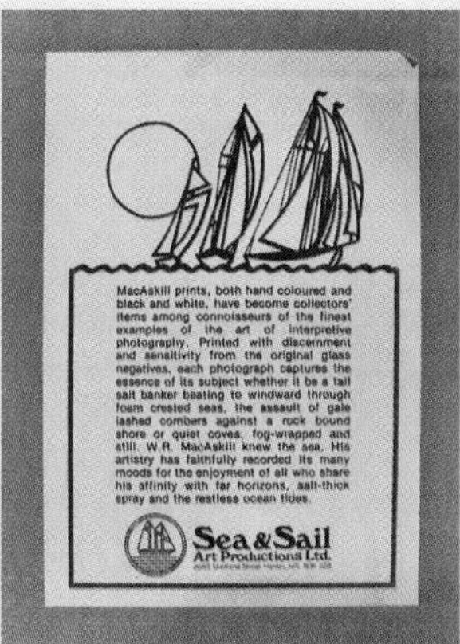

Newer paper label

National Art Ltd. logo, circa 1984

the Public Archives of Nova Scotia, where they remain today.

REGIONALITY
Canada; Halifax, Nova Scotia

REPRESENTATIVE TITLES & VALUE GUIDE
"Bluenose"
"Cape Le Rounde, C. B."
"Drying Sails"
"My Ship o' Dreams"
"Peggy's Cove Lighthouse"
"Rockbound Coast, Nova Scotia"
"Saga of the Sea"
"Schooners in Early Morning Mist"
"Sunset, Nova Scotia Coast"
Typical value range: $50.00 – 200.00+
Estimated value range: $25.00 – 50.00+

"Bluenose"

MacAskill

Have you ever seen a dusky-winged saltbanker ghosting out of the mist of Nova Scotia grey dawn . . . or watched a lofty barquentine [illegible] through the [illegible] off Chebucto Head, into the denser fog of marine oblivion? Have you scanned a maddened comber smashing the granite bastions of Peggy's. Or a lone, sou'westered schoonerman, standing starboard lookout, watching his lee rail plow the North Atlantic?

Today, saying you own a "MacAskill" is claiming possession of a collector's item in the world of photographic art . . . a masterpiece!

Poet John Masefield once wrote this finest of all marine photographers to ask a favor. The great fisherman-carriers of fore-and-aft sail were going the way of their square-rigged predecessors. Would the craftsman undertake to record the last of the schooners, in detail, so that future model-makers might more accurately reproduce them? Britain's Poet Laureate was asking no mere contribution to nautical history of a fond romantic. MacAskill was the complete master of his subject and his love. There was simply no one else able to render it captive in such unforgetable fashion.

MacAskill Pictures are available at . . .

MACASKILL-CROSBY PICTURES LTD.

HALIFAX SHOPPING CENTRE
HALIFAX, NOVA SCOTIA

WRITE FOR FREE CATALOGUE

MADE IN CANADA

Paper label

W. J. MacDONALD

BACKGROUND
Little background information on W. J. MACDONALD has been found. We have seen only one MacDonald picture over the years, and it was a western U.S. desert scene.

REGIONALITY
Western U.S.

REPRESENTATIVE TITLES & VALUE GUIDE
"Desert Sunset"
Estimated value range: $25.00 – 75.00

"Desert Sunrise"

ISLANDS OF PUGET SOUND
Series No. ~~200-3A~~/2-00
"ROSARIO BEACH"
Fidalgo Island
Copyright 1920 A. O. MACK

A. O. MACK

BACKGROUND

Little background information on A. O. MACK has been found. We have seen only one Mack picture over the years, and it was an exterior scene taken in the islands in Puget Sound, Washington. The picture carried a paper label that read "Rosario Beach, Fadalgo Island," which suggests to us that Mack was a Washington State photographer. And the simple fact that Mack anticipated selling enough copies of this particular title to have a paper label pre-printed in quantity suggests that Mack may have had a fairly sizable business in the area.

REGIONALITY

Northwest U.S; Washington State

REPRESENTATIVE TITLES & VALUE GUIDE

"Rosario Beach"
Estimated value range: $25.00 – 75.00

ROSSILER MACKINAE

BACKGROUND

Little background information on ROSSILER MACKINAE has been found. We have seen only one MacKinae picture over the years, and it was an exterior scene that provided no clue as to the picture's location or origin.

REGIONALITY

Unknown

REPRESENTATIVE TITLES & VALUE GUIDE

Untitled exterior
Estimated value range: $10.00 – 50.00

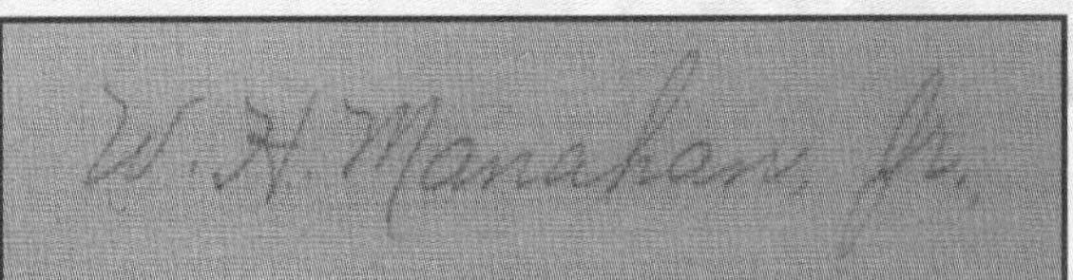

"In the Soul of Nature's Fir"

W.H. MANAHAN JR.

BACKGROUND

W.H. MAHAHAN JR. operated the Manahan Studio in Hillsboro, New Hampshire. We have only seen two Manahan pictures; one was signed "Manahan," and the other was signed "W. H. Manahan." Both were typical New England exterior scenes.

REGIONALITY

New England; New Hampshire

REPRESENTATIVE TITLES & VALUE GUIDE

"In the Soul of Nature's Fir"
Estimated value range: $25.00 – 50.00

J. H. MANN

BACKGROUND

Little background information on J. W. MANN has been found. Collector Edward J. Dennis IV reported seeing a J. W. Mann exterior scene titled "In the Adirondacks," which suggests that Mann probably worked in New York State.

REGIONALITY

New York

REPRESENTATIVE TITLES & VALUE GUIDE

"In the Adirondacks"
Estimated value range: $10.00 – 50.00

S. I. MARKEL

BACKGROUND

Little information has been found on S. I. MARKEL. We have only seen one Markel picture, and it was of the Lincoln Memorial in Washington DC, which suggests that Markel was a Washington DC photographer.

REGIONALITY

Washington DC

REPRESENTATIVE TITLES & VALUE GUIDE

Lincoln Memorial
Estimated value range: $25.00 – 50.00+

Charles Marshall

CHARLES MARSHALL

BACKGROUND

CHARLES MARSHALL was a photographer who worked out of Watertown, New York. We never saw a Marshall picture in circulation until several years ago, when we received a fairly large consignment of what we think were perhaps one-of-a-kind salesman's samples, which included approximately 15 – 20 Charles Marshall scenes. All were done in the Watertown, New York, area, and they included farm scenes, people scenes, and Thousand Island scenes. A paper label called his pictures "Face-Of-Nature Pictures, Genuine Hand-Painted Platinums, Direct From Nature." We suspect that Marshall was a regional photographer whose primary market was Thousand Island tourists. He may have tried to expand his market circa 1908 – 1912 by hiring a traveling sales representative to peddle his pictures outside of his native region. Hence the Pittsburgh-area salesman's sample find that found its way into our auctions. We have never seen a Charles Marshall either before, or since, this consignment was sold through several of our Auctions.

FACE-OF-NATURE PICTURES
Genuine Hand-Painted Platinums, direct from nature
By CHARLES MARSHALL
WATERTOWN, N. Y. U. S. A.

Paper label

REGIONALITY

New York; Watertown

Exterior scene

REPRESENTATIVE TITLES & VALUE GUIDE

"An Afternoon in May"
" 'Groves were God's Temples' "
"On the St. Lawrence"
"Summer Fleeces"
Typical value range: $50.00 – 200.00

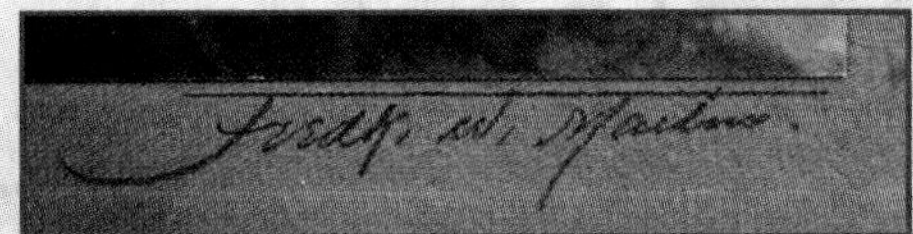

Southwestern U.S. desert

FREDERICK W. MARTIN

BACKGROUND

FRED MARTIN is a highly collectible photographer who worked out of Pasadena, California. Most of the Martin pictures that we have seen were taken either in or near the desert. The quality of Martin's work was comparable to that of most major photographers. His pictures were usually either signed "Frederick W. Martin" or "Fred'k. W. Martin." We have seen his signature signed either on the matting or directly onto the close-framed image. Fred Martin even produced a miniature hand-colored tourist postcard pack, which he titled *Gems of California Scenery.*

REGIONALITY

Southwest U.S.; Pasadena, California

REPRESENTATIVE TITLES & VALUE GUIDE

Assorted Southwest desert and landscape scenes
Typical value range: $50.00 – 150.00

Gems of California Scenery

RUSS MARTIN

BACKGROUND

RUSS MARTIN was a photographer who worked out of Prescott, Michigan. We have only seen one Russ Martin picture, and it was an exterior scene signed "Russ Martin."

REGIONALITY

Northcentral U.S.; Prescott, Michigan

REPRESENTATIVE TITLES & VALUE GUIDE

Exterior scene
Estimated value range: $10.00 – 50.00

GEORGE MASA (1881 – 1933)

BACKGROUND

Collector Jim Graves reported that he located some biographical information on a photographer named GEORGE MASA. Masa operated a studio called Asheville Photo Service in Asheville, North Carolina and operated that studio circa 1928 – 1933. Born in Japan in 1881, not much is known of his earlier life. He primarily photographed the lakes and mountains of Western North Carolina and the Smokey Mountains and his pictures were used both for hand-painted photos and postcards. A back-stamp used by Masa read "Photographed by Asheville Photo Service, Asheville NC." Apparently some of his pictures and materials have been preserved by the Pack Memorial Library in Asheville. After his death in 1933 his business was sold to E & E Fisher, and it is thought that E & E may have reissued some Masa photographs in lithograph format.

REGIONALITY

Southeast U.S.; Asheville, North Carolina

REPRESENTATIVE TITLES & VALUE GUIDE

Lake Lure, North Carolina
Estimated value range: $25.00 – 75.00

GUS A. MAVES

BACKGROUND

GUS A. MAVES was a photographer who worked out of Victoria, British Columbia, Canada and apparently lived in an area called Shoal Bay. Maves marketed his pictures as "Hand-Colored Art Gems."

REGIONALITY

Canada; Victoria, British Columbia

REPRESENTATIVE TITLES & VALUE GUIDE

Mount Malakat, Victoria, British Colombia
Estimated value range: $25.00 – 75.00

McCLURE (first name not known)

BACKGROUND
Little background information on McClure has been found. We have seen only one McClure picture over the years and it was a close-framed Rocky Mountains scene and a copyright on the image indicated that McClure was from Denver, Colorado.

REGIONALITY
Western U.S.; Denver, Colorado

REPRESENTATIVE TITLES & VALUE GUIDE
Closed-Framed Rocky Mountains
Estimated value range: $25.00 – 50.00+

Close-framed Rocky Mountains

McCORKLE (first name not known)

BACKGROUND
McCorkle was another Portland, Maine photographer. He sold hand-painted photographs primarily taken in Maine and marketed his pictures as "The McCorkle Platinums" circa 1910 – 1920.

REGIONALITY
New England; Portland, Maine

REPRESENTATIVE TITLES & VALUE GUIDE
Exterior scene
Estimated value range: $25.00 – 50.00

New Glasgow, Nova Scotia

F. O. McLEOD

BACKGROUND
F. O. McLEOD was a Canadian photographer who worked out of Nova Scotia, Canada. We have seen a fair number of his pictures over the years and they are always very nicely colored. A paper we have seen called his pictures "Nova Scotia Scenes — Seas and Landscapes," and indicated that his studio was located at 163 Provost St., New Glasgow, Nova Scotia.

REGIONALITY
Canada; New Glasgow, Nova Scotia

Cape Breton, Nova Scotia

REPRESENTATIVE TITLES & VALUE GUIDE
"Land o' Lakes, Cape Breton"
"Pentecostal Tabernacle,
New Glasgow, Nova Scotia"
Typical value range:
$50.00 – 100.00+

Paper label

E. H. MERRILL

BACKGROUND
E. H. MERRILL operated his studio at 25?? Middle Street in Portland, Maine. This untitled exterior had an oval Merrill backstamp, with the street number partially illegible.

REGIONALITY
New England; Portland, Maine

REPRESENTATIVE TITLES & VALUE GUIDE
Untitled exterior
Estimated value range: $10.00 – 50.00

MEYERS (first name not known)

BACKGROUND
Little background information on Meyers has been found. We have seen only one Meyers picture over the years, and it was an Exterior scene which provided no clue as to its location or origin.

REGIONALITY
Unknown

REPRESENTATIVE TITLES & VALUE GUIDE
Untitled exterior scene
Estimated value range: $10.00 – 50.00

MILE HIGH PHOTO STUDIO

BACKGROUND
The Mile High Photo Studio was based in Denver, Colorado. We have seen only one Mile High picture over the years, and it was a Rocky Mountains, Colorado, scene containing a paper label confirming its location.

Paper label

REGIONALITY
Western U.S.; Denver, Colorado

REPRESENTATIVE TITLES & VALUE GUIDE
Rocky Mountains, Colorado
Estimated value range: $50.00 – 75.00

Crater Lake, Oregon

MILLER PHOTO CO.

BACKGROUND
Little background information on the Miller Photo Company has been found. We have seen only one Miller Photo Co. picture over the years, and it was a circa 1920 Crater Lake, Oregon scene.

REGIONALITY
Northwest U.S.; Crater Lake, Oregon

REPRESENTATIVE TITLES & VALUE GUIDE
Crater Lake, Oregon
Estimated value range: $25.00 – 75.00

H. T. MITCHELL

BACKGROUND
H. T. MITCHELL was a relatively early photographer who worked out of Pawtucket Falls, Rhode Island. We have only seen one Mitchell Exterior scene and it was dated 1896.

REGIONALITY
New England; Pawtucket Falls, Rhode Island

REPRESENTATIVE TITLES & VALUE GUIDE
Exterior scene
Estimated value range: $10.00 – 50.00

"Bretton Woods"

Moehring

MOEHRING (first name not known)

BACKGROUND
MOEHRING was a New England photographer who we believe worked out of New Hampshire. His work was comparable to the major photographers and, unless you look very closely, it is very easy to confuse his signature with the Wallace Nutting signature. On more than one occasion we have stopped to look at what we thought was a Nutting but which in reality was a Moehring.

REGIONALITY
New England; New Hampshire

REPRESENTATIVE TITLES & VALUE GUIDE
"Bretton Woods"
"Decked for Spring"
Estimated value range: $25.00 – 75.00

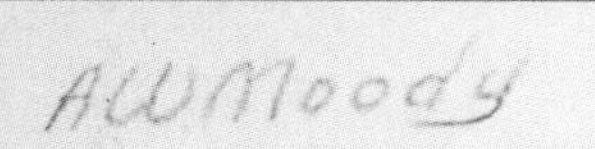

A. W. MOODY

BACKGROUND
A. W. MOODY operated Moody's Studio in New Hampshire. Most Moody pictures that we have seen were taken at or near Newfound Lake in New Hampshire.

REGIONALITY
New England; New Hampshire

REPRESENTATIVE TITLES & VALUE GUIDE
"The Ledges, Newfound Lake, Bristol, N.H."
Typical value range: $25.00 – 75.00

"The Ledges, Newfound Lake, Bristol, N.H."

KARL EVERTON MOON (1879 – 1948)

Carl Everton Moon
(1879 – 1948)

BACKGROUND

KARL EVERTON MOON was born in Wilmington, Ohio. After serving in the Ohio National Guard, he decided to pursue a career in photography and apprenticed under a series of photographers in Ohio, West Virginia, and Texas. Inspired by J. Fenimore Cooper's *Last of the Mohigans*, Moon had become interested in Native American at an early age. In 1903 he opened a studio in Albuquerque, New Mexico, where he began his photographic art studies of America's southwestern Indians. In 1905, Moon started a partnership with Thomas Keleher Jr., and their photographic studio was said to be one of the best equipped in the Southwest. In 1906, Moon was invited to exhibit his photographic work at the National Museum in Washington DC. His work was also shown at the American Museum of Natural History in New York and at the Cosmos Club in Washington DC.

Karl Moon became better known when he became the art director for the Fred Harvey Company (see Fred Harvey/Fred Harvey Company) and as photographer for the Santa Fe Railroad. Widely known for his hand-painted photographs of American Indians, Moon also was an accomplished painter, studying for six years with famed American landscape artist Thomas Moran. By 1914, Moon had left the employ of Fred Harvey and moved his family to Pasadena, California, where he continued to paint and write about Native Americans.

"Vincenti"

We have never had the opportunity to sell a Karl Moon photograph through our auctions.

REGIONALITY

Southwestern U.S.

REPRESENTATIVE TITLES & VALUE GUIDE

"The Arrow Maker"
"Grey Hawk"
"Last of His People"
"A Navajo Boy"
"Navajo Mother and Papoose"
"Open Country, Taos Village"
"A Warrior's Bride"
Estimated value range: $500.00 – 3,000.00+

"Navaho Boy"

RECOMMENDED READING

In Search of the Wild Indian: Photographs and Still Life Works by Carl And Grace Moon, by Tom Driebe, published through the Maurose Publishing Company. Tom Driebe has also published assorted Carl Moon calendars, note cards, and postcards.

Also marked "(c) EW Simpson" on the image

"Gathering Flowers," signed "by Moran"

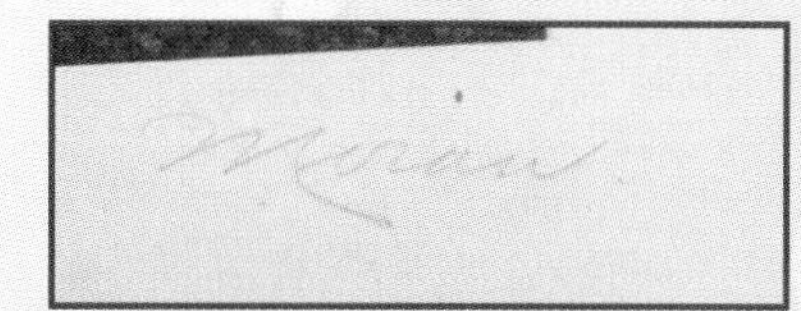

MORAN (first name not known)

BACKGROUND
MORAN is another one of those names that is difficult to explain. We have seen pictures signed "Moran", "by Moran", and we have even seen a picture marked "(c) EW Simpson" on the actual image above a "by Moran" pencil signature. To make things even more confusing, we have long suspected that Moran and Villar may be the same photographer, based upon the similarity of the 1930s-style garden scenes, but have been unable to confirm this. We have been unable to determine the specific location of any Moran pictures.

REGIONALITY
Unknown

REPRESENTATIVE TITLES & VALUE GUIDE
"A Cooling Drink"
"Gathering Flowers"
"Midst the Flowers"
Typical value range: $50.00 – 75.00+

E. A. MUELLER

BACKGROUND
Little background information on E. A. Mueller has been found. We have seen only one Mueller picture over the years, and it was a photo of a Native American chief and was signed "E. A. Mueller, 1925," which suggested to us that Mueller was probably from the southwestern U.S.

REGIONALITY
Southwest U.S.

REPRESENTATIVE TITLES & VALUE GUIDE
Native American chief
Estimated value range: $75.00 – 150.00

MURRAY (first name not known)

BACKGROUND
Little background information on MURRAY has been found. We have seen only one Murray picture over the years and it was an exterior scene that provided no clues as to its location or origin.

REGIONALITY
Unknown

REPRESENTATIVE TITLES & VALUE GUIDE
Exterior scene
Estimated value range: $10.00 – 50.00

MURREY (first name not known)

BACKGROUND
Little background information on MURREY has been found. We have seen only one Murrey picture over the years, and it was an exterior scene that provided no clues as to its location or origin.

REGIONALITY
Unknown

REPRESENTATIVE TITLES & VALUE GUIDE
Exterior scene
Estimated value range: $10.00 – 50.00+

DOLORES NELSON

BACKGROUND
Little background information on DOLORES NELSON has been found. We have seen only one Dolores Nelson picture over the years and it was an exterior scene providing no clue as to its location or origin. We found no connection between Dolores Nelson and Lyman Nelson.

REGIONALITY
Unknown

REPRESENTATIVE TITLES & VALUE GUIDE
Exterior scene
Estimated value range: $10.00 – 50.00+

LYMAN NELSON

BACKGROUND
Little background information on LYMAN NELSON has been found. We have seen only one Lyman Nelson picture over the years, and it was an exterior scene. We do know that Lyman Nelson was an early Portland, Maine, photographer whose business was purchased by Fred Thompson circa 1900 – 1905. We found no connection between Lyman Nelson and Dolores Nelson.

REGIONALITY
New England; Portland, Maine

REPRESENTATIVE TITLES & VALUE GUIDE
Exterior scene
Estimated value range: $25.00 – 50.00+

"The Old Mill Road"

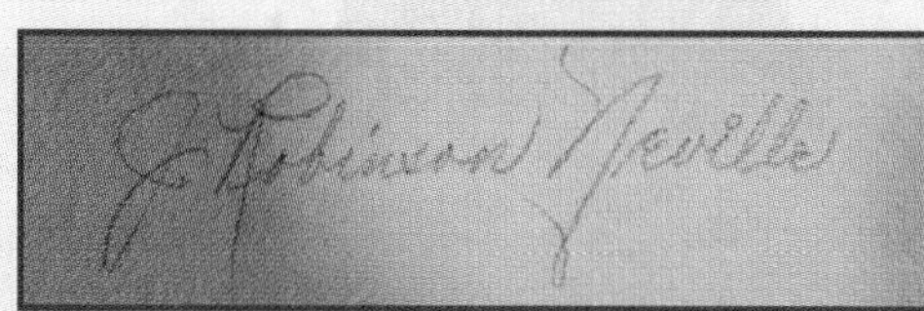

J. ROBINSON NEVILLE

BACKGROUND

J. ROBINSON NEVILLE was a photographer from Brockton, Massachusetts, although we have also seen quite a few Neville scenes taken in New Hampshire as well. All Neville pictures that we have seen have been exterior scenes. Sometimes they are signed "Neville," sometimes "J. Robinson Neville," and occasionally "J. R. Neville." The cover of an original picture box reads, "We guarantee that these scenes of Beautiful New England are genuine photographs artistically colored by hand, originating from the studios of J. Robinson Neville, Brockton Mass."

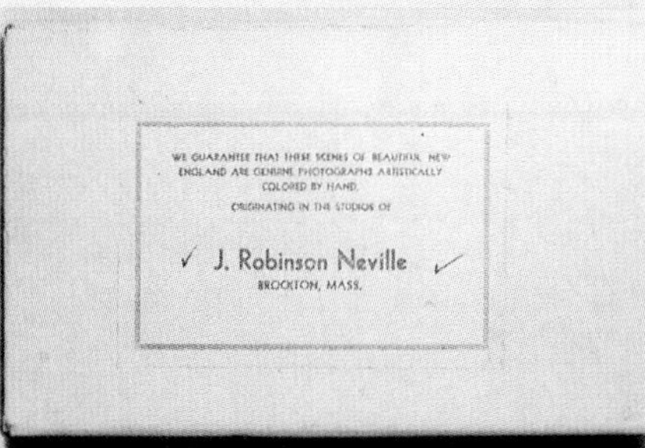

J. Robinson Neville original box

REGIONALITY

New England; Brockton, Massachusetts

REPRESENTATIVE TITLES & VALUE GUIDE

"Autumn in New England"
"Lilacs and Bride Wreath"
"The Old Mill Road"
"Spanning the River"
Typical value range: $50.00 – 100.00+

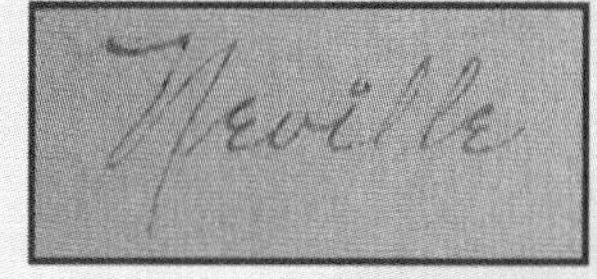

NEWCOMBE (first name not known)

BACKGROUND

Little background information on NEWCOMBE has been found. We have seen only one Newcombe picture over the years, and it was an exterior scene that provided no clues as to its location or origin.

REGIONALITY

Unknown

REPRESENTATIVE TITLES & VALUE GUIDE

Exterior scene
Estimated value range: $10.00 – 50.00+

"Lake Winnepesauke Grace"

MEREDITH NICK

BACKGROUND

Little background information on MEREDITH NICK has been found. We have seen only one Nick picture over the years, and it was an exterior scene taken at Lake Winnepesauke in New Hampshire, which suggests that Nick was a New Hampshire photographer.

REGIONALITY

New England; New Hampshire

REPRESENTATIVE TITLES & VALUE GUIDE

"Lake Winnepesauke Grace"
Estimated value range: $10.00 – 50.00+

Canadian Rockies

GEORGE NOBLE

BACKGROUND

GEORGE NOBLE is a highly collectible photographer from Banff, in the Canadian Rockies. We have seen a fair number of his pictures, and they usually contain a small, scribbled "Noble" pencil signature lower right beneath the image. Sometimes, because the signature is barely legible, you may be able to locate a Noble at a discounted price. The colors on Noble pictures are frequently colorful and bright. George Nobel died circa 1950.

REGIONALITY

Canada; Banff, Alberta

REPRESENTATIVE TITLES & VALUE GUIDE

Banff, Canadian Rockies
Typical value range: $75.00 – 150.00+

"The Rock Garden"

"An Historic Hallway"

MARY HARROD NORTHEND

BACKGROUND

Our experience with MARY HARROD NORTHEND work is an interesting story. We had never seen a Northend picture until around 2002, when a consignor brought in perhaps 20 – 25 unframed pictures for auction. Each was titled, pencil signed "Mary Harrod Northend," and carried an impressed "Mary Harrod Northend, Copyright" lower right in the image. The quality and detail on each of these pictures was excellent, and we suspected that the pictures consigned to us had probably been saleman's samples circa 1900 – 1910. We later learned that the Society for the Preservation of New England Antiquities (SPNEA) also had at least one Mary Harrod Northend picture in its archives.

REGIONALITY

New England

REPRESENTATIVE TITLES & VALUE GUIDE

"A Consultation"
"An Historic Hallway"
"The Home of Old China"
"Neptune's Realm"
"Old Wood Work"
"The Picturesque Tea House"
"A Quaint Old Dining Room"
"The Rock Garden"
"The Vine Clad Pergola"
Typical value range: $50.00 – $150.00+

BERTHA NOYERS

BACKGROUND

Little background information on BERTHA NOYERS has been found. We have seen only one Noyers picture over the years, and it was an exterior scene that provided no clues as to its location or origin.

REGIONALITY

Unknown

REPRESENTATIVE TITLES & VALUE GUIDE

Exterior scene
Estimated value range: $10.00 – 50.00+

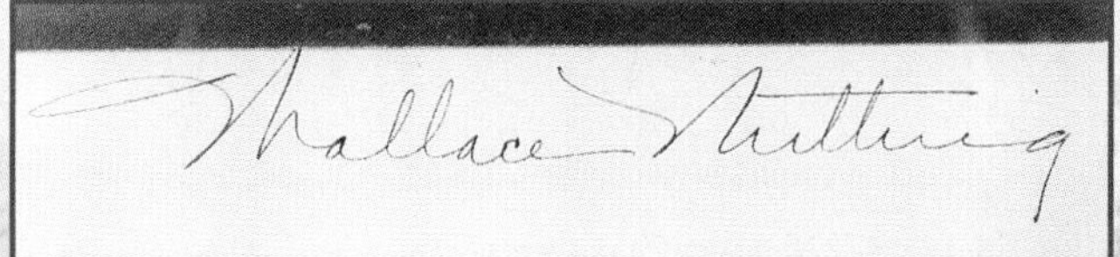

WALLACE NUTTING (1861 – 1941)

"...about ten million of my pictures hang in American homes..."
Wallace Nutting, circa 1936

Wallace Nutting, circa 1936

BACKGROUND

WALLACE NUTTING retired from the ministry in 1904, due to ill health. As part of his recovery, he began touring the New England countryside by carriage or car, taking photographs of rural America. Nutting was one of the first to recognize that the American scene was rapidly changing, that industrialization was altering the way America looked, and that our pure and picturesque country would never look the same again. He seemed to feel it his divine calling to record the beauty of America for future generations.

Beginning first in Vermont, then Massachusetts and Connecticut, and eventually the rest of New England, Nutting photographed country lanes, streams, orchards, lakes, and mountains. Wallace Nutting would take the photograph, assign a title, and instruct his colorists how it should be hand tinted. Each picture that met Nutting's high standards of color, composition, and taste would be affixed to its matting and signed by his employees with the famous Wallace Nutting name. (He hardly ever signed any pictures himself.) Those pictures that did not meet his strict standards were destroyed.

Architectural scene, "The Eames House"

His most popular and best-selling images included exterior scenes (apple blossoms, country lanes, orchards, streams, and the rural American countryside), interior scenes (usually featuring a colonial woman working near a hearth), and foreign scenes (typically thatch-roofed cottages). His poorest-selling pictures, which have become today's rarest and most highly collectible Nutting pictures, are classified as miscellaneous unusual scenes and include animals, architecture, children, floral still lifes, men, seascapes, and snow scenes.

"Old Mother Hubbard"
Wallace Nutting auction record of $8,910.00 at our 2002 auction

Beginning first with exterior scenes in New England, Nutting eventually traveled throughout the United States and Europe, taking photographs in 26 states and 17 foreign countries between 1900 and 1935. Overall, he took more than 50,000 pictures, 10,000 of which he felt met his high standards. The balance was destroyed.

It was around 1905 that Nutting began taking his first interior pictures. Supposedly, one day while it was raining outside, Mrs. Nutting suggested that he take a more "personable" picture indoors. So he set up a colonial scene, had an employee dress up in a colonial fashion, and took several different pictures. These sold relatively easily, which encouraged him to expand into this area.

Seascape, "Sea Ledges"

Nutting's love of antiques, his passion for the pilgrim period, and his unquestionable desire to turn a profit led him to eventually purchase and restore five colonial homes:

* Webb House, Wethersfield, Connecticut
* Wentworth-Gardner House, Portsmouth, New Hampshire
* Cutler-Bartlett House, Newburyport, Maine
* Hazen-Garrison House, Haverill, Maine
* Saugus Iron Works (Broadhearth), Saugus, Maine

Nutting purchased these homes because he felt each represented a different period of early colonial American style and taste. It was at these houses and at his own home, Nuttinghame (Southbury, Connecticut) and Nuttingholme (Framingham, Massachusetts), that the majority of his interior pictures were taken.

Misc. unusual scene, floral, iris and lilies

Nutting's desire to provide the most correct and appropriate settings for his Interior scenes led him in his quest to gather one of the best collections of early American furniture ever assembled. He would use the best examples of early American furniture in his interior scenes and, when he couldn't find the best, he would reproduce it.

Working in Southbury from 1905 to 1912, and then in Framingham from 1912 until his death in 1941, Nutting sold literally millions of his hand-colored photographs. He claims to have sold around 10,000,000 pictures, although knowing his habit of exaggerated salesmanship, that number is probably somewhat high.

Whatever the true number, it was large. Wallace Nutting pictures were sometimes called "poor man's prints." Sold throughout the first quarter of the twentieth century, well before the invention of color photography, these pictures initially sold for literally pennies. His market was primarily the middle- and lower-middle-class households of New England, those households that could not afford finer forms of art. Because of their low prices, Wallace Nutting pictures were purchased in large numbers, and by 1925, hardly an American middle-class household was without one. They were purchased as gifts for weddings, showers, holidays, birthdays, and for just about any other reason imaginable.

Animal scene, "A Triple Team"

Nutting sold many pictures directly through his studios where he also provided his own framing. But he also sold his pictures through many other outlets as well: department stores, drug stores, and gift shops, all around the country. He even had full-time salesmen on the road whose sole job was to sell his pictures to these retail establishments (salesmen whom, he claims, sold enough pictures to retire quite handsomely themselves).

The height of Wallace Nutting picture popularity was 1915 – 1925. During this time, Nutting had nearly 100 colorists in his employ, along with another 100 employees who acted as framers, matters, salesmen, management, and assorted administrative office personnel. Let there be no mistake about it, Wallace Nutting pictures were big business.

But by the late 1920s, people began to tire of Nutting pictures. As with any other fashion or style, tastes began to change. Wallace Nutting pictures became passé, and sales showed a steady decline. Even the introduction of different matting styles, greeting cards, pentype silhouettes, and lower priced machine-produced process prints could not rejuvenate sales.

The Wall Street crash of 1929 and the following depression all but sealed the fate of the Wallace Nutting picture business. Few new pictures were introduced after 1930, and Nutting basically sold pictures remaining in existing inventory throughout the 1930s.

Wallace Nutting died on July 19, 1941. Although the picture studio remained open for several years after his death, the output was inconsequential after the mid-1930s.

Exterior scene, "The Old Homestead"

SUBJECT MATTER OF WALLACE NUTTING PICTURES
There are four primary categories of Wallace Nutting pictures:

Exterior Scenes
These are the standard outdoor pastoral scenes, including apple blossoms, birches and other trees, streams, rivers, lakes, ponds, hillsides and mountains. Exterior scenes account for approximately 85% of all Wallace Nutting pictures that will be found, and are the most popular type of Wallace Nutting pictures today.

Interior scene, "Christmas Gifts"

Interior Scenes
These are usually the colonial indoor scenes, typically featuring a woman dressed in a colonial outfit and working around a fireplace. Interior scenes account for approximately 10% of all Wallace Nutting pictures.

Foreign Pictures
Wallace Nutting traveled to Europe on three separate occasions and took pictures in 16 different countries, although pictures taken in England, Ireland, and Italy are the ones that will most commonly be found.

Foreign scene, "The Bay at Amalfi"

Miscellaneous Unusual Scenes
This category includes seascapes, men, children, architectural scenes, florals, snow scenes, animals, and basically any pictures that do not fit into any of the above three categories. Foreign and miscellaneous unusual scenes combined account for approximately 5% or less of all Wallace Nutting pictures, are generally the most desirable to Wallace Nutting collectors, and usually account for the highest prices paid at auction.

Untitled Pictures
Most Wallace Nutting pictures had titles placed under the lower-left corner of the picture. On pictures 10" x 12" or smaller, the title was usually eliminated because it would not easily or tastefully fit beside the Wallace Nutting signature. When there is no title next to the signature, the picture is called an untitled picture and, as a general rule, is worth less than a comparable picture with a title.

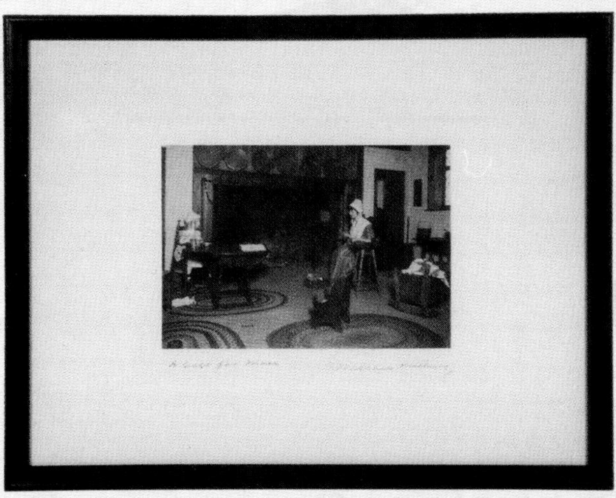

Misc. unusual scene, child, "A Call for More"

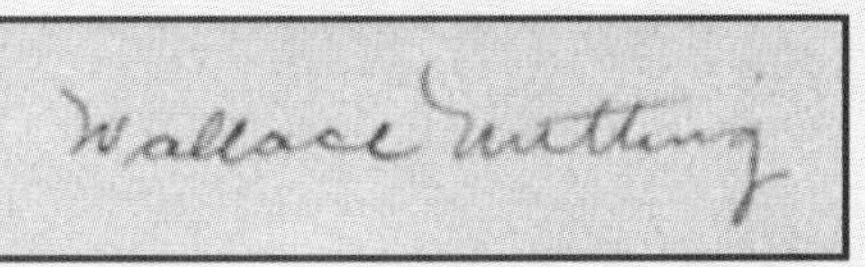

Pencil signature, dates a Wallace Nutting picture 1900 – 1910

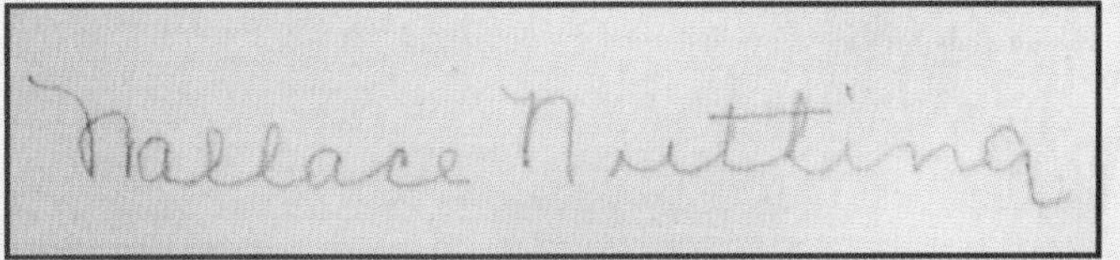

Pen signature, dates a Wallace Nutting picture 1900 – 1930+

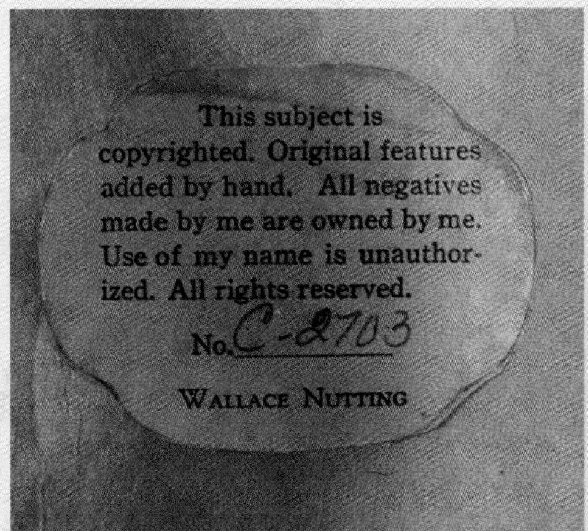

This subject is copyrighted. Original features added by hand. All negatives made by me are owned by me. Use of my name is unauthorized. All rights reserved.

No. C-2703

WALLACE NUTTING

Copyright label, dates a Nutting picture 1930 – 1940

Originality of Signatures

Wallace Nutting signed relatively few of his pictures. Rather, the Wallace Nutting signature was applied by more than 50 different colorists over a 35+ year period. If the signature is not original and authentic, or if the signature has been re-signed at a later date, the value will drop considerably. The ability to recognize authentic vs. re-signed pictures is probably the most difficult part of Wallace Nutting collecting and, although beyond the scope of this chapter, it is something that you must be aware of.

IDENTIFYING AND DATING WALLACE NUTTING PICTURES

Wallace Nutting hand-colored pictures usually date between 1900 and 1941. You should understand that just because a picture has a copyright marking on the picture (e.g., "copyright by Wallace Nutting, 1909" or "(c) W.N. '09"), that doesn't necessarily mean that the picture dates from 1909. Rather, that year represents only the year that the picture was copyrighted by Wallace Nutting. Your individual picture, although produced from the negative marked "1909," may have been colored and sold anywhere from 1909 to 1941.

However, there are several general guidelines that can help to further identify and date Wallace Nutting pictures:

Pencil Signature

A pencil signature typically dates the picture as 1900 – 1910. Fewer than 10% of all Nutting pictures will have a pencil signature.

Pen Signature

A pen signature typically dates the picture as 1910 – 1941. Most Wallace Nutting pictures will be signed in ink. The specific signature or signature style can help date the individual picture.

Black or Colored Border around the Picture

The colored border represents a different matting style introduced by Nutting in an attempt to rejuvenate declining picture sales. A black border will usually date a picture as circa 1930.

Original Copyright Label

An original Wallace Nutting copyright label on the backing paper will typically date the picture as circa 1930 – 1940.

Very Bright Colors

The earlier pictures were more lightly or subtly colored. Brightly colored pictures represent a different style in coloration and will usually date the picture as 1930 or later.

Process Print

All Process Prints will be dated as from 1938 or 1942.

PROCESS PRINTS

Between 1938 and 1942, twelve of Nutting's more popular titles were issued in machine-produced pictures that he called Process

Prints. In 1938, eight Process Prints titles were issued, with four more released in 1942. All Process Prints pictures measure 12" x 15", and if matted, the 12" x 15" print was placed on a 16" x 20" mat, with the signature eliminated, and the title was moved from the lower left corner to the lower right. Any backing label that contains "Process" means that the picture is a Process Print. The Process Print titles include:

Authentic Wallace Nutting Process Pictures must bear this label. All others are unauthorized.
No. 2710

Process Print copyright label

* "All Sunshine"
* "Among October Birches"
* "A Barre Brook"
* "Bonny Dale"
* "Decked as a Bride"
* "A Garden of Larkspur"
* "A Little River"
* "Nethercote"
* "October Glories"
* "Primrose Cottage"
* "Red, White, and Blue"
* "A Sheltered Brook"

REPRODUCTION ALERT

You should be aware that there have been several generations of Wallace Nutting reproductions and fakes. Most are very easy to detect and all have very minimal value to collectors.

Untitled exterior scene

Pirate Prints

Pirate prints first appeared in the 1920s, when a competing company began machine reproducing some of Nutting's most popular titles. They even left the original Nutting title under the lower left corner of the picture, although they removed the Wallace Nutting name from the lower right corner. Nutting successfully sued in court to stop them, but not until several thousand pirate prints had been released. On a pirate print, small symmetrical dots can be detected with a magnifying glass. Oftentimes, unscrupulous individuals have signed the Wallace Nutting name back on to these prints.

Re-Signed Hand-Colored Pictures

It is not uncommon for someone to have taken a pencil-signed picture of one of the lesser-known or unknown photographers, erased the original name, and signed the Wallace Nutting name. Not a big problem, but it has occurred.

Reproductions & fakes

1970s Photographs of Photographs

In the 1970s, a company took photographs of some original Wallace Nutting pictures and placed them on matting, adding the titles and the Wallace Nutting signatures. This series was sold by a popular reproduction house, and because the pictures are photographs, they fail the symmetrical dot test. Typically these reproductions had glossy photos with dark tints, thin paper matting, purplish signatures, and new frames. However, over the past 20 years many new frames were replaced by older frames to make the pictures appear original. These photos are fairly easy to detect once you know what to look for.

Snow scene

Color Laser or Xerox copies

Color laser or Xerox copies are becoming more prevalent. They are typically shiny, glossy pictures, with new mats, and re-signed signatures. The frames are usually old.

Process Prints

Although originally issued by Wallace Nutting, these machine-produced prints are often sold to unsuspecting buyers as being hand colored. On a Process Print, small symmetrical dots can be detected with a magnifying glass.

1990s Photographs of Photographs

A new series of fakes appeared on a limited basis in the early 1990s, again photographs of photographs, but this time of very unusual scenes, with pictures that fit the titles. The pictures that were so unusual that many people assumed they were Nutting when, in fact, they were not. These were also very limited in scope.

Calendar Pages

Also in the 1990s, several lovely Wallace Nutting calendars appeared, with a different picture for each month. Sometimes you will see these pictures cut down, placed in frames, and sold as original. On a calendar print, small symmetrical dots can be detected with a magnifying glass.

Man scene, "The Capture of a Red Coat"

REGIONALITY

New England; Framingham, Massachusetts; Foreign; Most states

REPRESENTATIVE TITLES & VALUE GUIDE

Common untitled exterior scenes: $50.00 – 125.00
Common titled exterior scenes: $75.00 – 250.00
Common untitled interior scenes: $75.00 – 150.00
Common titled interior scenes: $100.00 – 350.00
Common foreign scenes: $75.00 – 300.00
Common misc. unusual scenes: $75.00 – 300.00
Rarest and best pictures: $25.000 – 4,000.00+

(These ranges assume pictures to be in very good 4.0 grading condition. Values can drop considerably if the mat or image is damaged.)

Black border, dates a Wallace Nutting picture 1930 – 1940

RECOMMENDED READING

* *The Collector's Guide to Wallace Nutting Pictures: Identification & Values,* by Michael Ivankovich, the #1 selling book on Wallace Nutting pictures, which will help you to place a ballpark value on any Wallace Nutting picture. 160 pages, $18.95.

* *Collector's Value Guide to Early 20th Century American Prints,* by Michael Ivankovich, contains an extensive chapter on Wallace Nutting. 256 pages, $19.95

* *The Wallace Nutting Expansible Catalog,* a reprint of Nutting's 1915 salesmen's catalog, featuring nearly 1,000 Wallace Nutting pictures, the best Nutting visual reference book in print. 160 pages, $14.95.

* *The Alphabetical & Numerical Index to Wallace Nutting Pictures,* by Michael Ivankovich, listing over 1,000 Wallace Nutting picture titles and including the location where most pictures were taken. 310 pages. (This book is out of print and only available through the secondary book market.)

RECOMMENDED WEBSITE

www.wnutting.com: The Wallace Nutting Gallery, featuring information on upcoming Wallace Nutting auctions & events, a frequently updated Pictures for Sale page, Nutting collecting tips, Q&As, various Nutting trivia, and help in obtaining a value for your Nutting pictures.

M. L. OAKES

BACKGROUND
We believe that M. L. OAKES is also the Oakes Art Prints company that was based in San Diego, California. Certainly the subject matter in the above picture suggests San Diego. We have seen a picture pencil signed "M. L. Oakes." We have also seen several postcards that had comparable San Diego–type subject matter. One was marked "Oakes Art Prints, The Rock Lover's Shop, 5th & C Streets, San Diego Cal." The other was marked "Oakes Art Prints," 1552 5th St, San Diego Cal."

REGIONALITY
Western U.S.; San Diego, California

REPRESENTATIVE TITLES & VALUE GUIDE
Puento Cabrillo
Estimated value range: $50.00 – 100.00+

Oakes Art Prints, The Rock Lovers Shop
5th & C Streets San Diego, Cal.

Oakes Art Prints postcard marking

"Puento Cabrillo"

FRANK OAKES
OAKES FOTO

BACKGROUND
We believe that this OAKES FOTO was not made by the Oakes Art Prints company that was based in San Diego, California, but rather by Frank Oakes. No other information was found.

REGIONALITY
Western U.S.

REPRESENTATIVE TITLES & VALUE GUIDE
Untitled western U.S.; Perhaps Bryce Canyon, Utah
Estimated value range: $50.00 – 100.00+

Western U.S. scene

N. A. PARKER

BACKGROUND
Little background information on N. A. PARKER has been found. We have seen only one Parker picture over the years, and it was an exterior scene that provided no clue as to its location or origin.

REGIONALITY
Unknown

REPRESENTATIVE TITLES & VALUE GUIDE
Exterior scene
Estimated value range: $10.00 – 50.00+

PATCH (first name not known)

BACKGROUND
Little background information on PATCH has been found. We have seen only one Patch picture over the years, and it was an exterior scene that indicated it was produced by Patch's Studio in Randolph, Vermont.

REGIONALITY
New England; Randolph, Vermont

REPRESENTATIVE TITLES & VALUE GUIDE
"The Flume, White Mts."
Estimated value range: $10.00 – 50.00+

PATTERSON (first name not known)

BACKGROUND

Little background information on PATTERSON has been found. We have seen only one Patterson picture over the years, and it was taken at Crater Lake, Oregon, which suggests that Patterson was probably from the Crater Lake area.

REGIONALITY

Northwest U.S.; Crater Lake, Oregon

REPRESENTATIVE TITLES & VALUE GUIDE

"Crater Lake"
Estimated value range: $25.00 – 75.00+

Crater Lake OR

C. A. PAYNE

BACKGROUND

Little background information on C. A. PAYNE has been found. We have seen several C. A. Payne pictures over the years, and each was taken at Watkins Glen, New York. We strongly suspect that C. A. Payne was somehow related to or connected with George S. Payne, also of Watkins Glen, New York.

REGIONALITY

New York State

REPRESENTATIVE TITLES & VALUE GUIDE

"Watkins Glen"
Typical value range: $25.00 – 75.00+

Watkins Glen NY

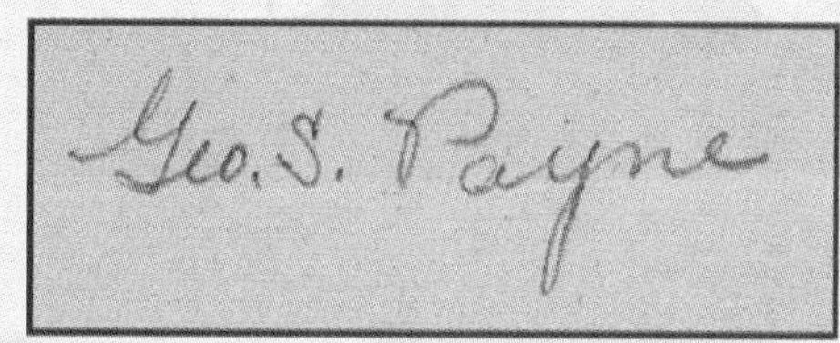

GEORGE S. PAYNE
THE PAYNE STUDIOS

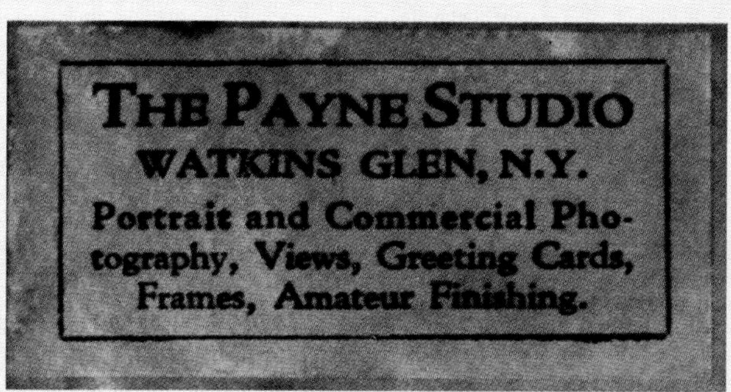

Paper label

BACKGROUND

GEORGE S. PAYNE operated the Payne Studio in Watkins Glen, New York. We have seen several Payne Studio pictures over the years, and each was taken at Watkins Glen. A paper label found on one picture read "The Payne Studio, Watkins Glen NY, Portraits and Commercial Photography, Views, Greeting Cards, Frames, Amateur Finishing." We strongly suspect that George S. Payne was somehow related to or connected with C. A. Payne, also of Watkins Glen.

REGIONALITY

New York State

REPRESENTATIVE TITLES & VALUE GUIDE

"Watkins Glen"
Typical value range: $25.00 – 75.00+

OWEN PERRY

BACKGROUND

Little background information on OWEN PERRY has been found. We have seen several Owen Perry pictures over the years, and all were exterior scenes. We do know that Owen Perry worked out of Portland, Maine, and that his studio was purchased by Fred Thompson circa 1900 – 1905.

REGIONALITY

New England; Portland, Maine

REPRESENTATIVE TITLES & VALUE GUIDE

Exterior scene
Estimated value range: $25.00 – 50.00+

Geo B Petty

GEORGE B. PETTY

"Choir Boy"

BACKGROUND

Whereas many photographers selling hand-colored photography during the early twentieth century resided in New England, GEORGE BROWN PETTY III used Chicago as his base of operations. Although we are uncertain of his date of birth or much about his early life, we have learned that his family roots can be traced back to England and Ireland.

We know that George Petty married Sarah Elizabeth Edwards, the daughter of Judge Wakeman Edwards, at Greyfriars, the Edwards family estate in Abbeville, Louisiana on December 3, 1890. Immediately after the wedding George and Lizzie moved to Lafayette, Louisiana, a larger and up-and-coming town.

Lizzie returned to Greyfriars for the births of their two children, Elizabeth (1891) and George IV (1894). Right around this time, Petty moved Lizzie and the family to Chicago, which at that time was the second largest and most rapidly expanding city in America. In Chicago, George Petty opened a photographic studio that eventually earned him considerable success.

Although Petty sold many hand-colored exterior scenes that were similar in style to those of Wallace Nutting, David Davidson, Fred Thompson, Charles Sawyer, and the other leading sellers of hand-colored photography of the time, he also expanded into areas never touched upon by other photographers. We have seen his pictures featuring young boys and girls, grandmothers, Madonnas, and a series of other family and home-oriented themes. Most of these themes include children in heart-warming scenes such as fishing, singing, and playing with Grandma. And although we have never personally seen one, we have heard that he even sold hand-colored nudes.

"Who Is It, Grandma?"

Most Petty hand-colored photographs are marked "(c) George B. Petty, Chicago," have a pencil signature that reads either "George B. Petty" or "Geo. B. Petty" lower right beneath the image, and are titled lower left. Frankly, we have not seen a large quantity of George Petty pictures in circulation over the past 20 years, which suggests to us that Petty was not necessarily a major producer of hand-colored photography from 1910 to 1925.

As a young boy, Petty's son, George Brown Petty IV, spent a great deal of time in his father's photography studio. In addition to learning about photography and hand painting,

"The Little Fisherman"

young Petty began to master the delicate workings of the airbrush. What may come as a surprise to many is that Petty's son, George Brown Petty IV, went on to a highly acclaimed career of his own when he moved beyond hand-painted photography into the field of pin-up art. So as you may have already guessed, young George Petty, who was later simply known as Petty, was the man responsible for creating the famous Petty Girl pin-ups for *Esquire Magazine* during the 1930s.

In 1916, George Brown Petty III developed a gall bladder blockage. Although this is relatively minor problem by today's medical standards, back then the gall bladder was considered inoperable. Death followed a few days later.

Young Petty assumed control of his father's business upon the elder's death, but found that he had no desire to be a shopkeeper. He closed the shop later in 1916, and pursued his career as a pin-up artist.

REGIONALITY
Northcentral U.S.; Chicago, Illinois

REPRESENTATIVE TITLES & VALUE GUIDE
"Choir Boy"
"The Little Fisherman"
"Low Bridge"
"The Old Rail Fence"
"Who Is It, Grandma?"
Typical value range: $50.00 – 150.00.

"The Old Rail Fence"

PHELPS (first name not known)

BACKGROUND
Little background information on Phelps has been found other than that Phelps was based in Gloucester, Massachusetts. We have seen only one Phelps picture over the years, and it was an exterior scene.

REGIONALITY
New England; Gloucester, Massachusetts

REPRESENTATIVE TITLES & VALUE GUIDE
Exterior scene
Estimated value range: $10.00 – 50.00+

A. EMERY PHINNEY

"Echo Lake, Franconia NH"

BACKGROUND

We have seen several PHINNEY pictures over the years, and all were taken in New Hampshire. We had been unable to locate a first or middle name until collector Jim Graves reported that he had picked up a picture titled "Mt. Washington from Jackson NH" that indicated that it had been taken by "A. Emery Phinney."

REGIONALITY

New England; New Hampshire

REPRESENTATIVE TITLES & VALUE GUIDE

"Autumn"
"Crawford Notch Road"
"Echo Lake, Franconia NH"
"In Crawford Notch, White Mountains, NH"
"Mt. Washington from Jackson NH"
Typical value range: $25.00 – 75.00+

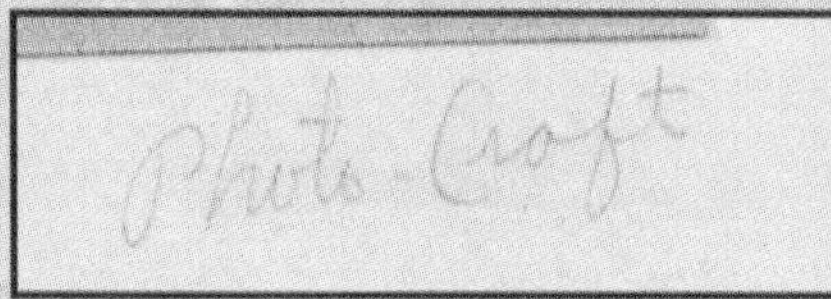

PHOTO-CRAFT

California landscape

BACKGROUND

PHOTO-CRAFT was a photography studio based in Riverside, California. We have only seen one picture by this company and it featured a mountain outside of Riverside. It was signed "Photo-Craft." We do not think this "Photo-Craft" has any connection with the "Photocraft Shop" in Colorado.

REGIONALITY

Western U.S.; Riverside, California

REPRESENTATIVE TITLES & VALUE GUIDE

Exterior scene
Typical value range: $25.00 – 75.00+

THE PHOTOCRAFT SHOP

BACKGROUND

The PHOTOCRAFT SHOP was a photographic studio based in Colorado Springs, Colorado. We have only seen one picture by this company, and it was a Rocky Mountain scene and included a Photocraft Shop paper label on the back. In our opinion, this Photocraft Shop has no connection with "Photo-Craft" from California.

REGIONALITY

Western U.S.; Colorado Springs, Colorado

REPRESENTATIVE TITLES & VALUE GUIDE

Exterior scene
Estimated value range: $25.00 – 75.00

CHAS. A. PLUMER

BACKGROUND

Little background information on CHAS. A. PLUMER has been found other than that Plumer was based in Boston, Massachusetts. We have seen only one Plumer picture over the years, and it was an exterior scene.

REGIONALITY

New England; Boston, Massachusetts

REPRESENTATIVE TITLES & VALUE GUIDE

Exterior scene
Estimated value range: $10.00 – 50.00+

PRANG ART CO. (also TABER-PRANG ART CO.)

BACKGROUND

LOUIS PRANG (1824 – 1909) was born in Europe and immigrated to the United States circa 1850. He became trained as a lithographer and settled in Boston, where he later became a printer and publisher. Shortly after the Civil War, he began issuing chromolithographs, and during the 1870s, he started publishing color lithographs of famous paintings.

Prang is perhaps best known for popularizing the Christmas card as we know it today. Although he didn't necessarily invent the Christmas card, he was instrumental in promoting the greeting card movement in America, and his lithograph shop produced Christmas cards every year, beginning in 1856. As cheaper card imitations began to flood the market, Prang decided to cease card production around 1890 rather than lower his high standards.

Somewhere after the turn of the century, Prang & Company became the Taber-Prang Art Company and was based in Springfield, Massachusetts. Although best know as a distributor of color lithographs, Taber-Prang did produce a limited number of hand-colored photographs (see Willis A. Deane in this chapter).

REGIONALITY

New England

REPRESENTATIVE TITLES & VALUE GUIDE

Overhanging Pine
Estimated value range: $25.00 – 100.00.

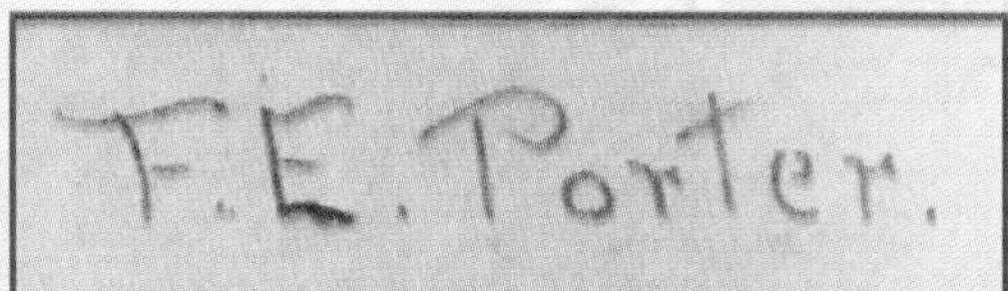

Exterior scene

F. E. PORTER

BACKGROUND

Little background information on F. E. PORTER has been found. We have seen only one Porter picture over the years, and it was an exterior scene that, we believe, was taken in New England.

REGIONALITY

New England

REPRESENTATIVE TITLES & VALUE GUIDE

Exterior scene
Estimated value range: $10.00 – 50.00+

This picture is a Camden Water Color from the
POTTER STUDIO, CAMDEN, MAINE.
Duplicates can be obtained by ordering Number 256

Exterior scene

POTTER STUDIO

BACKGROUND

The POTTER STUDIO was based in Camden, Maine, and specialized in exterior views taken in and around Camden. A paper label on the back read, "This picture is a Camden Watercolor from the Potter Studio, Camden, Maine. Duplicates can be obtained by ordering number 256."

REGIONALITY

New England; Camden, Maine

REPRESENTATIVE TITLES & VALUE GUIDE

Exterior scene
Estimated value range: $25.00 – 50.00+

Exterior scene

K. F. PRATT

BACKGROUND

Little background information on K. F. Pratt has been found. We have seen only one Pratt picture over the years, and it was an exterior scene taken in Warner, New Hampshire.

REGIONALITY

New England; New Hampshire

REPRESENTATIVE TITLES & VALUE GUIDE

"Snow Bound River, Warner N.H."
Estimated value range: $25.00 – 50.00+

A. E. PRICE

BACKGROUND

A. E. PRICE was a photographer from the Pacific Northwest. We have seen only one Price picture over the years, and it was a Mt. Rainier scene taken in Washington State.

REGIONALITY

Northwestern U.S.; Washington State

REPRESENTATIVE TITLES & VALUE GUIDE

Mt. Rainier
Estimated value range: $50.00 – 75.00

Close-framed Mt. Rainier

PURDYS STUDIO
WELLS, MINN.

Exterior scene

PURDY'S STUDIO

BACKGROUND
The PURDY STUDIO was located in Wells, Minnesota. We have seen only one Purdy Studio picture over the years, and it was an exterior scene.

REGIONALITY
North Central U.S.; Wells, Minnesota

REPRESENTATIVE TITLES & VALUE GUIDE
Exterior scene
Estimated value range: $25.00 – 50.00

"Valley Forge"

F. Radel

F. RADEL

BACKGROUND
F. RADEL was a photographer based in Phoenixville, Pennsylvania, who worked almost exclusively in Pennsylvania. Most Radel pictures we have seen were taken in the Philadelphia area, and a few were taken as far away as the Pocono Mountains. We have seen a significant increase in interest in Radel pictures recently, especially in the Philadelphia area.

REGIONALITY
Phoenixville, Pennsylvania

REPRESENTATIVE TITLES & VALUE GUIDE
"Buckwood Inn, Shawnee-on-the-Delaware"
"Valley Forge"
Typical value range: $50.00 – 150.00+

"Buckwood Inn, Shawnee-on-the-Delaware"

Paper label

Radel's Oil Colored Pictures

Are actual photographs taken of beauty spots of historic places. They are printed on the best photograph paper, each being colored by hand. We are continually adding new and beautiful subjects for your selection.

RADEL STUDIO
Phoenixville, Pa.

No.......... Name ....

L. M. RANK

BACKGROUND

L. M. RANK was a photographer from Canada. We have seen only one Rank picture over the years, and it was a Lake Louise picture, which suggests to us that Rank was from the Canadian Rockies.

REGIONALITY

Canada; Lake Louise

REPRESENTATIVE TITLES & VALUE GUIDE

Lake Louise
Estimated value range: $25.00 – 75.00+

P. H. READ

BACKGROUND

P. H. READ was a Canadian photographer. We have only seen one Read picture over the years, and it was taken in Prince Edward Island, Nova Scotia, Canada, which suggests that he was a Canadian photographer.

REGIONALITY

Canada; Prince Edward Island

REPRESENTATIVE TITLES & VALUE GUIDE

Prince Edward Island
Estimated value range: $50.00 – 75.00+

P. REYNOLDS

BACKGROUND

Little background information on P. REYNOLDS has been found. We have seen only one Reynolds picture over the years, and it was an exterior scene that provided no clue as to its location or origin.

REGIONALITY

Unknown

REPRESENTATIVE TITLES & VALUE GUIDE

Exterior scene
Estimated value range: $10.00 – 50.00+

RICHARDSON (first name not known)
THE RICHARDSON STUDIO

BACKGROUND
The RICHARDSON STUDIO was a photographic studio based in Newport, Vermont. We have seen only one Richardson picture over the years, and it was an exterior scene that, we believe, was taken in Vermont.

REGIONALITY
New England; Vermont

REPRESENTATIVE TITLES & VALUE GUIDE
Exterior scene
Estimated value range: $10.00 – 50.00+

Close-framed mountain, South Dakota

FRANK RISE
RISE STUDIO

BACKGROUND
FRANK RISE operated The Rise Studio in Rapid City, South Dakota, circa 1927. We have been unable to learn a great deal about Rise Studio other than that it was a photo refinisher that sold hand-painted photographs of South Dakota tourist destinations such as the Badlands and Mt. Rushmore. We have also located evidence that the Rise Studio took a picture of Charles Lindberg, dated September 6, 1927, just five days after Lindberg's stop in Pierre, South Dakota.

REGIONALITY
North Central U.S.; Rapid City, South Dakota

REPRESENTATIVE TITLES & VALUE GUIDE
Mt. Rushmore
Badlands, South Carolina
Close-framed mountain
Estimated value range: $50.00 – 100.00+

Mt. Rushmore, South Dakota

Paper label

Winter scene

Paper label

FREDERICK G. ROBBINS

BACKGROUND
FREDERICK G. ROBBINS operated the F. G. Robbins Art Co. at 30 Warlock Street in New Britian, Connecticut. We have seen several Frederick Robbins pictures over the years, and all were New England exterior scenes.

REGIONALITY
New England; New Britain, Connecticut

REPRESENTATIVE TITLES & VALUE GUIDE
Untitled exterior, birches
Untitled exterior, icy waterfalls
Estimated value range: $25.00 – 50.00+

H. A. ROBBINS

BACKGROUND
Little background information on H. A. ROBBINS has been found. We have seen only one H. A. Robbins picture over the years, and it was a seascape taken in Rhode Island, which suggests that Robbins may have been a Rhode Island photographer.

REGIONALITY
New England; Rhode Island

REPRESENTATIVE TITLES & VALUE GUIDE
"Rhode Island Coast"
Estimated value range: $25.00 – 50.00+

Seascape

WILMA ROBERTS

BACKGROUND

Collector Anders (Andy) Anderson has reported that WILMA ROBERTS of The Dalles, Oregon, hand painted and sold pictures for more than 60 years. She also hand painted the pictures of Benjamin Gifford (see Benjamin A. Gifford in this chapter) after 1939.

REGIONALITY

Pacific Northwest; The Dalles, Oregon

REPRESENTATIVE TITLES & VALUE GUIDE

Assorted Pacific Northwest scenes
Estimated value range: $25.00 – 50.00+

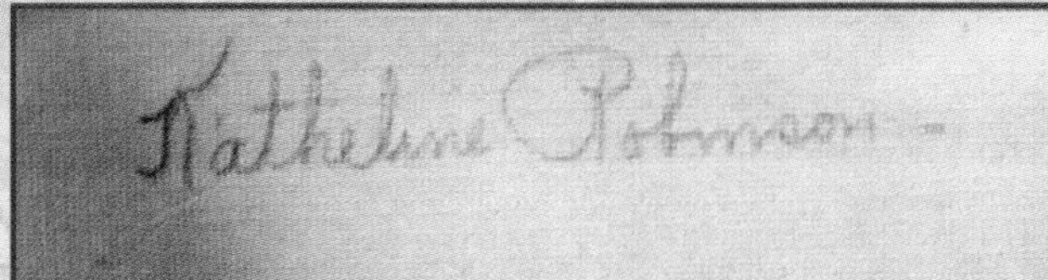

Miami Beach

KATHLEEN ROBINSON

BACKGROUND

Little background information on KATHLEEN ROBINSON has been found. We have seen only one Robinson picture over the years, and it was a seascape taken in Miami Beach, Florida, which suggests that Robinson was probably a Florida photographer.

REGIONALITY

Florida; Miami

REPRESENTATIVE TITLES & VALUE GUIDE

"Miami Beach"
Estimated value range: $50.00 – 100.00+

ROEGE (first name not known)

BACKGROUND

Little background information on ROEGE has been found. We have seen only one Roege picture over the years, and it was taken in Central Park in New York City, which suggests that Roege may have been a New York City photographer.

REGIONALITY

New York City

REPRESENTATIVE TITLES & VALUE GUIDE

Central Park
Estimated value range: $25.00 – 50.00+

STANLEY ROGERS

BACKGROUND
Little background information on STANLEY ROGERS has been found. Each of the Rogers pictures we have seen was taken at Gay Head, on Martha's Vineyard, Massachusetts, which suggests that Rogers was probably a Massachusetts photographer.

REGIONALITY
New England; Massachusetts

REPRESENTATIVE TITLES & VALUE GUIDE
Gay Head
Estimated value range: $50.00 – 100.00+

ROM

BACKGROUND
Little background information on ROM has been found. We have seen only one Rom picture over the years, an exterior scene taken on a lake, and it provided no clue as to its location or origin.

REGIONALITY
Unknown

REPRESENTATIVE TITLES & VALUE GUIDE
Untitled exterior
Estimated value range: $25.00 – 50.00+

Untitled lake scene

EDMUND HOMER "BUG" ROYCE (1883 – 1967)

BACKGROUND

EDMUND HOMER ROYCE, affectionately known as "Bug" to his friends, was born at 55 Bank Street in St. Albans, Vermont, on April 8, 1883. He died in the same house about 84 years later. Royce spent many of his early years dabbling as a part-time photographer after he had earned his first camera at the age of 10 by selling magazine subscriptions to local friends and family. He continued his love of photography for more than 55 years.

Photography remained a hobby in Royce's early years, but his true profession was that of stationary shopkeeper. He operated a store in St. Albans, Vermont, between 1909 and 1930. He retired from the business in 1930 and began to pursue his first love, photography. Just as Wallace Nutting felt it his calling to preserve the unblemished yet rapidly changing New England countryside for future generations, Royce found a calling of his own recording one of Vermont's rapidly vanishing treasures, its covered bridges. Vermont once had nearly 600 covered bridges around the state, but the great flood of 1927 destroyed all but 200 of them. With nearly 400 beautiful and historic covered bridges gone so quickly, Royce decided that it was his calling to photograph all of Vermont's remaining covered bridges for future generations.

Edmund Homer "Bug" Royce (1883 – 1967)

Royce began in 1930, and went on to document nearly 185 of Vermont's remaining covered bridges. He traveled literally thousands of miles across Vermont in search of covered bridges, while also managing to photograph thousands of images of Vermont's beautiful Green Mountains and beautiful landscapes along the way.

Once Royce had nearly all of Vermont's covered bridges preserved in his photographic file, he published *The Covered Bridge*, which included 100 of his best covered bridge images, in collaboration with Herbert Wheatley Congdon. The book's popularity led to two reprintings.

Close-framed covered bridge scene

In 1951, Royce was given the rare honor of being awarded a one-man photographic show at the Eastman-Kodak Exhibition in Grand Central Station, New York. Titled The Vermont Scene, this exhibition featured 48 of Royce's best covered bridge and landscape scenes. His work also appeared in *U.S. Camera* magazine, a national photographic magazine, and in an illustrated article on Vermont's covered bridges that appeared in *Kodakery*, a Kodak trade publication.

Royce was a fourth generation Vermonter, and his grandfather, Homer Royce, had been a U.S congressman and later the Chief Justice of the Vermont Supreme Court, and another relative, Steven Royce, had served as Vermont's governor during the middle of the nineteenth century.

Royce himself married a woman named June and became active in local community affairs. He served as president of the St. Albans

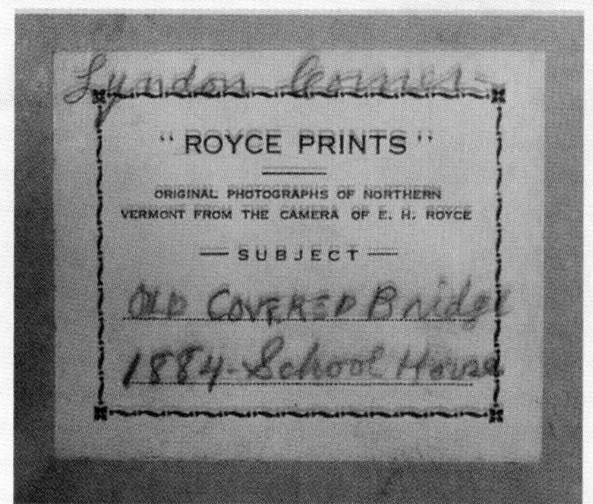

Paper label

Chamber of Commerce and president of the local Owls Club, and he was a board member of the Congregational Church.

Edmund Homer Royce died on March 26, 1967.

REGIONALITY
New England; St. Albans, Vermont

REPRESENTATIVE TITLES & VALUE GUIDE
Assorted Vermont covered bridge scenes
Assorted Vermont exterior scenes
Estimated value range: $50.00 – 150.00+

HAL RUMEL

BACKGROUND
Little background information on HAL RUMEL has been found. We have seen only two Rumel pictures over the years, one from Zion National Park and the other from Bryce Canyon, which suggests that Rumel may have been a Utah photographer.

REGIONALITY
Western U.S.; Utah

REPRESENTATIVE TITLES & VALUE GUIDE
Bryce Canyon
Zion National Park
Estimated value range: $25.00 – 50.00+

SANBORN (first name not known)

BACKGROUND
Little background information on SANBORN has been found. We have seen only one Sanborn picture over the years, and it was of Mt. Baldy, which suggests that Sanborn may have been from the Canadian Rockies.

REGIONALITY
Canada; Canadian Rockies

REPRESENTATIVE TITLES & VALUE GUIDE
"Mt. Baldy Reflected in Grand Lake"
Estimated value range: $25.00 – 75.00

"Mt. Baldy Reflected in Grand Lake"

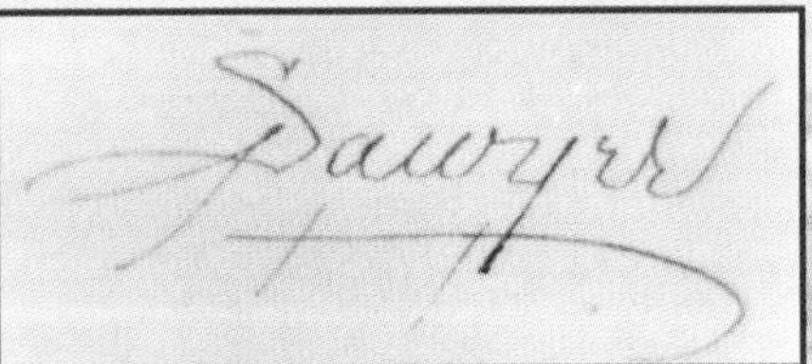

CHARLES HENRY SAWYER (1868 – 1954)

Charles Henry Sawyer, circa 1901 – 1902
(courtesy of Carol Gray & Doug Peters)

BACKGROUND

It has been said that the hand-colored photographs of CHARLES H. SAWYER did more to publicize the beautiful New England scenery than all New Hampshire state promotional materials and resort hotel literature combined. That statement may very well be true, because the Sawyer Picture Co. operated significantly longer than the businesses of Wallace Nutting, David Davidson, or Fred Thompson.

Charles H. Sawyer formed the Sawyer Picture Company in 1903, beginning in his family home of Norridgewock, Maine. Prior to that he had been a crayon portrait artist in, of all places, Providence, Rhode Island, the lifelong home of David Davidson, and the home of Wallace Nutting between 1894 and 1904. After a short stay there, he moved to Farmington, Maine, in 1904, where he did much of his earlier work.

During the earliest years of the business, Charles Sawyer did all of the work himself. He was not only the photographer, but the darkroom man, colorist, framer, and salesman. As he expanded over the next several years, he began to add staff.

Sawyer, rare circa 1905 maple sugaring scene

By 1912, business had grown to where he needed new and different views to increase the size of his picture inventory. Thanks in part to the recently invented automobile, Sawyer began traveling to the White Mountains of New Hampshire. By 1915, he had photographed such famous White Mountain locations as Franconia Notch, the Flume, The Old Man of the Mountain, and, perhaps his most famous subject, Echo Lake. With his business continuing to grow over the next several years, in 1920 Sawyer decided to move to larger quarters in Concord, New Hampshire. This not only moved him closer to his primary source of pictures, the White Mountains, but also closer to the large and commercially important Boston market.

Also in 1920, Sawyer hired Gladys Towle, a colorist who eventually worked with him for over the next 50 years. In order to ease the transition from Maine to New Hampshire, Sawyer had temporarily brought several colorists with him from Farmington to help train his new colorists in Concord. It was the Farmington colorists that initially trained Gladys Towle.

The peak period for the Sawyer Art Company seems to have been during the 1920s. At this time he had a staff of 11 colorists, along with an additional staff of framers, darkroom men, and associated office personnel. In the earlier and later years, Sawyer's staff was considerably smaller.

The Sawyer Pictures
HAND PAINTED
No. Price
STUDIO
Farmington, - Maine

Very early Farmington, Maine, paper label, circa 1905 – 1910

Lake Louise, Canada

Just as we have been able to establish a definite connection between Wallace Nutting, David Davidson, and Fred Thompson, we have also found that Charles Sawyer actually worked with Nutting for about one year. Although we have been unable to determine the exact date, it appears that Sawyer possibly worked for Nutting around 1902 or 1903, while Nutting was still in Providence and before he went into business for himself.

One early Nutting Maine picture was entitled "Original Dennison Plant, Brunswick, Maine." Sawyer was selling the exact same picture, with a slightly different title. One story has it that Sawyer stole the negative while he was working for Nutting and took it with him when he struck out on his own. Knowing Nutting's tendency to sue through the courts when he felt he was wronged (e.g., the pirated prints), we doubt that Nutting would have let someone steal one of his pictures, commercially market it, and get away with it.

Later Concord, New Hampshire paper label, circa 1930 – 1935

Another story has it that Sawyer took the Dennison plant picture while working for Nutting and sold it under the Nutting name while employed by Nutting. Then, when he left, Sawyer was allowed to take all of his own negatives with him, along with the right to continue marketing them.

Whatever the correct story, there is no doubt that both Nutting and Sawyer were marketing the same picture with slightly different titles. And to complicate matters further, we have also seen this Dennison plant title sold over the David Davidson signature as well.

Concord, New Hampshire, paper label, circa 1920 – 1925

Sawyer marketed various other pictures that looked remarkably similar to Nutting's. For example, we have seen a Sawyer exterior scene that looks almost exactly like one of Nutting's best-selling New Hampshire exterior scenes, "A Little River."

However, despite certain similarities in styles, subject matter, and titles, we have never seen anything to contradict the belief that Nutting and Sawyer were anything more than friendly competitors.

Mackeral Cove

Sawyer used a process similar to Nutting's in the early years, but altered it in later years as styles and tastes changed. Platinum paper was eventually replaced by paper called Satista, which contained mostly silver and very little platinum. Later, that was replaced by a gelatine-coated paper made by Eastman & Defender. Sawyer pictures have a distinctive coloring, that accentuate the oranges and browns, and the coloring grew significantly brighter in later years.

It is important to note that Sawyer focused almost exclusively on exterior scenes. In nearly 20 years of buying, selling, and seeking out Sawyer pictures, we have only seen one colonial interior title, "Pilgrim Mothers," and we have only seen a few examples of that particular title, indicating to us that Sawyer sold very few interior scenes.

Known Photographers

By the 1950s, White Mountain pictures were still being sold to tourists by the Sawyer Art Company. The early matted, hand-colored platinum pictures, mounted under glass, were replaced by colored pictures that were covered with a special lacquer and framed without glass. Sawyer lacquered pictures without glass are later pictures dating from the 1950s to the 1970s and are not very popular with collectors.

We have never seen any Sawyer process or facsimile prints.

The primary outlets for Sawyer pictures were gift shops, hotels, stationary stores, and jewelry stores, in that order. The gift shops and hotels were primarily seasonal, catering to tourists. The stationary and jewelry stores were year-round, with local New Hampshire residents the primary customers. Pretty much anyone having a birthday, shower, wedding, or other special event was a prime candidate to receive a Sawyer picture as a gift.

Because the Sawyer Pictures Company was part of the increasing White Mountain area tourist trade, it developed a series of items designed to appeal exclusively to tourists. Greeting cards, mirrors, calendars, miniature picture postcard packs, even wooden trivets, all with a beautiful Sawyer White Mountains picture, were produced.

Charles Henry Sawyer, circa 1960
(courtesy of Carol Gray & Doug Peters)

The Sawyer Pictures Company finally closed its doors in the 1970s, after nearly 70 years of selling its hand-colored pictures to the American public. Today, although Sawyer pictures are popular in most areas, New Hampshire is the heart of Sawyer pictures and is where Sawyer pictures are currently the hottest.

Gladys Trowle, Sawyer's long-time colorist, passed away in 1997.

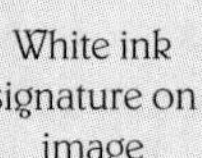

White ink signature on image

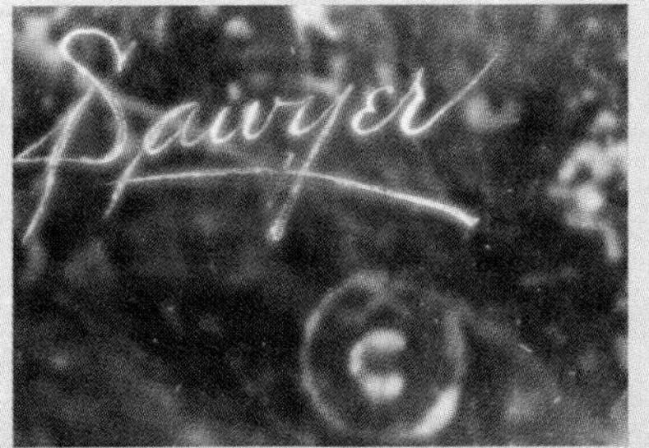

Reproduction Alert: As this book goes to press, we are unaware of any hand-colored Sawyer pictures being reproduced on a large scale. However, in recent years we have seen an increasing number of original Sawyer pictures that have been either remounted and re-signed, or signed on the picture in white ink. (Note that 99% of white ink signatures are authentic; however, we have seen a limited number of recently signed pictures with newer white ink applied.) Apparently a significant volume of loose, unmounted, and unframed Sawyer pictures came into the market during the mid-1990s. As these loose pictures have become dispersed through Sawyer collectors and the antique trade, certain individuals have starting remounting, re-signing, and framing some of these pictures, frequently signing the matting with a signature that looks very much like the authentic Sawyer signature. Sometimes these pictures are sold as being re-signed; sometimes no mention is made of the recently applied signature. This is not a major widespread problem, but it is something you should be aware of. We have also seen some black and white Sawyer reprints recently, usually of rarer scenes, which apparently were reproduced from original Sawyer glass negatives. We know of some antique dealers who unknowingly purchased them as original. And of course, you must always be on the lookout for color Xerox reproductions.

California mission

Portland Head Light

REGIONALITY
New England; New Hampshire; some western U.S.

REPRESENTATIVE TITLES & VALUE GUIDE
Common exterior scenes: $50.00 – 175.00
Common western U.S. & Canada scenes: $100.00 – 250.00
Interior scene, "Pilgrim Mothers": $250.00 – 500.00+
Rarest and best pictures: $250.00 – 1,000.00+
(These ranges assume pictures to be in very good 4.0 grading condition. Values can drop considerably if the mat or image is damaged.)

RECOMMENDED READING
The Hand-Painted Photographs of Charles Henry Sawyer, by Carol Begley Gray, Michael Ivankovich, and John Peters. Also see the Charles Sawyer chapter in *Collector's Value Guide to Early 20th Century American Prints* (Collector Books, by Michael Ivankovich), which includes a listing of many more known Sawyer titles. Also see our Exploring Early 20th c. Prints column on our website:
www.michaelivankovich.com

HAROLD BOARDMAN SAWYER (d. 1980)

Harold Boardman Sawyer
(courtesy of Carol Gray & Doug Peters)

BACKGROUND
Charles H. Sawyer was later joined by his son, HAROLD B. SAWYER, who continued to operate the Sawyer Pictures Company. They frequently traveled together, taking pictures throughout New England, New York, California, Washington State, and several national parks in the American West and the Canadian Rockies.

Although Harold continued to market many hand-painted pictures originally taken by his father in traditional matted and close-framed styles, as costs climbed over the years he looked for ways to reduce expenses. One approach he took was to sell close-framed pictures that were literally painted with a coat of lacquer and framed without glass. These pictures today are called lacquered pictures by collectors and rarely command the higher prices of his father's earlier pictures. However, for true Sawyer collectors, many rarities can be found in the lacquer format that never appeared in earlier years. And we have even seen some collectors reframing lacquered pictures in older frames and under glass.

When Harold Boardman Sawyer died in 1980, the Sawyer Pictures Co. finally closed its doors for good.

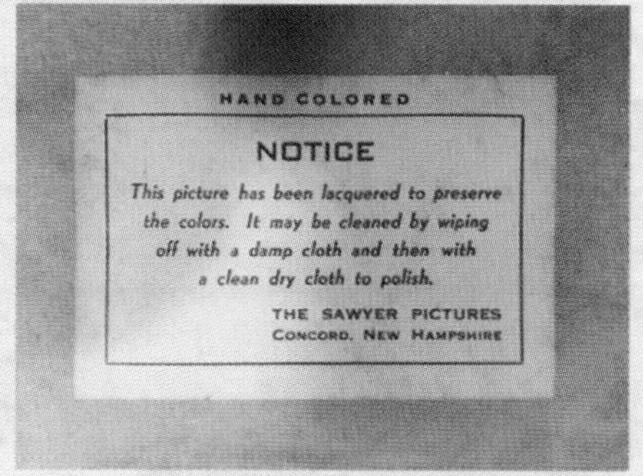

HAND COLORED

NOTICE

This picture has been lacquered to preserve the colors. It may be cleaned by wiping off with a damp cloth and then with a clean dry cloth to polish.

THE SAWYER PICTURES
CONCORD, NEW HAMPSHIRE

Lacquered exterior, paper label, circa 1960 – 1970s

REGIONALITY
New England; New Hampshire

REPRESENTATIVE TITLES & VALUE GUIDE
Common exterior scenes: $50.00 – 175.00
Common western U.S. & Canada scenes: $100.00 – 250.00
Lacquered pictures: $25.00 – 100.00+
Rarest and best pictures: $250.00 – 1,000.00+
(These ranges assume pictures to be in very good 4.0 grading condition. Values can drop considerably if the mat or image is damaged.)

RECOMMENDED READING

The Hand-Painted Photographs of Charles Henry Sawyer, by Carol Begley Gray, Michael Ivankovich, and John Peters. Also see the Charles Sawyer chapter in *Collector's Value Guide to Early 20th Century American Prints* (Collector Books, by Michael Ivankovich), which includes a listing of many more known Sawyer titles. Also see our Exploring Early 20th century Prints column on our website: www.michaelivankovich.com

Newfound Lake title-specific paper label, circa 1930s

Newfound Lake

Who from living things
Dost love to 'scape to that beatitude
Which from converse with secret nature springs,
Fly to this green and shady solitude,
High hills, blue lakes, and everlasting woods.
— Harry Hibbard

THE SAWYER PICTURES.
Concord, New Hampshire.

Bridge of flowers pin,

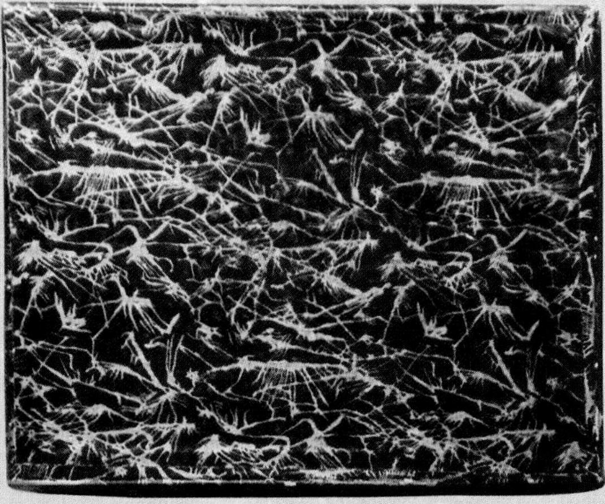

Later exterior scene, still in original box

Lacquered exterior, without glass, circa 1960 – 1970s

Assorted tourist oddities, circa 1930s

Crater Lake

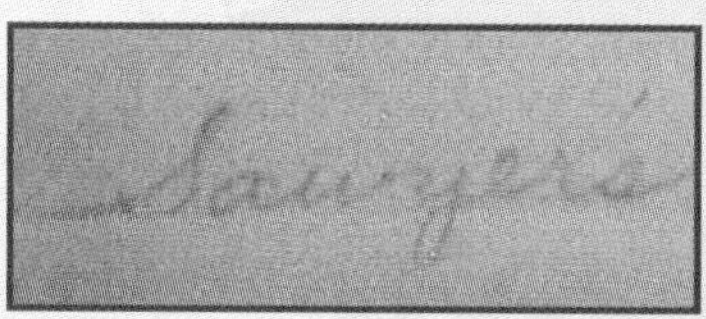

SAWYERS

BACKGROUND

Not to be confused with Charles or Harold Sawyer, a different company named SAWYERS sold pictures of Crater Lake in Oregon. We have seen several Sawyers pictures over the years, and all were from Crater Lake. Each picture was signed "Sawyers," which many collectors have confused with "Sawyer." The Crater Lake subject matter suggests that Sawyers was probably from the Pacific Northwest.

REGIONALITY

Northwest U.S; Oregon

REPRESENTATIVE TITLES & VALUE GUIDE

Crater Lake

Estimated value range: $50.00 – 100.00+

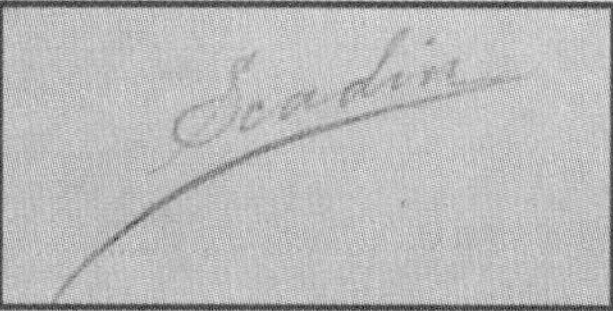

R. HENRY SCADIN (1861 – 1923)

BACKGROUND

Collectors Jim and Clair Graves have passed along to us some considerable research on R. HENRY SCADIN. Both a photographer and a horticulturalist, Scadin was born in Michigan on September 18, 1861. Details of his early life are limited, but it is known that he grew up on the family farm in Webster, Michigan, attended the Spencerian Business College in Detroit in 1884, and then returned to Webster to work on the family farm. In 1884 he married Kate Queal, and together they had two children, both of whom died at an early age. Corn and wheat farming apparently never agreed with Scadin, but at an early age he did develop a love for raising fruit.

R. Henry Scadin (1861 – 1923)

Somewhere around 1890 or 1891 Scadin became interested in photography and, while on a trip to Florida, had some early success in selling his pictures to visiting tourists. Around 1895 or 1896, Scadin and Kate discovered North Carolina and apparently fell in love with the area. He did some photographic work at the Toxaway Company and photographed a series of lakes and resorts in the area. Around this time a third child, a son, was born.

Moving to Sapphire, North Carolina, Scadin set up a photography shop. In addition to selling his hand-painted photos, he offered family, wedding, and portrait photography, and he developed film for amateur photographers. Over the next 10 years, Scadin moved several times between North Carolina, Michigan, and New England, but it seems he always moved back to North Carolina.

In his remaining years, Scadin continued to cultivate his orchards and sell his hand-colored photographs, both in North Carolina and in Vermont, which had become home to his son.

R. Henry Scadin died on May 9, 1923.

On February 5, 1980, the University of North Carolina at Asheville acquired the R. Henry Scadin Photographic Collection, which includes 1,200 glass plates and 43 diaries compiled by Scadin between 1890 and 1923. This collection has been extensively cataloged and further information is available at the Ramsey Library at UNCA.

Exterior scene

REGIONALITY
Southeast U.S.; North Carolina

REPRESENTATIVE TITLES & VALUE GUIDE
Exterior scene
Estimated value range: $25.00 – 50.00+

FREDERICK B. SCHEETZ

BACKGROUND
FREDERICK B. SCHEETZ was a Pennsylvania photographer who did considerable work in the Philadelphia area. Most Scheetz pictures we have seen were taken on the Wissahickon Creek and in Fairmont Park. Most pictures we have seen were pencil-signed "Fred'k B. Scheetz." We have seen a significant increase in interest in Scheetz pictures recently, especially in the Philadelphia area.

"The Wissahickon at Valley Green"

REGIONALITY
Pennsylvania; Philadelphia

REPRESENTATIVE TITLES & VALUE GUIDE
"Cresheim Creek"
"Fairmont Park"
"Near Devil's Pool"
"The Valley Green"
"The Wissahickon at Valley Green"
"Wissahickon Waters"
Typical value range: $50.00 – 150.00+

Exterior scene

SCHLESINGER BROTHERS

BACKGROUND

Little background information on SCHLESINGER BROTHERS has been found. We have seen only one Schlesinger Brothers picture over the years, and it was a typical exterior scene. The "Schlesinger Bros. N.Y." signature on the image suggests that the company was located in New York State.

REGIONALITY

New York State

REPRESENTATIVE TITLES & VALUE GUIDE

Exterior scene
Estimated value range: $25.00 – 50.00

WALTER SHELDON

BACKGROUND

Little background information on WALTER SHELDON has been found. We have seen only one Sheldon picture over the years, and it was a typical exterior scene that gave no clue as to its location or origin.

REGIONALITY

Unknown

REPRESENTATIVE TITLES & VALUE GUIDE

"Wannamaker Falls"
Estimated value range: $25.00 – 50.00+

GUY L. SHOREY

Guy Shorey logo

BACKGROUND

Guy Shorey operated the Shorey Studios in Gorham, New Hampshire. In addition to hand-painted photos, the Shorey Studios also sold picture postcards and even offered photographic services that included publishing high school yearbooks. Shorey Studios apparently used several different trademarks, one of which included the Old Man of the Mountain.

REGIONALITY

New England; New Hampshire

REPRESENTATIVE TITLES & VALUE GUIDE

"Mt. Adams from the Glen"
"Mt. Chocorua over Chocorua Lake"
"Mt. Washington over Peabody River"
"New Hampshire Birches"
"Old Man of the Mountain"
Estimated value range: $50.00 – 150.00+

Typical New Hampshire scenes

RECOMMENDED READING

Among the White Hills: The Life and Times of Guy L. Shorey, by Guy A. Gosselin and Susan B. Hawkins (Shorey's daughter).

J. W. SHOTT

BACKGROUND

Little background information on J. W. SHOTT has been found. Collector Jerry Hechler reported seeing a J. W. Shott titled "Nature's Arch" that provided no clue as to its location or origin.

REGIONALITY

Unknown

REPRESENTATIVE TITLES & VALUE GUIDE

"Nature's Arch"
Estimated value range: $10.00 – 50.00

"Girl in Garden"

E. W. SIMPSON

BACKGROUND

E. W. SIMPSON is another one of those names that is difficult to explain. We have seen hand-painted pictures marked "(c) E. W. Simpson" on the actual image, mounted above a "Moran" pencil signature. To make things even more confusing, we have long suspected that Moran and Villar may be the same photographer, based upon the similarity of the 1930s-style garden scenes, and now we have seen the "E. W. Simpson" signature on similar pictures. Are Simpson, Moran, and Villar the same person? We have been unable to determine the specific location of any Simpson pictures, and have found no connection between E. W. Simpson and R. E. Simpson.

REGIONALITY

Unknown

REPRESENTATIVE TITLES & VALUE GUIDE

"Girl in Garden"
Estimated value range: $25.00 – 75.00+

R. E. SIMPSON

BACKGROUND

Little background information on R. E. SIMPSON has been found. We have seen only one R. E. Simpson picture over the years, and it was a Florida scene. We have been unable to determine the specific location of any Simpson pictures, and have found no connection between R. E. Simpson and E. W. Simpson.

REGIONALITY

Florida

REPRESENTATIVE TITLES & VALUE GUIDE

Untitled Florida scene
Estimated value range: $25.00 – 75.00

"Lake Sunnapee from Brightwood"

SLADE (first name not known)

BACKGROUND
Little background information on SLADE has been found. We have seen only one Slade picture over the years, and it was a typical exterior scene that was taken at Lake Sunnapee, New Hampshire.

REGIONALITY
New England; New Hampshire

REPRESENTATIVE TITLES & VALUE GUIDE
"Lake Sunappee from Brightwood"
Estimated value range: $25.00 – 50.00+

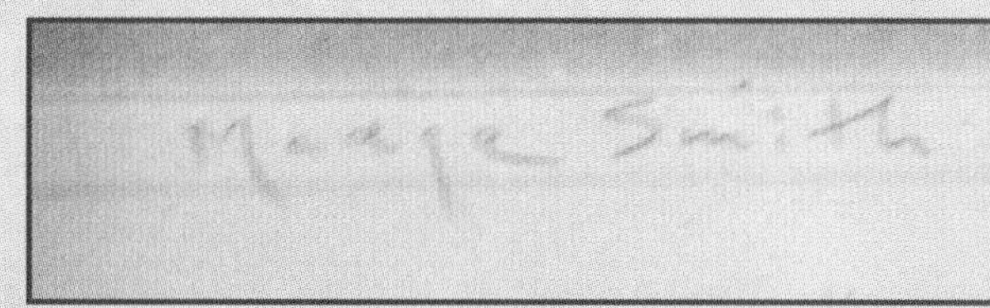

Snow scene, New Brunswick, Canada

MADGE E. SMITH

BACKGROUND
Little background information on MADGE E. SMITH has been found. We have seen only one Madge E. Smith picture over the years, and it was a snow scene taken in New Brunswick, Canada, which suggests that Madge E. Smith was a Canadian photographer. We have seen no connection between Madge Smith and R. S. Smith.

REGIONALITY
Canada; New Brunswick

REPRESENTATIVE TITLES & VALUE GUIDE
New Brunswick, Canada
Estimated value range: $25.00 – 75.00+

R. S. SMITH

BACKGROUND

Little background information on R. S. SMITH has been found. We have seen only one R. S. Smith picture over the years and it was taken in Nova Scotia, Canada, suggesting that R. S. Smith was a Canadian photographer. We have seen no connection between R. S. Smith and Madge Smith.

REGIONALITY

Canada; Nova Scotia

REPRESENTATIVE TITLES & VALUE GUIDE

Nova Scotia, Canada
Estimated value range: $25.00 – 75.00+

EDWARD G. SNOW

BACKGROUND

Little background information on EDWARD G. SNOW has been found. We have seen several Snow pictures over the years that seem to date circa 1915 – 1920, and each picture looked like it had been taken in New England. Also, the quality of each Snow picture that we have seen was comparable in quality and color to those of the other major photographers.

REGIONALITY

New England

REPRESENTATIVE TITLES & VALUE GUIDE

"Sunday Morning"
"Waiting"
Estimated value range: $50.00 – 100.00+

"Sunday Morning"

J. FRED SPALDING

"Lake Louise, Alberta"

BACKGROUND

J. FRED SPALDING operated The Camera Products Company, 1731 Dunbar St., Vancouver, British Columbia, Canada, and sold a wide variety of pictures taken in or near the Canadian Rockies. We have probably seen more Spalding pictures taken at Jasper National Park than taken anywhere else. His pictures often carried a Camera Products paper label or backstamp. His pictures were often pencil signed "(c) J. Fred Spalding" and were typically quite colorful. In our opinion Spalding is one of the more collectible Canadian photographers.

REGIONALITY

Canada; Vancouver, British Columbia

REPRESENTATIVE TITLES & VALUE GUIDE

"Mt. Edith Cavell, Jasper Park"
"The Athabasca River, Jasper Park"
"Lake Louise, Alberta"
Estimated value range: $75.00 – 200.00+

T. ROY SPILLER

BACKGROUND

Little background information on T. ROY SPILLER has been found. We have only seen one Spiller picture, which dated circa 1920 – 1925. It was an exterior scene and gave no clue as to its location or origin.

REGIONALITY

Unknown

REPRESENTATIVE TITLES & VALUE GUIDE

Exterior scene
Estimated value range: $10.00 – 50.00

D. SPURWAY

BACKGROUND

Little background information on D. SPURWAY has been found. We have only seen one Spurway picture, which dated circa 1941. It was taken in the Canadian Rockies, which suggests that Spurway was a Canadian photographer.

REGIONALITY

Canada

REPRESENTATIVE TITLES & VALUE GUIDE

Canadian Rockies
Estimated value range: $25.00 – 75.00

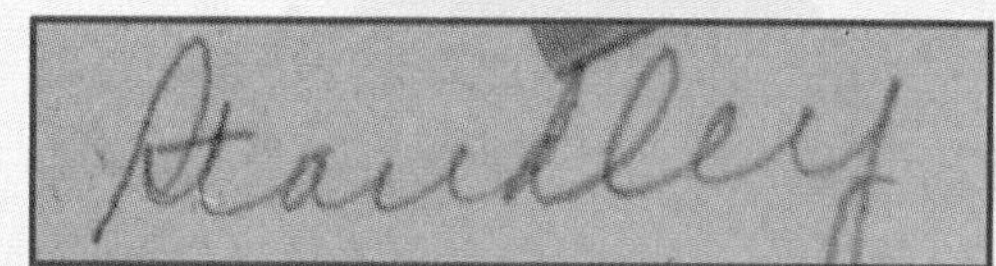

HARRY LANDIS STANDLEY (1881 – 1951)

BACKGROUND

Born in Arkansas City, Kansas, on July 28, 1881, HARRY LANDIS STANDLEY moved with his family to Pueblo, Colorado, when he was only seven. They eventually moved to Cripple Creek and later to Colorado Springs while he was still in his younger years. This is when he was first exposed to the depth and beauty of the Rocky Mountains.

Harry Landis Standley (1881 – 1951)

Standley first became interested in photography as a teenager, just before the turn of the century. After apprenticing under several local photographers, he opened his first photography shop in Colorado Springs in 1901, at the age of 20. As he gained experience over the next 20 years, his business grew. And as he prospered, Standley moved his growing photography business to several different locations within Colorado Springs before finally settling into his permanent business address at 224 North Tejon Street in 1921.

Like nearly everyone else who has experienced them, Standley fell in love with Colorado's Rocky Mountains. For more than 50 years, he roamed the upper mountains and lower countryside carrying his heavy photographic equipment, photographing the lakes, streams, canyons, green valleys, and of course, the snow-capped mountains. In the earlier years he carried a Pony Premo #6 (5" x 7") view camera, a tripod stand, and his usual daily supply of heavy glass negative plates. As the years progressed, photographic technology greatly improved and his equipment load was significantly lightened as he traveled the back roads of Colorado looking for new places and things to photograph.

At the age of 40, Standley was able to combine his passion for photography and his love of the Colorado outdoors with a totally new undertaking, mountain climbing. And what started out as a hobby soon turned into a passion. Before long, Standley had not only photographed all of Colorado's 14,000 peaks — he is believed to have been only the eighth man in history to have climbed all of Colorado's 14,000 peaks as well.

Standley's passion for climbing enabled him to meet many of Colorado's other early climbers, and in 1923 he became one of the five founding members of the AdAmAn Club, an exclusive hiking group that climbed Pike's Peak each New Year's Eve to set off a fireworks display, much to the delight of the Colorado Springs residents below.

Standley's hand-colored pictures were widely sold throughout Colorado, especially to tourists and visitors to the Pike's Peak and Estes Park regions. They were primarily sold through his photography shop and through assorted other tourist and gift shop locations. Travelers always enjoy bringing home a memory of their vacation trip, and what better way to fondly remember a special trip to Colorado than a beautiful and elegant Standley picture? As a result, Standley pictures hung in houses throughout America, as well as in houses as far away as England, France, Switzerland, and Germany.

Colorado scene

Aside from the distinctive subject matter of Colorado's beautiful Rocky Mountains, several other characteristics seem to typify Standley pictures:

1) The word *Colorado* is usually the last word in the title.
2) The signature is usually written in pencil.
3) Often, the signature is written at a drastic 45-degree angle, thus giving the Standley signature a completely different look from those of other photographers.

Sold primarily as tourist gifts, Standley pictures were not necessarily meant to last forever. As a result, many of the signatures and titles have become quite faded over the years, and it is not uncommon for the Standley attribution to go unrecognized today.

In addition to his commercial sales, Standley's work was recognized professionally as well. In 1947, the Fine Arts Center featured a one-man show of his scenic mountain views, and this same show was also well received at the Art Institute of Dayton, Ohio.

After nearly 50 years in the photography business, in 1947, Standley sold his business to Stanley Balcomb and John Turner. Yet he continued to work for the new owners on a part-time basis, and was actually in the office the day prior to his death. Harry Landis Standley died of a heart attack on March 15, 1951. He never married, and his only known survivor was a sister, Hilda Standley.

REGIONALITY
Western U.S.; Colorado Springs, Colorado

Colorado scene

REPRESENTATIVE TITLES & VALUE GUIDE
"Big Thompson Canon, Colorado"
"Dream Lake, Rocky Mt. National Park, Colorado"
"Long's Peak and Bear Lakes, Estes Park, Colorado"
"Long's Peak and Colorado Divide, Estes Park, Colorado"
"Lower Twin Lake and Twin Peaks, near Leadville, Colorado"
"Mt. Evans from Echo Lake, Colorado"
"Odessa Lake, Colorado"
"Odessa Lake, Estes Park, Colorado"
"Pikes Peak and Gateway to the Garden of the Gods, Colorado"
"Royal Gorge from Canon City, Colorado"
"Seven Falls, Colorado"
"Snowmass Lake from Outlet, Colorado"
"Wildcat Point, Lookout Mountain, Boulevard, Colorado"
Typical value range: $50.00 – 200.00+

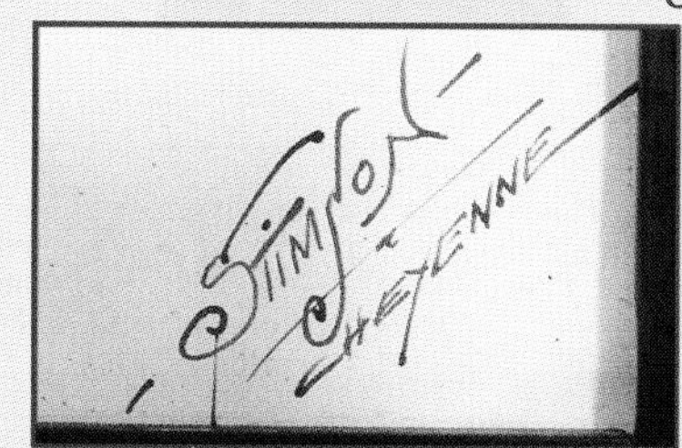

JOSEPH ELAM STIMSON (1870 – 1952)

Monogram

BACKGROUND

JOSEPH ELAM STIMSON was born at Brandy Station, Virginia, on May 18, 1870. His parents were William and Jennie Stimson, and he was one of eight children; he had six brothers and one sister. Stimson spent most of his early childhood in the southern Appalachian Mountains of South Carolina. When he was thirteen, the family moved to Pawnee City, Nebraska.

In 1886 Stimson left for Appleton, Wisconsin, where he began work as a photographer's apprentice for his cousin, James Stimson. While in Appleton, Stimson learned the skills of portrait photography, and learned details of both the collodian or wet-plate process and the new dry-plate process. He moved to Cheyenne, Wyoming in 1889 at the suggestion of two brothers who worked for the Union Pacific Railroad, without a camera, a studio, or clientele. He bought the Cheyenne studio and equipment of Wyoming pioneer photographer, Charles Kirkland, and in July of 1889, Stimson began making portrait photography.

In 1901, Stimson was hired as a publicity photographer for the Union Pacific Railroad. The railroad needed quality scenic photographs to help change the image of the scandal-plagued railroad, and Stimson was given free rein to photograph anything that might draw investors to the railway. Besides the obvious subject of the railroad itself, Stimson was to photograph natural wonders, city scenes, farms and ranches, mining and irrigation projects, and anything else that might bring money to the new railroad.

Wyoming panoramic view

In 1894, Stimson married Anna Peterson and they went on to have three children, all girls. Establishing a solid business reputation in Cheyenne, Stimson traveled throughout Wyoming over the next five years photographing such sights as the Big Horn Mountains, Jackson Hill, the Tetons, and other scenic places. He compiled his scenic views into several albums and began selling prints from his negatives. It was these prints that brought Stimson to the attention of the Union Pacific Railroad. At this time, railroads were extremely interested in attracting passengers, travelers, and even investors. To accomplish this, the railroad used exotic western photography, often taken by Stimson, strategically placed in brochures, advertising, magazines, and calendars, and even on depot walls, to help popularize and glamorize the railroad. Between 1900 and 1910, Stimson used his camera to record the sights and beauty found in ten states along the Union Pacific Railroad.

Stimson, In his Model T Ford, circa 1908

By 1903, Stimson's reputation as a scenic photographer had grown to the point that he was asked by the state of Wyoming to provide five hundred Wyoming scenes that would be displayed at the Louisiana Purchase Exposition to be held the following year in St. Louis. The prints were to be hand colored, a skill that Stimson often exhibited before the advent of color film. He was awarded a silver medal for his views of mining and machinery, and two more silver medals for two other displays. By 1906, after only ten years in scenic work, Stimson had gained national recognition as a photographer and artist. In the decades that followed, he continued to produce thousands of photographs, including not only Wyoming scenes, but also Colorado, Nebraska, Kansas, Utah, Idaho, Nevada, and California spaces.

Stimson died in 1952 at the age of 82 and was buried in Cheyenne.

The Stimson Collection was acquired by the state of Wyoming in 1953 and consists of over 7,500 photographs, many of them on 8" x 10" glass-plate negatives. The collection also has several oversized hand-tinted prints, many framed by Stimson personally. This collection is available to the public through the Wyoming state archives. Copyright to the Stimson Collection is held by the Wyoming state archives.

REGIONALITY
Western U.S.; Cheyenne, Wyoming

REPRESENTATIVE TITLES & VALUE GUIDE
Grand Teton Mountains, Wyoming
Estimated value range: $100.00 – 500.00+

Delta Upsilon, Colgate University

PAUL STRAND

BACKGROUND
Little background information on PAUL STRAND has been found. We have only seen one Strand picture, which dated circa 1920 – 1925. It was a hand-painted scene of a fraternity house at Colgate University in Hamilton, New York, which suggests that Strand was from New York State.

REGIONALITY
New York state

REPRESENTATIVE TITLES & VALUE GUIDE
Colgate University
Estimated value range: $25.00 – 75.00

STOTT (first name not known)

BACKGROUND
Little background information on STOTT has been found. We have only seen one Stott picture over the years, an exterior scene that provided no clue as to its location or origin.

REGIONALITY
Unknown

REPRESENTATIVE TITLES & VALUE GUIDE
Exterior scene
Estimated value range: $10.00 – 50.00

W. R. SUMMERS

"Rock Bed of the Wissahickon"

BACKGROUND
W. R. SUMMERS was a Pennsylvania photographer who did considerable work in the Philadelphia, Pennsylvania, area. Most Summers pictures we have seen were taken in the Philadelphia area, with most that we have seen taken on the Wissahickon Creek. Most Summers pictures we have seen were signed "W. R. Summers." Based upon the number of Philadelphia-area Summers pictures we have seen, we believe that he was from Philadelphia. We have seen a significant increase in interest in Summers pictures recently, especially in the Philadelphia area.

REGIONALITY
Pennsylvania; Philadelphia

REPRESENTATIVE TITLES & VALUE GUIDE
"Rock Bed of the Wissahickon"
Wissahickon
Typical value range: $50.00 – 100.00+

FRED H. SUNBRISTIN

BACKGROUND
Collector Jim Graves has reported acquiring a picture by FRED H. SUNBRISTIN that was taken at Lake Louise in Alberta, Canada, which suggests that Sunbristin was a Canadian photographer.

REGIONALITY
Canada; Lake Louise, Alberta

REPRESENTATIVE TITLES & VALUE GUIDE
Lake Louise
Estimated value range: $25.00 – 75.00+

SUNSENE PHOTOS

BACKGROUND
Little is known about SUNSENE other than it sold a variety of Florida hand-colored photographs. The most common view we have seen is the world famous Bok Singing Tower and Bird Sanctuary, which was dedicated by Edward William Bok to the state of Florida in 1929. Some views simply include the Singing Tower, while other views include a different angle of the Singing Tower, with pink storks or other birds standing in the forefront. Our guess is that most Sunsene photos were sold through Florida gift shops to visiting tourists.

Most Sunsene hand-colored photographs can be identified by the "Sunsene Hand Colored" marking that usually appears in the lower right portion of the photograph. These are some of the least collectible Florida hand-colored photographs but they are still quite affordable, usually selling in the $25.00 – 50.00 range.

"The Singing Tower, Florida"

REGIONALITY
Florida

REPRESENTATIVE TITLES & VALUE GUIDE
Singing Tower scene
Typical value range: $25.00 – 50.00+

ESTHER SVENSON

BACKGROUND
Although we have seen relatively few Esther Svenson pictures on the open market over the years, Svenson's is an interesting story. For nearly 40 years, Esther Svenson of Framingham, Massachusetts, was Wallace Nutting's head colorist; she was one of his most trusted and faithful employees. While Nutting was busy publishing books, reproducing furniture, giving speeches, and tending to other parts of his business, Esther Svenson ran most of the day-to-day operations in Nutting's hand-painted picture business (which provided more revenue to Nutting than any other segment of his business).

Wallace Nutting died in 1941. When Mrs. Marietta Nutting died in 1944, she left much of the remaining business to Esther Svenson and Ernest John Donnelly, another longtime and trusted employee. Together they tried to continue running Wallace Nutting Pictures, but times had changed and the public had basically stopped buying hand-painted photographs in any large numbers by the mid-to-late 1940s. Donnelly sold his portion of the business to Esther Svenson in 1946, and Svenson continued to occasionally paint and sell Wallace Nutting pictures from her home, on an extremely limited basis, for the next 10 years.

Apparently Esther Svenson at some point took some of her own pictures, hand painted them, and sold them. However, based upon the limited number that we have seen over the years, this was a short-lived career for Svenson.

REGIONALITY
New England; Framingham, Massachusetts

REPRESENTATIVE TITLES & VALUE GUIDE
Exterior scene
Estimated value range: $25.00 – 75.00+

TABER-PRANG ART CO. (Also PRANG ART CO.)

BACKGROUND

LOUIS PRANG (1824 –1909) was born in Europe and immigrated to the United States circa 1850. He became trained as a lithographer and settled in Boston, where he later became a printer and publisher. Shortly after the Civil War, he began issuing chromolithographs, and during the 1870s, he started publishing color lithographs of famous paintings.

Prang is perhaps best known for popularizing the Christmas card as we know it today. Although he didn't necessarily invent the Christmas card, he was instrumental in promoting the greeting card movement in America, and his lithograph shop produced Christmas cards every year, beginning in 1856. As cheaper card imitations began to flood the market, Prang decided to cease card production around 1890 rather than lower his high standards.

Somewhere after the turn of the century, Prang & Company became the Taber-Prang Art Company and was based in Springfield, Massachusetts. Although best known as a distributor of color lithographs, Taber-Prang did produce a limited number of hand-colored photographs (see Willis A. Deane in this chapter).

REGIONALITY

New England

REPRESENTATIVE TITLES & VALUE GUIDE

"Overhanging Pine"
Estimated value range: $25.00 – 100.00

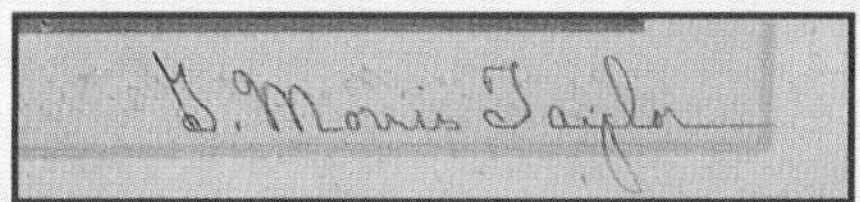

GILBERT MORRIS TAYLOR (1894 – 1967)

BACKGROUND

Collector Don (no last name on his e-mail) reported that GILBERT MORRIS TAYLOR was born in St. Paul, Minnesota, in 1894. While growing up in St. Paul, he also trained in photography there. His aunt, Charisa Bass, was a respected amateur photographer who trained in Paris in the 1890s. In 1924 Taylor set up a photography studio in Atlin, British Columbia, Canada, primarily due to its reputation as "Canada's Little Switzerland." Taylor specialized in selling hand-painted photographs of the Canadian Rockies to visiting tourists, and his pictures were typically signed "G. Morris Taylor." He also produced a series of pictorial postcards from the same region of Canada. Taylor's first marriage ended in divorce in the late 1920s. He had one son from that union. He married Helen Emelyn, of Portland, Oregon, and they moved to Jasper, Alberta, Canada, but kept the Atlin Studio open during the summer months. They eventually retired to Santa Barbara, California, after selling the Jasper business to Tom Johnson of Saskatoon, Saskatchawan, Canada. G. Morris Taylor died in 1967.

"Moligne Lake, Perfect Reflections, Jasper Park"

REGIONALITY

Canada; Jasper National Park, Alberta

REPRESENTATIVE TITLES & VALUE GUIDE

"Moligne Lake, Perfect Reflections, Jasper Park"
"Mt. Unwin, Moligne Lake, Jasper National Park"
Estimated value range: $50.00 – 100.00+

FLORENCE C. THOMPSON

Full pen signature

BACKGROUND

Most collectors of early twentieth century hand-colored photography are familiar with Fred Thompson, who was the fourth-largest-selling hand-colored picture photographer of the early twentieth century. But relatively few collectors are aware of FLORENCE THOMPSON — the other Thompson.

Little is known about Florence Thompson except that her studio was located at 62 State Street, Newburyport, Massachusettes. Her subject matter consisted of basic exterior and interior scenes, and although she did produce a limited number of miscellaneous unusual scenes, we are unaware of any foreign scenes by her. She did copyright various titles with the Library of Congress copyright office,

"The One Horse Shay"

Her signature typically comes in two forms, both script. One signature, "Florence Thompson," is easily recognizable because it provides you with her first name. The second signature, "Thompson," is not as identifiable because it only provides the last name, and for years collectors have thought that the script "Thompson" was actually a signature used by Fred Thompson.

So with few exceptions, when you see the block pencil "Thompson," it is Fred Thompson. When you see the script pencil "Thompson," it is Florence Thompson. We have never seen any evidence of any direct connection or relationship between the two Thompsons, so we would speculate that the Florence Thompson script signature was intentionally designed to more clearly differentiate her from the more famous Fred Thompson. We do know that she was "Mrs. Florence C. Thompson," and therefore, married.

REGIONALITY

New England; Newburyport, Massachusetts

REPRESENTATIVE TITLES & VALUE GUIDE

"A Different Lesson"
"The Incoming Tide"
"The One Horse Shay"
"Six Master"
Typical value range: $50.00 – 100.00

"Six Master"

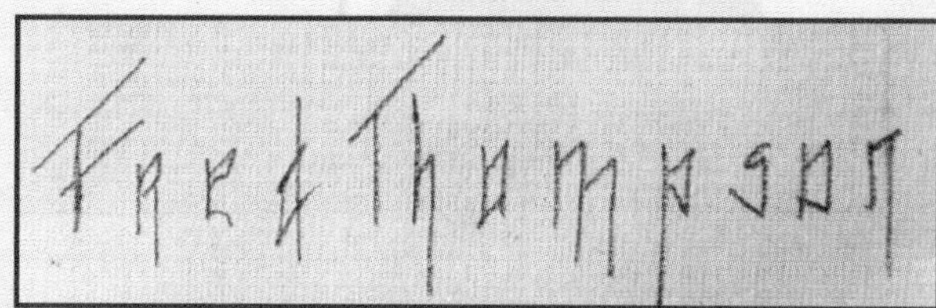

Frederick H. Thompson
(1844 – 1923)

FRED THOMPSON (1844 – 1923)

BACKGROUND

FREDERICK H. THOMPSON was another of New England's most popular photographers in the early 1900s. Born on Stevens Avenue in Deering Center (known today as Westbrook), Maine, on March 17, 1844, Frederick H. Thompson was 17 years older than Wallace Nutting. The son of the Reverend Zenas and Leonora Thompson, he attended local schools, including Bethel Academy, where his father also preached. Frederick H. Thompson was married for many years, although we have been unable to learn his wife's name. She died in 1904 of unknown causes.

Like Wallace Nutting, Frederick H. Thompson was a versatile businessman. In 1888, he and his brother, Zenas (named after their father), formed Zenas Thompson and Brother, a carriage manufacturing company in Portland, Maine. Their original carriage factory was located on Union Street in Portland, but it was destroyed by fire and later moved to Elm Street, also in Portland. This firm was sold in 1906, presumably due to competition from the growing automobile trade. In 1907, he purchased the Daisy Lunch Room in Portland, a small local restaurant, and changed its name to Thompson Spa.

"The Forks"

Frederick H. Thompson was also an avid amateur photographer and soon became a prominent member of both the Portland Camera Club and the Portland Society of Natural History. Like Wallace Nutting's, his hobby soon became an overwhelming compulsion and eventually turned into a business.

Somewhere around 1908, Frederick H. Thompson opened the Thompson Art Company, or TACO as it was called on many of his picture labels. Using a process very similar to Wallace Nutting's, Thompson traveled throughout Maine, New Hampshire, and northern Massachusetts taking what he referred to as nature pictures. These consisted of blossoms, birches, mountains, streams, and whatever else in the outdoors caught his eye.

Early Thompson
"TACO" paper label

In addition to his scenic outdoor views, the Thompson Art Company also became well-known for its colonial interior scenes. Using a formula similar to Nutting's, Thompson would locate the appropriate room setting, decorate it with period furniture and antique accessories, provide a female model with the typical long dress and bonnet, and photograph interiors views similar in style and quality to Nutting's. Catchy titles were applied to the pictures.

Known Photographers

There is no doubt that despite the fact that Frederick H. Thompson was significantly older than Wallace Nutting, Nutting was the innovator and Thompson was the follower. Just as we have seen a definite link between Nutting and David Davidson, there is also a connection between Nutting and Frederick H. Thompson. Although we have found nothing in writing connecting the two, it is obvious that Thompson visited Nutting on at least one occasion.

"Priscill and Prue"

If you look closely at Thompson's "Fireside Fancy Work" and Nutting's "An Elaborate Dinner," there is no doubt that both pictures were taken in the same room. Knowing that "An Elaborate Dinner" was taken in Nuttinghame, Nutting's Southbury home during the 1905 – 1912 period, "Fireside Fancy Work" would seem to confirm that Thompson visited Nutting at least once and, since Nutting allowed him to shoot that picture within his home, would seem to suggest that perhaps Nutting was providing photographic guidance to Thompson. Knowing that Nutting removed the ceiling in this room around 1907 in order to expose the beams and knowing that Fred Thompson died in 1909 would seem to isolate the Nutting-Thompson meeting in Southbury to the 1907 – 1909 time period.

Wallace Nutting, "An Elaborate Dinner"

On the whole, Thompson's interior scenes, although very good when compared to other photographers of that period, never surpassed Wallace Nutting's in terms of quality of furnishings and decorative authenticity. As we said earlier, Nutting's knowledge of fine antiques and his access to them enabled him to put together room settings that far surpassed those of his contemporaries.

Fred Thompson, "Fireside Fancy Work"

Like Nutting, Thompson expanded into other miscellaneous unusual areas as well. After his picture inventory became complete, with blossoms, birches, country lanes, streams, hillsides, and colonial interior scenes, Thompson began taking pictures of the Maine coastline, animals in the country, children (in scenes designed to appeal to mothers), men in colonial outfits, and other miscellaneous unusual scenes.

Some subjects worked quite well for Thompson. For example, "Portland Head," which features Portland's very famous seacoast lighthouse, sold very well for Thompson. During the early twentieth century the beautiful Maine coastline was a popular tourist destination, and nearly anyone who visited it wanted to take home a remembrance of it, and quite often a visitor would take home a Fred Thompson picture. Some of his sheep scenes also were good sellers.

TACO Nature Studies paper label

Although Maine tourists loved Thompson's Portland Head lighthouse picture, they apparently failed to fall in love with Thompson Old Fisherman pictures. From our perspective, "The Old Pilot" and "Toiler of the Sea" represents two of Thompson's very best and most distinctive photographs. The

"Toiler of the Sea'

subject matter is wonderful, and the clarity and detail are as good as those of any other hand-colored photographs we have seen. Yet, judging by the fact that these are two of the rarest Thompson pictures known, they apparently weren't very popular with Maine tourists and failed to sell many copies.

Other of Thompson's pictures did not sell very well. Just as Nutting experienced, the typical New Englander simply didn't want pictures of snow, men, cows and horses, or someone else's children hanging on the walls of their houses. Thompson tried them, they didn't sell, and today are considered to be collector's rarities.

But Fred Thompson also pursued several different areas that were rarely sold by other photographers. One example is close-up maritime pictures of schooners or sailing ships. As previously mentioned, Thompson catered to the visiting Maine tourists, and he learned that the photogenic tall-masted ships found in many Maine coastal ports became good sellers. They typified Maine to the tourists, and many people wanted such a picture to take home with them. Thompson photographed literally dozens of these sailing ships, and today they are probably the most popular Thompson pictures with collectors, rarely selling for less than $100.00.

"The Old Pilot"

Another subject that Thompson pursued was an area seemingly avoided by most other photographers: the American flag. America's 1917 – 1918 participation in World War I occurred during the peak period of early twentieth century hand-colored photography and, with patriotism at a fever pitch, you would have thought that most photographers would have tried to capitalize on it. Yet aside from Thompson, few did.

Still another area that Thompson pursued more than his competitors was "oddities." Thompson used the term to cover all his non-framed picture items, including calendars, small mirrors, tiny two-handled trays, glass paperweights, etc., each with a Fred Thompson hand-colored picture.

Thompson pictures were long regarded as some of the best pictures available and became known throughout the country, although their primary market was New England. The main marketing outlets, in addition to the studio, were gifts shops and department stores throughout southern and central Maine, especially along the seacoast. Fred Thompson pictures made excellent gifts and provided pleasant memories for the increasing number of vacationers traveling to Maine due to the advent of the automobile.

"Old Frigate"

What may come as a surprise to many people is that Frederick H. Thompson died a sudden, tragic, and unnatural death. On November 16, 1909, he was found dead in his studio. His death was ruled a suicide as a result of ingesting cyanide. Worry over business matters is believed to have been the cause of his suicide. He died at the age of 65.

The Thompson Art Company didn't end there, however. His son, Frederick M. Thompson, took control of the business upon his father's death and continued to run it until 1923. Therefore, the "Fred Thompson" that appears on so many hand-colored photographs actually refers to two Fred Thompsons, Frederick H. Thompson, the father, and Frederick M. Thompson, the son.

Frederick M. Thompson had attended Tufts University and didn't enter the Thompson Art Company until shortly before his father's death. Prior to his joining the family business, Frederick M. had worked in Cuba on an engineering project.

Although he knew little about photography prior to joining the company, he quickly became known as an expert in the business of nature prints. Not only did he continue selling his father's pictures, he added many new pictures to the Thompson Art Company line.

Throughout the next several years, he acquired several smaller studios in the Portland area (along with their complete line of pictures), including the Lamson Nature Print Company, the Owen Perry Company, and the Lyman Nelson Company.

Frederick M. Thompson died on November 24, 1923, at the age of 47. With his death, the doors of the Thompson Art Company were closed and no more Thompson pictures were sold.

REGIONALITY
New England; Portland, Maine

REPRESENTATIVE TITLES & VALUE GUIDE
"Apple Tree Road"
"Birch Bank"
"Brook in Winter"
"Fernbank"
"Fireside Fancy Work"
"Golden Trail"
"Lombardy Poplar"
"Maiden Reveries"
"Midsummer"
"Old Toll Bridge"
"Paring Apples"
"Portland Head"
"The Roller"
"White Head"
"Woodland Symphony"
Common untitled exterior scenes: $37.00 – 75.00
Common titled exterior scenes: $50.00 – 150.00
Common untitled interior scenes: $50.00 – 90.00
Common titled interior scenes: $75.00 – 200.00
Sailing schooners: $10.00 – 250.00+
Oddities: $50.00 – 150.00+
Best-of-the-best scenes: $250.00 – 750.00+

Early "Lamson Nature Prints" paper label

Oddities

Oddities backstamp

"Monument Square 1869" (hand-colored lithograph)

RECOMMENDED READING
See the Fred Thompson chapter in *Collector's Value Guide to Early 20th Century American Prints* (Collector Books, by Michael Ivankovich), which includes a listing of many known Thompson titles. Also see our Fred Thompson Exploring Early 20th C. Prints column on our website: www.michaelivankovich.com

THOMAS THOMPSON

BACKGROUND

Little background information on THOMAS THOMPSON has been found. We have only seen one Thomas Thompson picture, which dated circa 1920 – 1925. It was a basic exterior scene that provided no clue as to its location or origin.

REGIONALITY

Unknown

REPRESENTATIVE TITLES & VALUE GUIDE

Exterior scenes
Estimated value range: $10.00 – 50.00+

H. J. THORNE

BACKGROUND

H. J. THORNE was a photographer from Portland, Oregon. Active between 1898 and 1938, Thorne was a Mazama member and active mountain climber who hand painted his pictures in oils. He also sometimes used his pictures in a lectures series that he gave.

REGIONALITY

Northwest U.S.; Portland Oregon

REPRESENTATIVE TITLES & VALUE GUIDE

Western U.S. Scenes
Zion National Park
Estimated value range: $25.00 – 75.00+

American flag exterior scene

C. A. TILLINGHAST

BACKGROUND

The Reverend C. A. TILLINGHAST worked at 405 Potter Ave., Providence, Rhode Island. We have seen only a few Tillinghast hand-painted pictures over the years, and we have to wonder whether the Rev. Tillinghast knew the Rev. Wallace Nutting, who also preached in Providence, Rhode Island, around the same time.

REGIONALITY

New England; Providence, Rhode Island

REPRESENTATIVE TITLES & VALUE GUIDE

"Along the Brook"
Assorted untitled scenes
Estimated value range: $25.00 – 50.00+

Backstamp

Exterior scene

HENRY TROTH

BACKGROUND

Little background information on HENRY TROTH has been found. We have seen several Henry Troth pictures, which dated circa 1920 – 1925. One picture seemed to suggest that he was from Philadelphia, Pennsylvania, another was taken in Bermuda, and another was taken in Italy. Our best guess is that Troth was a photographer who was based in Philadelphia but traveled widely, taking and selling hand-painted photographs of the various places that he went to.

REGIONALITY

Unknown

REPRESENTATIVE TITLES & VALUE GUIDE

Exterior scene

Estimated value range: $25.00 – 75.00+

"Chioggia, Italy"

"Royal Palm, Bermuda"

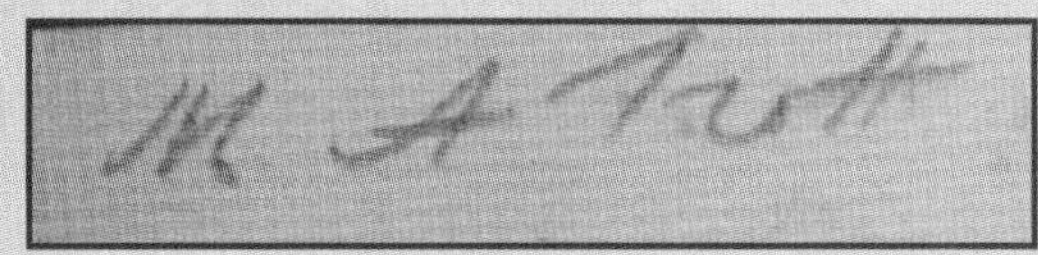

M. A. TROTT

BACKGROUND

M. A. TROTT was a photographer who specialized in Bermuda scenes. We have seen a variety of Trott pictures over the years, and all were taken in Bermuda and presumably sold as part of the Bermuda tourist trade circa 1920 – 1930s. "Bermuda" is part of most Trott titles.

REGIONALITY

Bermuda

REPRESENTATIVE TITLES & VALUE GUIDE

"Fairyland Gate, Bermuda"

"Royal Palm, Bermuda"

Estimated value range: $50.00 – 100.00+

F. HAYDEN TUCKER

BACKGROUND
Little background information on F. Hayden Tucker has been found. Collector Ted Davies reported seeing a F. Hayden Tucker scene titled "Collinwood" that gave no clues as to its origin or location.

REGIONALITY
Unknown

REPRESENTATIVE TITLES & VALUE GUIDE
Collinwood
Estimated value range: $10.00 – 50.00+

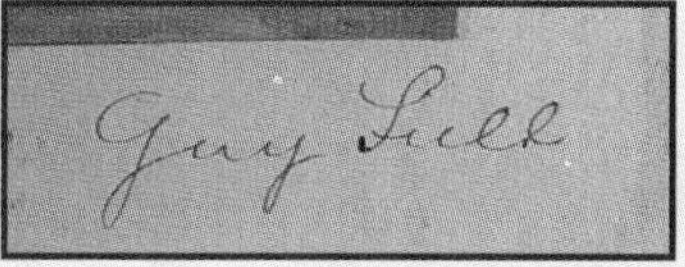

GUY TULL

BACKGROUND
Guy Tull was a photographer who, it seems, may have worked out of Massachusetts. We have seen a variety of Guy Tull pictures over the years, and all seem to have been taken in Massachusetts circa 1920 – 1930. We have found no firm connection between Guy Tull and Sanford Tull.

REGIONALITY
New England; Massachusetts

REPRESENTATIVE TITLES & VALUE GUIDE
Exterior scenes
"A Plymouth Doorway"
Estimated value range: $50.00 – 100.00+

"A Plymouth Doorway"

SANFORD TULL

BACKGROUND
Sanford Tull was a photographer who worked out of Massachusetts. We have seen a variety of Sanford Tull pictures over the years, and all seem to have been taken in Massachusetts, or at least New England, circa 1920 – 1930. We have also seen a paper label that states that Sanford Tull previously worked for Wallace Nutting. We have found no firm connection between Sanford Tull and Guy Tull.

REGIONALITY
New England; Massachusetts

REPRESENTATIVE TITLES & VALUE GUIDE
Exterior scenes
Manchester Byway
Estimated value range: $50.00 – 100.00+

TURNER (first name not known)

BACKGROUND

Little background information on TURNER has been found. We have only seen a few Turner pictures, which dated circa 1920 – 1925. All were interior scenes that seemed to have been taken in New England, and each picture was beautifully done and on a par with those of the major photographers.

REGIONALITY

New England

REPRESENTATIVE TITLES & VALUE GUIDE

" 'goin' to within' "
"Ready for the Reception"
Estimated value range: $25.00 – 75.00+

NELSON UNDERHILL

BACKGROUND

NELSON UNDERHILL was primarily an artist, not a photographer, but we have included him in this book because his work is often confused with hand-painted photographs. Like May Farini and Bessie Pease Gutmann and the Guttman & Gutmann Co., Nelson Underhill introduced a series of colonial scenes in an attempt to compete with Wallace Nutting's Colonial Revival interior scenes. Although they look like and are often confused with hand-painted photographs, actually the Nelson Underhill pictures we have seen have been color lithographs. We have found no clues regarding the location of Nelson Underhill.

REGIONALITY

New England

REPRESENTATIVE TITLES & VALUE GUIDE

"Dressing the Bride"
"Old Melody"
Estimated value range: $25.00 – 50.00+

"Dressing the Bride"

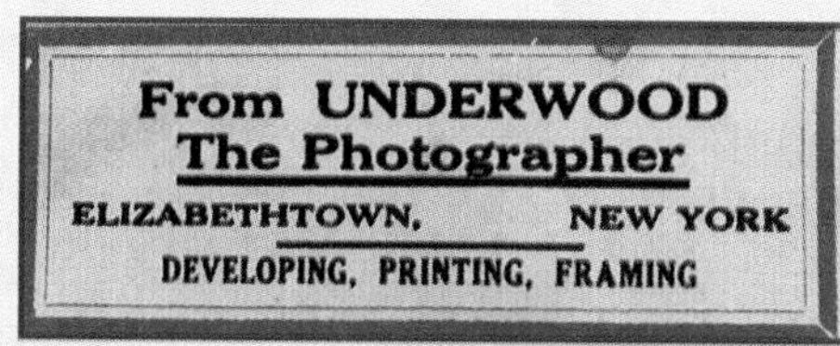
From UNDERWOOD
The Photographer
ELIZABETHTOWN, NEW YORK
DEVELOPING, PRINTING, FRAMING

UNDERWOOD (first name not known)

BACKGROUND

Little background information on UNDERWOOD has been found. We have only seen one Underwood picture, which dated circa 1920 – 1925. It was a basic exterior scene that included a paper label that read "From Underwood, The Photographer, Elizabethtown, New York, Developing, Printing, Framing." We have found no connection between "Underwood, The Photographer" and "Underwood & Underwood."

REGIONALITY

New York State; Elizabethtown

REPRESENTATIVE TITLES & VALUE GUIDE

Exterior scene
Estimated value range: $10.00 – 50.00+

UNDERWOOD & UNDERWOOD

BACKGROUND

Little background information on UNDERWOOD & UNDERWOOD has been found. We have only seen one Underwood & Underwood picture, which dated circa 1920 – 1925. It was a basic exterior scene that indicated it was from New York State. We have found no connection between "Underwood & Underwood" and "Underwood, The Photographer."

REGIONALITY

New York State

REPRESENTATIVE TITLES & VALUE GUIDE

Exterior scene
Estimated value range: $10.00 – 50.00+

R. MERITT VACY

BACKGROUND

Little background information on R. MERRITT VACY has been found. We have only seen one Vacy picture, which dated circa 1920 – 1925. It was a basic exterior scene, and it seemed to indicate that Vacy was from the Pocono Mountains region of Pennsylvania.

REGIONALITY

Pennsylvania; Pocono Mountains region

REPRESENTATIVE TITLES & VALUE GUIDE

Exterior scene
Estimated value range: $25.00 – 75.00+

J. W. VEITCH

BACKGROUND

Little background information on J. W. VEITCH has been found. We have only seen one Veitch picture, which dated circa 1920 – 1925. It was a beautifully colored western U.S. snow-capped mountain scene that suggested to us that Veitch worked somewhere in the Rocky Mountains region. This picture was signed "J. W. Veitch" in white ink directly upon the image.

Close-framed Rocky Mountains scene

REGIONALITY

Western U.S.; Rocky Mountains

REPRESENTATIVE TITLES & VALUE GUIDE

Close-framed Rocky Mountains scene
Estimated value range: $25.00 – 75.00+

JOHN G. VERKAMP

BACKGROUND

JOHN G. VERKAMP worked out of the Grand Canyon region of Arizona. We have seen a portfolio titled *Views of the Grand Canyon, Arizona* that included 12 hand-painted photogravures of the Grand Canyon. These portfolios were mass-produced for the tourist trade, but the color on each picture was applied by hand.

REGIONALITY

Southwestern U.S.; Grand Canyon, Arizona

REPRESENTATIVE TITLES & VALUE GUIDE

Views of the Grand Canyon, Arizona
Estimated value range, complete portfolio: $50.00 – 175.00+
Estimated value range, individual framed pages from portfolio: $10.00 – 50.00+

O. A. VIK

BACKGROUND

Little background information on O. A. VIK has been found. We have only seen one Vik picture, which dated circa 1920 – 1925. It was a beautifully colored scene from the South Dakota Badlands that suggested to us that Vik worked in South Dakota. This picture was signed "So. Dakota Badlands (c) O. A. Vik" in white ink directly upon the image.

REGIONALITY

Northcentral U.S.; South Dakota

REPRESENTATIVE TITLES & VALUE GUIDE

Close-framed South Dakota Badlands scene
Estimated value range: $50.00 – 100.00+

Close-framed South Dakota Badlands scene

VILLAR (first name not known)

BACKGROUND

VILLAR is another one of those names that is difficult to explain. We have seen many pictures signed "Villar," but have never seen a first name, have never seen any biographical information, and have never seen even a paper label or backstamp that could provide any information as to the location or origin of any Villar picture. To make things even more confusing, we have long suspected that Villar and Moran may be the same photographer based upon the similarity of the 1930s-style garden scenes, but have been unable to confirm this.

"The Steps to the Road"

REGIONALITY

Unknown

REPRESENTATIVE TITLES & VALUE GUIDE

"Day Dream"
"The Old Homestead"
"The Old Well"
"A Shady Nook"
"Shallow Waters"
"A Spring Pastoral"
"The Steps to the Road"
Typical value range:
$50.00 – 100.00+

"The Old Well"

J. R. WAPT

BACKGROUND

J. R. WAPT was a photographer who worked in the Bucks and Montgomery County areas of Pennsylvania. All Wapt pictures we have seen were taken in this two-county area, and each was signed "J. R. Wapt." We have seen a significant increase in interest in Wapt pictures recently, especially in the Bucks County/Montgomery County, Pennsylvania, area.

REGIONALITY

Pennsylvania; Bucks and Montgomery counties

REPRESENTATIVE TITLES & VALUE GUIDE

"The Delaware"
"Delaware River Turn"
"The Perkiomen"
Typical value range: $50.00 – 100.00+

"The Delaware"

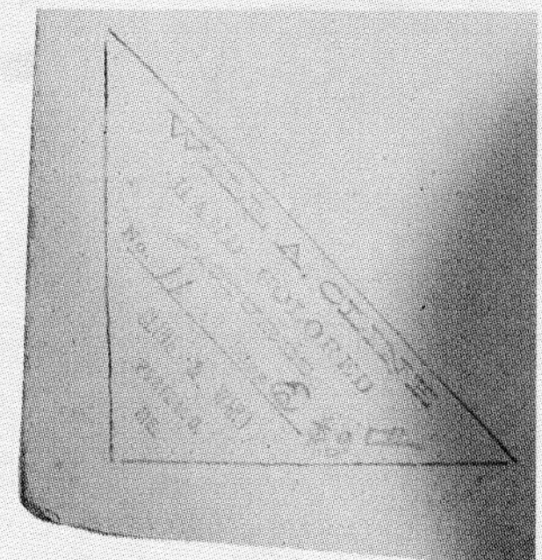

Backstamp

Maine Seascape

ARTHUR WARD

BACKGROUND

ARTHUR WARD was a partner of Will Cline in Portland, Maine. We have seen several Arthur Ward hand-colored photos that, when taken apart, carried one or two paper labels. One label read "Will A. Cline, Hand-Colored Pictures, Cline & Ward, Portland ME." The other read "Cline & Ward, Colored Photographs, Portland, Maine." The pictures dated circa 1910 – 1920 and the quality was very good. Most pictures we have seen were from southern Maine and presumably intended for the Maine tourist market.

REGIONALITY

New England; Portland, Maine

REPRESENTATIVE TITLES & VALUE GUIDE

"Flood Tide"
"Portland Head Light"
"Rocky Cliffs"
Typical value range: $50.00 – 100.00

K. J. WATERS

BACKGROUND

K. J. WATERS was a photographer who worked in Rainier National Park in Washington State. We have only seen one Waters picture, and it had "Emmons Glacier, Rainier National Park, (c) K. J. Waters" on the image.

REGIONALITY

Northwest U.S.; Washington State

REPRESENTATIVE TITLES & VALUE GUIDE

"Emmons Glacier"
Estimated value range: $25.00 – 75.00+

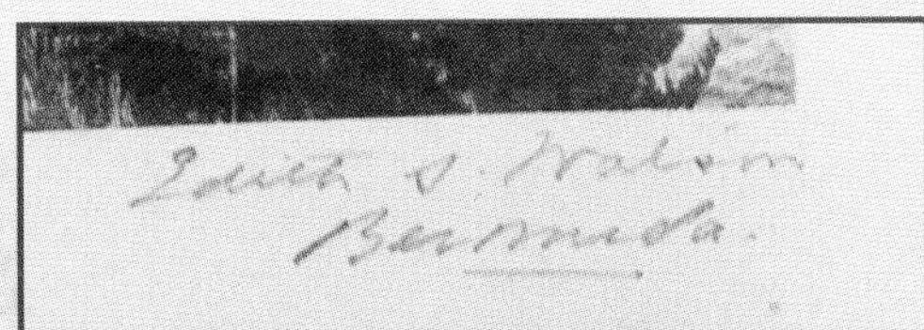

EDITH S. WATSON

Bermuda

BACKGROUND
EDITH WATSON was a photographer who did a considerable amount of work in Bermuda. All Watson pictures we have seen were taken in Bermuda and were signed "Edith Watson." Most of her pictures were brightly colored, to reflect the beautiful sunny days of Bermuda. We have also seen an Edith Watson included in a book titled *Women Photographers at National Geographic*, which mentions "Edith Watson's view of Cape Breton (Canada) Island early in the century." This would suggest that the scope of Edith Watson's work extended far beyond Bermuda.

REGIONALITY
Bermuda

REPRESENTATIVE TITLES & VALUE GUIDE
Bermuda
Bermuda seacoast
Bermuda triptych
Long Bay, Bermuda
Typical value range: $50.00 – 100.00+

"Lake Beauvert"

The Tekarra Gift Shoppe paper label

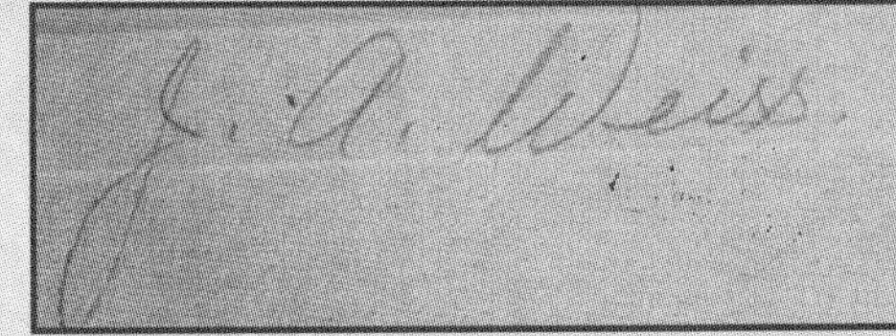

J. A. WEISS

BACKGROUND
J. A. WEISS was a photographer who worked in or near Jasper National Park in Alberta, Canada. All Weiss pictures we have seen were taken in Jasper National Park and were signed "J. A. Weiss." Collector Richard Turkiewicz has submitted a copy of a Weiss backstamp that read "Photographed and Copyrighted by J. A. Weiss, Jasper, Alta." We have also seen a paper label on several occasions that indicated that Weiss's pictures were distributed by The Tekarra Gift Shoppe in Jasper Park.

REGIONALITY
Canada; Jasper National Park, Alberta

REPRESENTATIVE TITLES & VALUE GUIDE
"Lake Beauvert"
"Lake Beauvert and Pyramid Mtn."
Estimated value range: $50.00 – 100.00+

"Square Tower House"

EDMUND WESTERVELT

BACKGROUND

EDMUND WESTERVELT was a photographer who worked mainly in New Mexico. Each Westervelt picture we have seen was taken in New Mexico and were signed "Edmund Westervelt." The composition, color, and detail of Westervelt's pictures were comparable to those of the major photographers.

REGIONALITY

Southwest U.S.; New Mexico

REPRESENTATIVE TITLES & VALUE GUIDE

"Square Tower House"
Typical value range: $50.00 – 100.00+

J. WESTHOUSE JR.

BACKGROUND

Little background information on J. WESTHOUSE JR. has been found. We have only seen one Westhouse picture, which dated circa 1920 – 1925. It was taken in New England, which suggests that Westhouse was probably a New England photographer.

REGIONALITY

New England

REPRESENTATIVE TITLES & VALUE GUIDE

Birch Borders
Estimated value range: $10.00 – 50.00

F. W. WESTWOOD

BACKGROUND

The late Ted Davies reported seeing a F. W. WESTWOOD scene titled "A Birch Road" that included a Westwood Studio Label from Meriden, Connecticut. Ted thought the image was taken at Pierce Hill, Connecticut.

REGIONALITY

New England; Meriden, Connecticut

REPRESENTATIVE TITLES & VALUE GUIDE

"A Birch Road"
Estimated value range: $10.00 – 50.00+

DONALD WHITE

BACKGROUND
DONALD WHITE was a photographer who worked out of Springfield, Vermont, and specialized in Vermont scenes, presumably for the tourist trade. The only Donald White picture we have seen included a paper label that read "Vermont Scene No. 1031, by Donald White, Springfield, Vermont". The fact that this paper label included a blank line where the picture number was hand written suggests that White carried a reasonably large inventory of Vermont scenes.

REGIONALITY
New England; Springfield, Vermont

REPRESENTATIVE TITLES & VALUE GUIDE
Vermont birches
Estimated value range: $25.00 – 50.00+

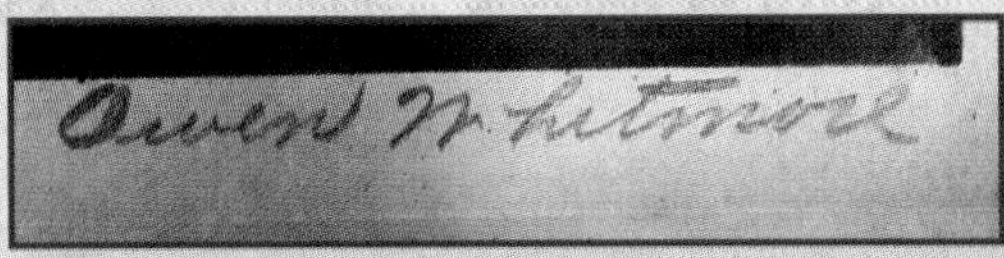

OWEN WHITMORE

BACKGROUND
Little background information on OWEN WHITMORE has been found. We have only seen one Whitmore picture, which dated circa 1925 – 1930. It was an interior scene, and the furniture used for it suggests that it was taken in New England.

REGIONALITY
New England

REPRESENTATIVE TITLES & VALUE GUIDE
"Her Fortune"
Estimated value range: $25.00 – 50.00+

"Her Fortune"

MARY C. WHITNEY

BACKGROUND
Little background information on MARY C. WHITNEY has been found. The late Ted Davies reported seeing a Mary C. Whitney scene titled "The Narrows" that gave no clue as to its origin or location.

REGIONALITY
Unknown

REPRESENTATIVE TITLES & VALUE GUIDE
"The Narrows"
Estimated value range: $10.00 – 50.00+

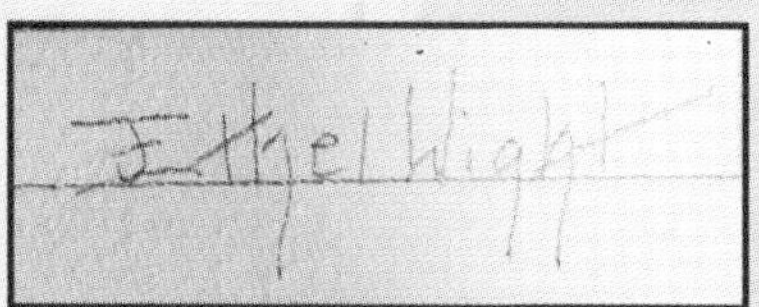

"Foggy Seas"

ETHEL WIGHT

BACKGROUND

Little background information on ETHEL WIGHT has been found. We have seen several Wight pictures, which dated circa 1920 – 1930. All were New England seascapes and outdoor scenes, and we believe that Wight was another Portland, Maine, photographer. Her pencil signature, in precise block letters, is strongly suggestive of the Fred Thompson signature, suggesting that she either copied the look of, or was somehow associated with, Fred Thompson in Portland, Maine. The quality of her work is excellent.

REGIONALITY

New England; Portland, Maine

REPRESENTATIVE TITLES & VALUE GUIDE

"Foggy Seas"
"Roadside Birches"
"Silvery Seas"
Typical value range: $50.00 – 75.00+

J. R. WILCOX

BACKGROUND

There is some debate whether J. R. WILCOX was a photographer who sold hand-painted photographs or an artist who sold hand-painted photographic reproductions of his paintings. Either way, Wilcox definitely worked in Florida. We have seen relatively few framed Wilcox pictures in circulation. Rather, most Wilcox pictures we have seen have been unframed and, quite often, associated with E. G. Barnhill hand-painted photos. There has been some speculation that Barnhill may have bought out the J. R. Wilcox Studio at some point and, when Barnhill's remaining photographic inventory was reintroduced into the marketplace, Wilcox's remaining pictures were included as well. In our opinion, Wilcox's work has limited appeal because its appearance is more impressionistic than realistic in contrast and tone.

REGIONALITY

Florida

REPRESENTATIVE TITLES & VALUE GUIDE

Various Florida palm and water scenes
Estimated value range: $25.00 – 50.00+

Florida scene

Florida scene

Wilcox, Florida scene

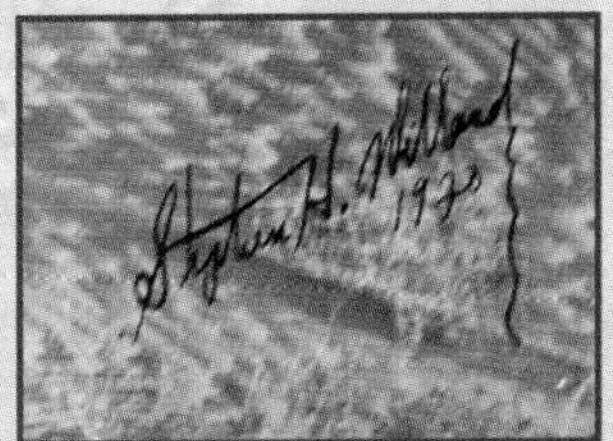

"Silence and Desolation"

SILENCE AND DESOLATION.

Title on image

STEPHEN H. WILLARD (1894 – 1965)

BACKGROUND

STEPHEN H. WILLARD was one of the Southwest's premier landscape photographers and perhaps America's best desert photographer. Born in 1894 in Earlville, Illinois, he moved with his parents to Corona, California, at the age of two. He received his first camera at age 16, and over the next several years expanded his photographic skills by taking pictures of California's mountain and desert regions.

From 1905 to 1920, Willard primarily operated a studio in Corona called Photos of the Colorado Desert. He was also in a partnership with Bear Valley Photographers (Wright M. Pierce). In 1912, his studio was located in a tent in Kings Canyon in the Sierra Mountains. This area later became the Kings Canyon National Park. During this time he was dating Virginia Best, whose father owned the concession rights in the valley. Although Willard tried to establish a studio in Yosemite National Park, he lost out to Ansel Adams, who went on to much considerable photographic acclaim.

In 1922, Willard and his wife, Beatrice, moved from Los Angeles to Palm Springs. In Palm Springs, Willard expanded his photographic inventory and began selling hand-painted images to visiting tourists through several outlets, including the Desert Inn Gallery in Palm Springs and the Palm Canyon Trading Post, which was managed by his wife. In 1923, Willard established a summer studio in Mammoth Lakes, California, and he used this as a base to photograph the Sierras, the White Mountains, and the deserts of Death Valley. His became the longest-running business in the area.

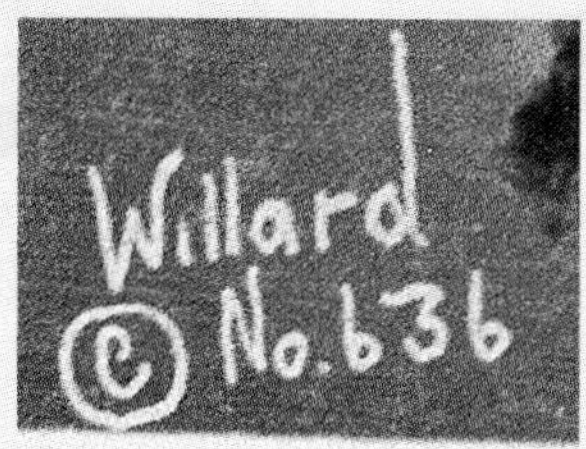

Copyright on image

NOT FOR REPRODUCTION
POSITIVELY NO RELEASE
STEPHEN H. WILLARD, Palm Springs, Ca

Backstamp #1

Reproduction Rights on All Copyrighted Photos
Must Be Obtained from
STEPHEN H. WILLARD, PALM SPRINGS, CAL.

Backstamp #2

In the 1930s, Willard was hired by the U.S. Borax Corporation to document Death Valley, and his photographic work played a key role in President Hoover's 1933 decision to add land to the park. In 1936, his photographs played an important role in the proposal and decision to create the Joshua Tree National Park.

In 1935, Willard built his own studio in what is known today as Morton's Botanical Garden on South Palm Drive Canyon in Palm Springs. Discouraged by the increasing development in the Coachella Valley and the gradual loss of his favorite photographic sites, Willard moved to the Owens Valley in the Great Basin Desert in 1947. Stephen Willard died there in 1965.

Unlike so many other photographers whose photographic collections were lost upon their death, Willard's daughter, Dr. Beatrice Willard, donated her father's lifetime collection of photographic prints, negatives, and hand-painted pictures to the Palm Springs Desert Museum, where they have been cataloged and exhibited. A 2001 Willard exhibition was titled Stephen Willard: California Desert Photography and featured images that included Joshua tree woodlands, desert fan palm oases, sand dunes, badlands, and the desert's steepest peak, Mount San Jacinto.

REGIONALITY

Southwestern United States; California

REPRESENTATIVE TITLES & VALUE GUIDE

"The Desert"
"The Sea of Desolation"
"Sentinels of the Desert"
Typical value range: $100.00 – 250.00+

Snow-capped mountains, southwestern U.S.

Desert scene, southwestern U.S.

"Clifton by the Sea, Calif."

ERNEST WILLIAMS

BACKGROUND
Little background information on ERNEST WILLIAMS has been found. We have only seen one Williams picture over the years, probably circa 1920 – 1925. It was a California seascape, which suggests that Williams was probably a California photographer.

REGIONALITY
Western U.S.; California

REPRESENTATIVE TITLES & VALUE GUIDE
"Clifton by the Sea, Calif."
Estimated value range: $25.00 – 75.00

WILLIAMS (first name not known)

BACKGROUND
WILLIAMS was a Hawaiian photographer whose work we have seen several times. The hand-painted pictures we have seen, dated circa 1925 – 1930, were signed "Williams, Honolulu," and included flowers and other local scenery that probably would have appealed to visiting tourists.

REGIONALITY
Hawaii; Honolulu

REPRESENTATIVE TITLES & VALUE GUIDE
Ponciana
Estimated value range: $25.00 – 75.00

GEORGE WILMOT

BACKGROUND
Muriel Everhart reported that GEORGE WILMOT was her mother's first husband and lived in Brooklyn, New York. She also reported that Wilmot worked extensively in the Hudson River Valley and in the New Jersey Palisades.

REGIONALITY
New York State; New Jersey

REPRESENTATIVE TITLES & VALUE GUIDE
Untitled exterior scene
Estimated value range: $10.00 – 50.00+

A. B. WILSON

BACKGROUND
A. B. WILSON was a New England photographer who worked circa 1905. We have only seen one A. B. Wilson exterior scene, and that picture suggested to us that Wilson was a New Hampshire photographer. Note that A. B. Wilson is not Alexander Wilson.

REGIONALITY
New England; New Hampshire

REPRESENTATIVE TITLES & VALUE GUIDE
White Mountain birches
Estimated value range: $25.00 – 50.00

ALEXANDER WILSON

BACKGROUND
Collector Don (no last name in e-mail) reported that Alexander Wilson was a photographer who worked in Chilliwack, British Columbia, Canada, circa 1928 – 1946. Don also reported that he had six Wilson pictures in his collection, and each seemed to be from the Chilliwack area. Note that Alexander Wilson is not A. B. Wilson.

REGIONALITY
Canada; Chilliwack, British Columbia

REPRESENTATIVE TITLES & VALUE GUIDE
Untitled exterior scene
Estimated value range: $50.00 – 100.00+

"Cultus Lake, Chilliwack BC"

Seascape

House scene

P. WINSLOW

BACKGROUND

P. WINSLOW was a New England photographer who, in our opinion, probably worked on Cape Cod. We have seen pictures signed both as "Winslow" and "P. Winslow," and most pictures have been seascapes, usually with sand dunes. The quality was typically very good.

REGIONALITY

New England; Massachusetts, probably Cape Cod

REPRESENTATIVE TITLES & VALUE GUIDE

Large house scene
Seascape
Typical value range: $50.00 – 100.00+

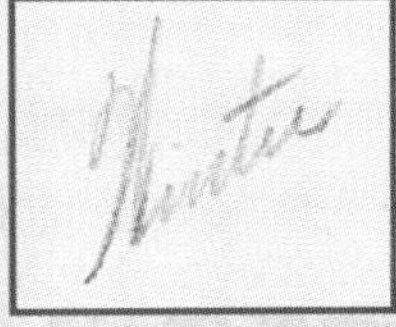

FRANK WINTER
WINTER PHOTO CO.

BACKGROUND

FRANK WINTER operated the Winter Photo Company in Portland, Oregon. Most of Winter's work that we have seen has been centered on or near the Columbia River. A backstamp that we have seen reads "Winter-Luetters Pictures, Hand-Colored, Winter Photo Co., 240 East 32nd Street, Portland Ore."

REGIONALITY

Northwest U.S.; Portland, Oregon

REPRESENTATIVE TITLES & VALUE GUIDE

"Columbia River Highway"
"Eagle Creek Bridge"
Estimated value range: $50.00 – 100.00+

Exterior scene

"Winter-Luetters Pictures"
HAND COLORED
WINTER PHOTO CO.
240 East 32nd Street
PORTLAND - ORE.

Backstamp

NED DAVID WITHAM

BACKGROUND

Jim Witham reported that N. D. WITHAM was actually his grandfather Ned David Witham. He reported that Witham was originally from Vermont, was a Methodist minister, and had a studio in Grantham, New Hampshire. Most of Witham's photographic work centered near the Connecticut River and the Little Sugar River near Claremont, New Hampshire, circa 1906. Witham also extensively photographed local logging operations there as well.

REGIONALITY

New England; New Hampshire

REPRESENTATIVE TITLES & VALUE GUIDE

Birch Lane
Estimated value range: $10.00 – 50.00+

RUFUS WOOD

BACKGROUND

RUFUS WOOD was a photographer who had a studio at 5 Main Street, Taunton, Massachusetts. We have only seen two exterior scenes by Wood, and both were seemingly taken in Massachusetts circa 1935 – 1940.

REGIONALITY

New England; Massachusetts

REPRESENTATIVE TITLES & VALUE GUIDE

Exterior blossom scene
Estimated value range: $10.00 – 50.00+

N. WORSHAK

BACKGROUND

Little background information on N. WORSHAK has been found. We have only seen one Worshak picture, which dated circa 1920 – 1925. It was taken in New England, which suggests that Worshak was a New England photographer.

REGIONALITY

New England

REPRESENTATIVE TITLES & VALUE GUIDE

"The Old North Shore"
Estimated value range: $10.00 – 50.00

WRIGHT (first name not known)

BACKGROUND
Little background information on WRIGHT has been found. We have only seen one Wright picture, which dated circa 1920 – 1925. It was taken in New England, which suggests that Wright was a New England photographer.

REGIONALITY
New England

REPRESENTATIVE TITLES & VALUE GUIDE
Exterior scene
Estimated value range: $10.00 – 50.00+

Bear River

PAUL YATES

BACKGROUND
PAUL YATES was a photographer who specialized in Nova Scotia scenes. All seem to have some form of water in them; scenes include lakes, bays, and the ocean. Large and small boats are also typically found in Yates's work. Signatures are usually in pencil, and we have seen both indented mat formats and image-over-gold-foil formats. Overall, the quality is very good.

REGIONALITY
Canada; Nova Scotia

REPRESENTATIVE TITLES & VALUE GUIDE
"Bear River"
"The Digby Wharves"
"The Milford Lakes"
Typical value range: $50.00 – 100.00+

"The Digby Wharves"

Chapter 7

Unknown Photographers

Looking to enter the hand-painted photography market without breaking the bank? Try collecting hand-painted photography by unknown photographers.

As we've already discussed, the biggest name in early twentieth century hand-painted photography is undoubtedly Wallace Nutting. His pictures are generally the most highly collectible and most expensive of all early twentieth century hand-painted photography, with prices for the best and rarest Nutting pictures running into the hundreds and even thousands of dollars.

Following Nutting both in popularity and collectibility today are David Davidson, Charles Sawyer, and Fred Thompson, who ranked two, three, and four, respectively, behind Nutting in total output. As the price of Nutting pictures has increased in recent years, so too have the prices of Davidson, Sawyer, and Thompson scenes, especially as more collectors have started collections exclusively focusing upon works by these three photographers. Prices for better and rarer Davidson-Sawyer-Thompson pictures can now typically run into the $100.00 – 300.00 range, and we have sold Fred Thompson and Charles Sawyer pictures for more than $800.00 each.

Following Nutting, Davidson, Sawyer, and Thompson are hand-colored photographs by the major regional photographers. Some of the names in this group: E. G. Barnhill, J. Carleton Bicknell, Hal Burrowes, Pedro Cacciola, Royal Carlock, J. Walter Collinge, Cleve Craswell, Norman Edson, Emma Freeman, H. Marshall Gardiner, W. H. Gardiner, J. M. Garrison, Gibson, James Harris, Byron Harmon, F. Jay Haynes, Jack Ellis Haynes, Charles Higgins, Frederick Hodges, Theo Hordczak, Fred Kiser, Kolb Brothers, Lamson Studios, Wallace R. MacAskill, Fred Martin, Carl Moon, George Petty, Edmond Royce, Harry Standley, Joseph Stimson, Florence Thompson, Stephen Willard, etc. Pictures by these photographers have all become increasingly collectible in recent years, especially in certain specific regions of the country.

Below the major regional photographers are all of the other named but less collectible photographers, with names such as Nelson, Gunn, Hennessy, Kattleman, and Lane. Yet as more is learned about some of these photographers, they may jump up into level #3 with the more important regional photographers.

Adorable child

All of which takes us to level #5 in the inverted pyramid of early twentieth century hand-painted picture photographers, hand-painted photographs by unknown photographers. This category is just what the name implies, black and white photographs that have been individually hand-painted but that are not directly attributable to any specific photographer. That is, no photographer's name appears anywhere on the picture, on the matting, or on the frame's paper backing.

Since collectors typically collect the name, and since there is no name here to collect, hand-painted photographs by unknown photographers are typically the least collectible and the least expensive of all early twentieth century hand-painted photography — which is what makes them so much fun to collect.

Who were these unknown photographers? They actually include a very broad spectrum of early twentieth century photographers. Most were amateurs who simply colored their own personal pictures as a hobby. Some actually became quite good at coloring their photographs, while others did an extremely poor job. Fortunately, those that did a poor job generally didn't produce many pictures that remain in circulation today.

Many were full-time or part-time professional photographers who, for lack of a better term, might be called Wallace Nutting wannabes. Some photographers saw that Nutting, Davidson, Sawyer, and Thompson were making money selling their work, and attempted to duplicate their style. Some focused exclusively on hand painting their pictures; others only colored pictures at the request of certain clients, rather than for the mass market.

And still other unknown photographers simply colored their work in order to beautify family photographs or mementos prior to the introduction of color photography. My parents' wedding photograph was actually my first introduction to hand-painted photography.

For whatever reason, each of these photographers neglected to add a name to his or her work.

Unknown Photographers

These photographers were primarily local, or at best regional, in their work. They sold their work either through area gift shops or other local outlets, and quite often gave their work away to friends and family as personal gifts.

What is available to collect? One of the most enjoyable aspects of collecting hand-painted photographs by unknown photographers is that the field is extremely broad. Of course there are the standard exterior scenes made so famous by Wallace Nutting, including pictures of lakes, blossoms, birches, streams, and country lanes. Yet this area is not highly collectible because the theme was so widely covered by better-known photographers.

Family photographs (children, parents, grandparents, brothers, sisters, aunts, uncles, cousins, or other family members, either in individual or group shots) is another broad area that is readily available to collect, yet one that is not highly sought after by most collectors. After all, how many people today are interested in owning pictures of someone else's family and ancestors?

Aside from condition, subject matter is usually the primary determinant of value. The more interesting the subject matter, the more highly collectible the picture is. Over the years, we have seen hand-colored pictures of cowboys and Indians; soldiers and sailors; naval battleships and destroyers; cars, trucks, and trains; motor boats and row boats; houses and castles; athletic teams and events; farms and farm animals; and much, much more, all of which are collectible to some segment.

Specific locations and events such as New York City, Boston, Philadelphia, or other major cities, Europe and Asia, Central Park and Estes Park, Florida beaches and the Pacific Ocean, 4-H fairs and state fairs, and World's Fairs and international expositions are all good examples of highly desirable pictures.

One especially broad collectible category is western U.S. hand-painted photography. The western national parks and deserts presented a huge area of interesting subject matter just waiting to be photographed and sold as hand-painted pictures. And the vacationers to these national parks and the surrounding areas were prime candidates for purchasing large quantities of these pictures. The Grand Canyon, Yosemite, Yellowstone, Zion, Bryce Canyon, Rocky Mountains, and the Arizona desert were all widely photographed, and pictures of them are highly collectible today. Photographers in Colorado, Utah, Arizona, New Mexico, California, Oregon, Washington, and Nevada all sold large numbers of hand-painted pictures to local residents and visiting tourists.

Perhaps the most highly sought-after pictures lie in the area of crossover collectibility, a term that refers to a single subject matter that may be of interest to several different groups of collectors. For example, we had in our collection a picture of a tugboat that had the word "Ford" clearly marked on its smokestack. A picture such as this would not only be desirable to collectors of hand-painted photography, but also to collectors of tugboats and collectors of Ford memorabilia. Another example of crossover collectibilty we have in our collection now is a picture with a hand-painted fire truck, circa 1910. This would appeal to truck collectors and collectors of fire-fighting memorabilia as well as collectors of hand-painted photography. The greater the number of potential collectors who may be interested in a specific picture, the greater the potential value.

Why do collectors collect hand-painted photographs by unknown photographers? Here are six quick reasons:

* These photos are still relatively easy to find. You can find them at antique shows, antique shops, flea markets, auctions, and sometimes even in auction box lots.

Someone else's relatives

* They are generally the least expensive type of hand-painted photography still available to collect. A general price range for these pictures is $5.00 – 100.00, usually under $50.00 and often under $25.00. However, better examples are already often bringing well over $100.00, and I don't expect the price to drop anytime soon.

* There is a very broad assortment of subject matter to collect. We covered this earlier, but you should be aware that there is enough diversity to appeal to most levels of collectors.

* Unlike the most popular pictures by the better known photographers, which often sold hundreds and sometimes thousands of copies, pictures by unknown photographers are usually one-of-a-kind pieces. Which means that each is probably unique; there probably isn't another one out there like it. Which also means that if you get the right piece, you can name your own price (once you find the right collector).

* Because they are generally one-of-a-kind pieces, and because they are generally less expensive to purchase, pictures by unknown photographers can offer a large potential upside for a relatively small investment.

* The crossover collectibility of them makes them even more fun and challenging to collect.

So if you are looking to enter a new area of collecting, hand-painted photographs by unknown photographers might just be for you. My advice? Set a reasonable budget and collect only what appeals to you. Most of these pictures are attractive and perfectly sized for any area in most homes. And perhaps most importantly, this category of collecting represents an area where you can still find some incredible bargains.

Memories from a western vacation

Youthful sporting memories

The World's Fair

Memories from a foreign vacation

Get out the vote! circa 1915

Railroading in days past

Chapter 8

Regionality

As we have already mentioned many times throughout this book, the primary difference between the Wallace Nutting market and the markets for all of the other Wallace Nutting–like photographers focuses upon one factor: regionality. All of the other factors — subject matter, grading, condition, size — remain the same for each market. But the single most important pricing variable beyond subject matter, grading, condition, and size will usually be regionality.

What we mean by this is that hand-painted pictures will usually be in higher demand, and will command higher prices, in the region where they originated. Conversely, the farther you move away from that region, generally the lower demand, and the lower the price. So what we will try to do for you here in chapter 8 is to break down and analyze the results of the research that we shared with you in chapter 6, by region.

New England, Atkinson, "Old Man of the Mts."

COLLECTING TIP

In most instances, the demand for hand-painted photography will be highest in the region where the picture originated.

Overall we have accounted for more than 300 different early twentieth century photographers of hand-painted pictures in this book. These include photographers whose pictures have passed through our auctions and through out retail business. It includes photographers whose work we have seen in our travels, and whose work has been reported to us by others. And it includes photographers whose work we have seen available on eBay and other Internet sites.

Is it complete? No. We know that we have missed some along the way. But we think it's pretty darn complete. Our list probably has more eastern vs. western U.S. photographers because, with our homebase being Pennsylvania, we obviously have greater access to more eastern pictures than western pictures. But frankly, our auctions have become national in nature, and we deal with large numbers of people all over the United States and Canada on a regular basis. So, in our opinion, if we haven't seen or heard about it a specific photographer over the years, then that photographer is probably a fairly minor player within the field.

What follows here is a summary analysis of the information contained in Chapter 6.

NEW ENGLAND

New England as a region had by far the largest number of photographers. Of the 311 we have documented, 112 (36.0%) were from New England. These New England states break down as shown in the following chart:

State	Number	Leading Photographer
Connecticut	3	Wallace Nutting (Southbury CT, 1905 – 1912)
Maine	21	Fred Thompson (Portland ME)
Massachusetts	23	Wallace Nutting (Framingham MA, 1912 – 1941)
New Hampshire	19	Charles Sawyer (Concord NH)
Rhode Island	3	David Davidson (Providence RI)
Vermont	10	Homer Royce (St. Albans VT)
Unknown New England state	33	N/A

The New England photographers break down as follows:

Connecticut

Wallace Nutting, Frederick G. Robbins, and F. W. Westwood.

Maine
J. Carleton Bicknell, Ralph L. Blood, Hal Burrowes, Call, Rudolph Cassens, Will A. Cline, E. T. Haling, Charles R. Higgins, J. B. Kahill, George C. Keep, Lamson Studios, LeBusch, McCorkle, E. H. Merrill, Lyman Nelson, Owen Perry, Potter Studio, Charles Sawyer, Fred Thompson, Arthur Ward, and Ethel Wight.

Massachusetts
Florian Baker, Pedro Cacciola, Cedric G. Chase, William Coffin, Winthrop F. Coffin, Consolidated Art Co., G. W. French, H. Marshall Gardiner, Garland, Edward Guy, Margaret Hennessy, LaBelle Studio, J. Robinson Neville, Wallace Nutting, Phelps, Chas. A. Plumer, Stanley Rogers, Esther Svenson, Florence Thompson, Guy Tull, Sanford Tull, P. Winslow, and Rufus Wood.

New Hampshire
Atkinson, Babcock, Brooks, W. H. Burke, C. D. Currier, Homes, Edgar Burdett Leet, W. H. Mahahan Jr., Moehring, A. W. Moody, Meredith Nick, A. Emery Phinney, K. F. Pratt, Charles Sawyer, Harold Boardman Sawyer, Guy Shorey, Slade, A. B. Wilson, and Ned David Witham.

Rhode Island
David Davidson, H. T. Mitchell, and H. A. Robbins.

Vermont
Bill Brehmer, Mrs. N. Corlis, Willis A. Deane, Mack Derek, Van Derk, Lester Farnum, Patch, Richardson Studio, Homer Royce, and Donald White.

Unknown New England States
Oscar Allen, J. P. Anthony, I. Austin, Baker Art Gallery, Wallace Baldwin, Bernie, Brown, E. Brown, Burnham, Depue Brothers, P. Erikson, E. L. Foote, George Forest, Gandara, Gibson, Gideon, Thomas C. Hawkes, Hendrickson, Woodbury E. Hunt, Nick Hutchinson, Hyde, Kabel, Victor Kahill, Ralph Kimball, Knoffe, David Leand, Mary Harrod Northend, F. E. Porter, Edward Snow, J. Westhouse Jr., Owen Whitmore, N. Worshak, and Wright.

In our opinion, there are several distinct reasons New England had such a large concentration of photographers who were selling hand-colored photos at this time.

* New England's population was larger than most other areas in the country, which provided a larger market for this product.

* New England was a nearby tourist destination for a large portion of America's population, and tourists increased the market size for this product.

* With New England's larger population, with the larger demand due to its population and tourist base, more photographers were needed in New England than in other parts of the country.

New Hampshire's White Mountains, Vermont's Green Mountains, and the southern Maine coast were all commonly photographed areas. Many non-specified locations such as streams, rivers, lakes, mountains, country roads, etc., were also frequently photographed.

Perhaps the number one surprise in New England hand-painted photography is the lack of Boston pictures that are found. With all of Boston's historical sites, we would have expected a larger volume of Boston pictures to have surfaced, but relatively few have.

Portland, Maine, Charles Sawyer, Portland Head Lighthouse

PORTLAND, MAINE

We've always asserted that Portland, Maine, was a hotbed for early twentieth century photographers, yet even we were surprised by how many Portland photographers we were able to document. Of the 311 photographers that we documented, a surprising 15 (or 4.8%) were based in that one city. These include J. Carleton Bicknell, Ralph L. Blood, Hal Burrowes, Will A. Cline, J. B. Cahill, George C. Keep, Lamson Studios, LeBusch, McCorkle, E. H. Merrill, Lyman Nelson, Owen Perry, Fred Thompson, Arthur Ward, and Ethel Wight.

We're not sure why Portland was so rich with photographers. Many of them seem to be pre-1910, and our guess is that Portland was more of a tourist destination circa 1900 – 1910 than it was circa 1925 – 1940. As the automobile improved in reliability, southern Maine locales may have been replaced by more remote locations as primary tourist destinations for many New Englanders.

Portland Head Lighthouse was the most commonly photographed scene in Portland, and more pictures of it were sold to visiting tourists than were pictures of any other single location.

In our opinion, the top four Portland photographers in terms of total photographic output would have been 1) Fred Thompson, 2) J. Carleton Bicknell, 3) Lamson Studios, and 4) Hal Burrowes.

Florida, Sunsene Pictures, the Singing Tower

FLORIDA

Although Florida has long been a popular tourist destination, we were surprised by how few hand-colored picture photographers seemed to work there. Of the 311 photographers we documented, only 13 (or 4.2%) were based in that entire state. That's 13 for an entire state verses 16 for the single city of Portland, Maine. These 13 include Esmund G. Barnhill, H. Marshall Gardiner, W. H. Gardiner, Gunn, James Harris, Wesley Jackson, Lamoreaux, Wallace Nutting, Kathleen Robinson, R. E. Simpson, Sunsene, Fred Thompson, and J. R. Wilcox.

With Florida being such a warm-weather tourist destination, we expected to see a higher concentration of photographers marketing their pictures there, but that didn't seem to be the case. On the other hand, we have seen a large number of hand-painted pictures by unknown photographers taken in Florida, which suggests that many amateur photographers took their cameras with them on winter vacation and photographed Florida's beauties for their own enjoyment.

St. Augustine was the most commonly photographed city in Florida. With such popular sights as the Oldest House, the Fountain of Youth, Charlotte Street, and Ft. Marion, large numbers of these pictures were sold. Surprisingly few pictures from Miami or Miami Beach have surfaced. And somewhat even more surprisingly, we have seen more with non-specific location scenes (palm trees, sandy beaches, warm-weather streams, sunsets, etc.) than we have seen with specific locations (Miami, Orlando, St. Petersburg, Winter Park, the Everglades, etc.).

In our opinion, the top four Florida photographers in terms of total photographic output were 1) James Harris (St. Augustine), 2) Esmund Barnhill (St. Petersburg), 3) W. H. Gardiner (Daytona), and 4) Sunsene (Bok Singing Tower).

Wallace Nutting and Fred Thompson sold very few Florida pictures, and we have seen surprisingly few H. Marshall Gardiner Florida pictures, even though he did have a studio in Florida.

Pennsylvania, Wallace Nutting, "A Perkiomen October"

MIDDLE-ATLANTIC STATES

The Middle-Atlantic states had a fair, but not large, number of photographers during this period. Of the 311 photographers we have documented, 26 (8.4%) were from New Jersey, New York, or Pennsylvania. The Middle-Atlantic states break down as shown in the following chart:

State	Number	Leading Photographer
New Jersey	4	James Harris (Lake Hopatcong NJ)
New York	14	Frederick B. Hodges (Rome NY)
Pennsylvainia	8	F. Radel (Phoenixville PA)

The Middle-Atlantic photographers break down as follows:

New Jersey
Paul R. Collier, Bessie Pease Gutmann, James Harris, and Jean Woolman Kirkbride.

New York
Burnell Studio, A. G. Cheney, Frederick A. Hodges, Frederick B. Hodges, J. W. Mann, Charles Marshall, C. A. Payne, George S. Payne, Roege, Schlesinger Brothers, Paul Strand, Underwood & Underwood, Underwood, and George Wilmot.

Pennsylvania
C. Delancy Allen, C. M. Gilbert, Joseph Hudson, F. Radel, Frederick Scheetz, W. R. Summers, R. Merritt Vacy, and J. R. Wapt.

There were some surprises here as well. For example, in New

York State there were surprisingly few hand-painted pictures taken in New York City, the Finger Lakes, the Catskill Mountains, Niagara Falls, or the Adirondack Mountains. We saw practically no pictures taken anywhere along the New Jersey shore (including Atlantic City), and we saw practically no pictures taken of Philadelphia landmarks, the Poconos region, or Pennsylvania Dutch-Amish Country, for example. No hand-painted pictures at all were found from Baltimore or Annapolis, Maryland. All of these locations seemed ripe for tourist-oriented hand-painted pictures and practically none have surfaced.

Washington DC, Royal Carlock, Washington Monument

WASHINGTON DC

Washington DC has long been a popular tourist destination with Americans, and even in the slow Depression years, the government employment offered to local residents and a steady stream of tourists resulted in strong picture sales for DC photographers, even when sales dipped for non-DC photographers during this period. Of the 311 photographers that we documented, 6 (1.9%) were based in Washington DC.

The Washington DC photographers include C. O. Buckingham, Campbell Art Co., Royal Carlock, Oakley Clark, Theo Horydczak, and S. I. Markel.

In our opinion, the top three selling Washington DC photographers were: 1) Royal Carlock, 2) C.O. Buckingham, and 3) Theo Horydczak.

Perhaps the most interesting thing about the Washington DC photographers is that they were not nearly as affected by the Great Depression as were most non-DC photographers, who suffered through these years. Apparently many local residents still had government jobs, and visiting tourists still wanted to take home a hand-painted photograph from Washington DC.

Pacific Northwest, Asahel Curtis, Mt. Rainier, Washington

PACIFIC NORTHWEST

The Pacific Northwest states had a fair, but not large, number of photographers during this period. Of the 311 we have documented, 19 (5.9%) were from Alaska, Oregon, and Washington State. The Pacific Northwest states break down as shown in the following chart:

State	Number	Leading Photographer
Alaska	3	E. Andrews (Douglas, AK)
Oregon	8	Fred Kiser (Crater Lake OR)
Washington	8	Norman Edson (Vashon Island WA)

The Pacific Northwest photographers break down as follows:

Alaska
E. Andrews, George L. Johnson, and Heath Arlo Ives.

Oregon
Benjamin A. Gifford, R.J. Gifford, Fred H. Kiser, Patterson, Wilma Roberts, Sawyers, H. J. Thorne, and Winter.

Washington State
J. Bert Barton, Asahel Curtis, Norman Edson, J. Boyd Ellis, A. O. Mack, A. E. Price, and K. J. Waters.

Mt. Rainier was the most commonly photographed location, probably followed by Mt. Hood and then the Columbia River region.

Western United States, Charles Sawyer, Yosemite National Park

WESTERN U.S.

The western U.S. had a fair number of photographers during this period. Of the 311 we have documented, 37 (11.7%) were from Arizona, California, Colorado, Idaho, Montana, Utah, Wyoming, and various unknown western States. The western U.S. breaks down as shown in the following chart:

State	Number	Leading Photographer
Arizona	3	Kolb Brothers (Grand Canyon AZ)
California	12	Stephen Willard (Palm Springs CA)
Colorado	7	Harry Landis Standley (Colorado Springs CO)
Idaho	1	Stanley L. Anderson (Rexburg ID)
Montana	1	T. J. Hileman (Glacier Nat. Park MT)
Utah	1	Hal Rumel (Zion & Bryce Parks UT)
Wyoming	4	F. Jay Haynes (Yellowston Nat. Park WY)
Unknown States	8	J. M. Garrison (Unknown, but probably CA)

The Western U.S. photographers break down as follows:

Arizona
Fred Harvey, Kelly Studio, and Kolb Brothers.

California
Bagnall, Bear Photo, C. W. Briggs, Hal H. Campbell, J. W. Collinge, Emma B. Freeman, Kamera Art Studios Inc., Frederick W. Martin, M. L. Oakes, Photo-Craft, Stephen Willard, and Ernest Williams.

Colorado
C. D. Ford, Carl F. Hildreth, Kirwan, McClure, Mile High Photo Studio, Photocraft Shop, and Harry Landis Standley.

Idaho
Stanley L. Anderson.

Montana
T. J. Hileman.

Utah
Hal Rumel.

Wyoming
W. Brewer, F. Jay Haynes, Jack Ellis Haynes, and Joseph Elam Stimson.

Western State Not Known
Eve S. Bradley, L. Cooper, Leo Furback, J. M. Garrison, Fred Harvey, W. J. MacDonald, Frank Oakes, and J. W. Veitch.

Not surprisingly, California had the largest number of photographers. National parks (Yellowstone, Glacier, Yosemite, and Estes), the Rocky Mountains, and southwestern deserts were among the most photographed western locations. Somewhat surprisingly, few hand-painted photographs from major cities such as San Francisco or Los Angeles have been seen.

Northcentral states, Rise Studio, South Dakota

NORTHCENTRAL U. S.

The Northcentral U.S. was fairly light in photographers during this period. Of the 311 we have documented, only 9 (2.9%) were from Illinois, Michigan, Minnesota, or South Dakota. The northcentral states break down as shown in the following chart:

State	Number	Leading Photographer
Illinois	1	George Petty (Chicago IL)
Michigan	2	W. H. Gardiner (Mackinack Island MI)
Minnesota	4	F. Jay Haynes (St. Paul MN)
South Dakota	2	Rise Studio (Rapid City SD)

The Northcentral photographers break down as follows:

Illinois
George Petty.

Michigan
W. H. Gardiner and Russ Martin.

Minnesota
F. Jay Haynes, Jack Ellis Haynes, K. P. Howarth, and Purdy's Studio.

South Dakota
Rise Studio and O. A. Vik.

There was relatively little hand painting of photographs in the northcentral portion of the U.S. Gardiner specialized in Mackinac Island, Michigan, and Mt. Rushmore and the Badlands were widely photographed in South Dakota.

Other states, location unknown

OTHER STATES

There was relatively little hand painting of photographs throughout the rest of the country. Of the 311 photographers we have documented, only 5 (1.6%) were from outside the regions already reviewed above. These states break down as shown on the following chart:

State	Number
Georgia	1
Louisiana	1
Mississippi	1
North Carolina	2

The photographers from these states break down as follows:

Georgia
DeGroot.

Louisiana
Barnett Crowley.

Mississippi or Alabama
Eddy.

North Carolina
George Masa and R. Henry Scadin.

Canada,
Charles Sawyer, "Lake Louise"

CANADA

Canada had a fair number of photographers during this period. Of the 311 we have documented, 23 (7.4%) were from throughout Canada. The Canadian photographers break down as shown in the following chart:

Province	Number	Leading Photographer
Alberta	8	Byron Harmon (Banff, Alberta)
British Columbia	4	J. Fred Spalding (Vancouver, British Columbia)
New Brunswick	2	Madge Smith (New Brunswick)
Nova Scotia	5	Wallace R. MacAskill (Halifax, Nova Scotia)
Prince Edward Island	2	Oliver Cleveland Craswell (Prince Edward Island)
Quebec	1	Hayward Studios (Montreal, Quebec)

The Canadian photographers break down as follows:

Alberta
Associated Screen News, Byron Harmon, Lane's Studio, George Noble, L. M. Rank, Fred H. Sunbristin, Gilbert Morris Taylor, and J. A. Weiss.

British Columbia
Gus A. Maves, Sanborn, J. Fred Spalding, and Alexander Wilson.

New Brunswick
F. E. Garrett and Madge Smith.

Nova Scotia
Galloway, Wallace R. MacAskill, McLeod, R. S. Smith, and Paul Yates.

Prince Edward Island
Oliver Cleveland Craswell and P. H. Read.

Quebec
Hayward Studios.

Province Not Known
D. Spurway.

Although Canada had 23 documented photographers for the entire country, this is relatively small when compared to the 16 that we documented for the city of Portland, Maine, alone. Canada's photographers were pretty much spread throughout the country with the Canadian Rockies, the Banff area, Jasper National Park, and the Maritime Provinces of eastern Canada being the most photographed locales. The location used for the best-selling pictures was Lake Louise in the Canadian Rockies.

Non–United States or Canada, H. Marshall Gardiner, Bermuda

NON–UNITED STATES OR CANADA

The number of photographers we found from outside the U.S. and Canada were miniscule. Of the 311 we have documented, 10 (3.2%) were from the Bahamas, Bermuda, Cuba, and England, with 70% of these being from Bermuda. These photographers break down as shown in the follwing chart:

Foriegn Country	Number	Leading Photographer
Bahamas	8	Frederick S. Armbrister (Nassau, Bahamas)
Bermuda	4	H. Marshall Gardiner (Bermuda)
Cuba	2	American Studios (Havana, Cuba)
England	5	Harvey Studios (England)

The non–United States or Canada photographers break down as follows:

Bahamas
Frederick S. Armbrister.

Bermuda
Mark Alan, R. Dowly, H. Marshall Gardiner, A. H. Hayward, Stuart Hayward, M. A. Trott, and Edith Watson.

Cuba
American Photo Studios.

England
Harvey Studio.

Region not known

REGION NOT KNOWN

This category represents photographers we simply could learn nothing about. Most often the problem was that we just had a last name or a first initial, and were unable to pinpoint any specific region.

The photographers whose regions are not known break down as follows:

S. L. Blair, E. A. Bragg, Linda Cattell, Colart, R. J. Cooper, Gould, H. S. Hannum, C. Hazen, Hemenway, A. S. Homer, W. F. Jackson, Kattleman, Knaffle & Co., Krabel, Lake, Deck Lane, Lang, Lawrence, M. Lightstrum, Rossiler MacKinae, Meyers, Moran, Murray, Murrey, Dolores Nelson, Newcombe, Bertha Noyers, N. A. Parker, P. Reynolds, ROM, Walter Sheldon, J. W. Shott, E. W. Simpson, T. Roy Spiller, Stott, Thomas Thompson, Henry Troth, F. Hayden Tucker, Nelson Underhill, Villar, and Mary C. Whitney.

Chapter 9

Some Final Topics and Thoughts

HAND-PAINTED POSTCARDS

In 1898, Congress passed a law authorizing the manufacture and use of "private mailing cards," later known as postcards. With the telephone not yet invented, postcards became a primary means of casual communication. Machine-printed postcards were the vast majority of the millions of postcards that were produced. But many photographers were also selling hand-painted postcards. As you read through the various photographer biographies in chapter 6, you will see that many of them were selling hand-painted postcards in addition to hand-painted pictures. Without a doubt, the hand-painted postcards were infinitely superior to the machine-printed cards in terms of quality and desirability, and were preferred by most individuals. However, the higher labor costs associated with hand painted postcards usually pushed the price beyond the practical means of all but the wealthiest people. Hand-painted postcards were popular not only in the United States, but also in Europe and elsewhere.

Hand-painted postcard

Hand-painted postcard

HAND-PAINTED TRAVEL PORTFOLIOS

Another highly collectible and seemingly undervalued area within this field includes the many travel portfolios that were sold with hand-colored pictures. Most travel portfolios you will see include machine-produced, offset lithographic prints. But occasionally, if you look hard enough, you can find portfolios that contain hand-painted photogravures. A photogravure is not a photograph that has been individually developed from a negative. Rather, a photogravure is a print of a photograph that has been reproduced by lithographic means. However, the fact that one has been hand colored adds a premium to the value. Oftentimes, hand-painted portfolios can be purchased at the same price as those that were machine produced and the break-up value will far exceed the purchase price.

Hand-painted travel portfolios

STEREOSCOPIC CARDS

Stereoscopic cards were also widely hand painted. Like picture postcards, most were machine printed, but hand-painting provided better and more realistic three-dimensional effects, and you can still locate many hand-painted stereoscopic cards in your travels.

Hand-painted stereoscopic cards

To date, we have seen the following hand-colored travel portfolios:

- *Glacier National Park*
- *Grand Canyon National Park, Arizona*
- *Mackinac Island*
- *Panama Pacific International Exhibition: San Francisco 1915*
- *Rainier National Park: Mountain Glacier Wonderland*
- *San Francisco: The Queen City*
- *Scenes of Estes Park and the Rocky Mountain National Park of Colorado*
- *Scenes Through the Canadian Rockies*
- *The Canadian Rockies*
- *The Columbia Highway: America's Greatest Scenic Drive*
- *The Grand Canyon of Arizona*
- *Views of Grand Canyon, Arizona*

COLLECTING TIP

Postcards, stereoscopic cards, travel portfolios, and many other photographic items were hand painted during the late ninteenth and early twentieth centuries.

HAND-PAINTED JAPANESE PHOTOGRAPHS

Over the years we have seen two different types of Japanese hand-colored pictures. The first type are the standard hand-painted photos. These are the basic platinum prints, developed in a darkroom, from an original glass negative, and then hand-painted, framed, and sold, presumably to tourists visiting Japan. We have seen relatively few of these.

The second type of Japanese hand-painted photo, although somewhat more common, is absolutely beautiful. These photos are generally city or temple views, often of Nikko, Japan. They are often found unframed, and prices can vary from $10.00 – 15.00 from one dealer to $200.00 – 300.00 from another dealer, for exactly the same image.

HAND-PAINTED PHOTOGRAPHS OF NATIVE AMERICANS

There are several different types of hand-colored photographs of Native Americans. The first are hand-colored images taken by some of America's premier photographers of Native Americans. Edward Curtis and Carl Moon are two photographers who come to mind. The value of hand-colored pictures by artists such as these are predicated more upon the name of the photographer than on the subject matter, and are beyond the scope of this book.

The second type of hand-painted photographs of Native Americans are those more oriented to tourists. These were often by lesser-known or unknown photographers and were sold to visiting tourists at trading posts, Indian reservations, and retail shops throughout the American Southwest.

Perhaps some of the most interesting hand-painted pictures of Native American we have seen involve images from the Museum of Natural History. Apparently, around 1920 someone purchased a series of black and white reprints, taken from the negatives of original views by famous southwestern U.S. photographers, from the Museum of Natural History. Each photo contained a backstamp confirming this. Anyway, someone took each of these black and white images and beautifully hand painted them, making each perhaps a one-of-a-kind piece.

Native American

Japanese temple

Japanese landscape

SOME FINAL THOUGHTS AND OBSERVATIONS

* Hand-painted photographs were generally sold as gifts or tourist memorabilia rather than fine art.

* Relatively few photographers were able to generate a sufficient income solely from the sale of hand-painted photographs. Most had to generate additional income from related endeavors such as portrait photography, commercial photography, postcard photography, and photofinishing and film developing.

* There were surprisingly few photographs from America's major cities such as New York, Boston, Philadelphia, Chicago, New Orleans, San Francisco, Los Angeles, etc. The one exception was Washington DC, where many hand-painted pictures were taken and sold.

* Despite the high level of patriotism during the 1914 – 1918 World War I period, relatively few photographers ever succeeded in capitalizing on the patriotic theme, and few ever even included an American flag in their pictures.

* Significantly more photographers colored their pictures with watercolors than with oils.

* Whereas Native Americans are frequently found in hand-painted photographs, extremely few African Americans will ever be found in hand-colored photos.

* Although collectors typically collect the name, hand-painted photographs by unknown photographers can be the most fun to collect, because you can locate much broader diversity of subject matter at relatively inexpensive prices.

* Certain photographers are extremely undervalued today. The key to successful collecting today is to be ahead of the curve. Try to identify those photographers with the most collectible potential, or from the most potentially collectible areas, before the majority of other collectors catch on. Happy hunting!

Chapter 10

Conservation and Preservation

Special Note: This chapter is being reprinted, nearly in its entirety, from a book titled The Hand-Painted Photographs of Charles Henry Sawyer. Although Mike is listed as one of the co-authors in that book, his contribution to that book came solely in the form of writing the five-point grading system and providing current pricing. This chapter about conserving and preserving hand-painted photographs was prepared by Doug Peters, one of the other co-authors of that book. Doug has given us permission to reprint this chapter in its entirely, which we have done, making only the minor modifications necessary to adapt that text to fit this new book. Our special thanks go to Carol Gray and Doug Peters for allowing us to use this material. Anyone interested in ordering the Charles Sawyer book can do so via our website at www.michaelivankovich.com. Also, please note that the conservation opinions offered in this chapter are related to, and limited to, hand-painted photographs of the early twentieth century. They do not apply to all other forms of art or prints.

Some of the tools needed for conserving and preserving hand-painted photographs

INTRODUCTION

The adverse effects of water, humidity and light were known during the time of Charles Sawyer, Wallace Nutting, and many of their early twentieth century photographic colleagues. The adverse effects of acidic papers and backing materials were not known or understood.

Although "paper" had been used for thousands of years as a support material for writing, drawing, and painting, little was understood of the chemistry involved in the paper degradation process. Wood slats, acid-contaminated cardboard, and poster-boards were commonly used, and indeed were the standard materials used during the years that these early twentieth century photographers worked. Today we understand that the yellowing of paper and the process of brittling and degradation are most commonly caused by acids inherent in or used in the process of making paper. Wood and wood slats naturally contain acid. Papers made from wood pulp, unless stripped of the acid, contain acids that ultimately destroy the materials they are in, or injure materials in close enough proximity to be damaged by leaching acid.

The long-term survivability of hand-painted photographs requires the removal of all acid-based materials that can be removed without destroying an image itself. Acid is probably the number one enemy of the hand-painted photograph. Its presence in mounting and backing materials requires the dismantling and reframing of painted photographs, using the acid-free supports and backing materials commonly available today. Hand-painted photography purists who insist on virgin pictures (i.e., unopened pictures with the original backing paper still intact, acidic though it may be) will find themselves building a collection that is slowly destroying itself.

Water is another enemy of the hand-painted photograph. Water, liquids (e.g., Windex), dampness, and the molds that grow in damp environments are more immediate and fast-acting in their destruction of the fine painted photograph than the slower and more insidious acids.

Paper-based works of art need to be kept in a climactically controlled environment. Although the range of temperature may be a wide range, excessive humidity can cause cockling (waffling/distortion) of framed painted images. It also causes metallic inclusions in the paper to oxidize (rust). This process is called *foxing*. Humidity also speeds up the process of acid leaching. Finally, humidity, in the presence of mold spores (as in basements), may cause mold to grow on the image or mat mounting. Direct sunlight and strong indirect light may, depending on the type of paint used, cause the general or selective fading of colors on the painted photograph.

Hand-painted photographs should be hung in low, non-direct light environments. In many ways, on the scale of durability, stone sculpture and hand-painted photographs are on opposite ends of the continuum. Recognizing and respecting the fragility of this medium is vital to its survival and value preservation.

CONSERVATION ISSUES RELATING TO HAND-PAINTED PHOTOGRAPHS, MOUNTING, AND FRAMES

Charles Sawyer and the other photographers used glass negatives to print black and white (and sepia, which were not painted) photographic images, which they then painted and/or colored. Earlier images were platinum prints; later images are gelatin-silver.

These painted photographs were then mounted on paperboard, using glue sheets. These mat-mounted images were then placed directly in frames behind glass, with or without a mat mount. Over the years, this presentation was then backed by wood panel slats, cardboard, or heavy paper board. In later years (1960s – 1970s), a heavy mat-mounted image was sometimes sprayed with a protective coating of lacquer and framed without glass, backboard, or cardboard.

Opening original sealed and stamped hand-painted photographs is a must-do conservation recommendation.

1) Backing sheets should be replaced.

2) The wood slats or high-acid cardboard backing materials should be replaced with acid-free mat board or other acid-free rigid board. Unless this step is taken, over time, these high-acid materials will leach into the matting and damage the mat or the painted photographs they are supporting.

3) Frame — save, clean, and reuse.

4) Glass should be saved, cleaned, and reused; replace only if broken. Use of special glass, e.g., UV, is not appreciated by collectors, and has a tendency to reduce the short-term value. Collectors prefer the antique look provided by the irregular surface of old glass.

5) The paperboard that supports hand-painted photographs was not acid-free in the early twentieth century. Nothing can be done about this without removing the painted photograph from the mat (AND THIS SHOULD NOT BE DONE). Because the title and signature of the artist are on the mat, separating the image from its heat-mounted mat would destroy the image's value. In cases of extreme damage, a professional conservator should be consulted.

6) Water stains are commonly found on most pictures that one might see in today's antique shops. As the prices for these images escalate, it may soon be cost effective to hire professional paper conservators to tone down water stains. Although in some instances a professional can make a water stain "almost disappear," water stains cannot be easily removed. Amateur attempts at bleaching or coloring the mat or repainting a stain on a painted image almost always end in disaster.

7) Water stains and other injuries to the mat can be disguised by placing a new mat on top of the damaged mat. This is called *overmatting*. One can usually assume that any overmatted image was overmatted to disguise damage to the underlying mat.

8) On older papers containing chemical and metal impurities, over time, these impurities can cause discoloration (age spots) and, where metal contaminants are found, especially when the paper has been exposed to humidity, we find rust spots. Foxing cannot be treated by amateurs. Foxing is a natural paper degradation process not completely understood. It seems linked to moisture and metallic inclusions in the paper support. During earlier times of paper production, metal and chemical contaminants remained in the finished product. Today's fine art papers are stripped of impurities. They are also more likely to be made from cotton than cellulose.

9) Close-framed painted photographs are prone to *cockling* (waffling). Cockled papers can be professionally flattened. The most common cause of cockling is a tight frame and/or dampness. To solve this problem, the frame needs to be routed out to make more space for the image. To retain value, the photograph and mount should not be cut down from their original dimensions.

15 STEPS TO THE CLEANING AND RESTORATION OF HAND-PAINTED PHOTOGRAPHS

Tools needed: 1) needle-nose pliers, 2) soft brush, 3) hair dryer, 4) sprig gun or nail punch, 5) X-Acto knife, 6) Windex, 7) paper towels, 8) Old English scratch cleaner, 9) acid-free paper, 10) double-sided tape or Elmer's Glue, 11) new backing paper, 12) drill, 13) eye screws and wire, 14) Murphy's Oil Soap, and 15) archival-quality document cleaning pad.

This is actually more safely done by a professional framer who is informed about conservation issues, but if you are the more adventuresome type, this process isn't all that hard and can be very effective in conserving and preserving your collection.

Step 1) Remove the original backing paper, if any remains. If the backing paper contains labels, stamps, printed or other informational material, save that backing for reuse in the last step of the cleaning and restoration process.

Step 2) Remove and save the original nails with needle-nose pliers. Where possible, the original nails should be reused in the same holes.

Step 3) Carefully remove the glass from the frame. Clean both sides of the glass thoroughly. Set the glass in a safe place, and look next to the frame.

Step 4) Because the frame is 60 – 100 years old, it is probably covered with smoke, oil, and grease residues. Take a fine brush, dipped in a diluted solution of Murphy's Oil Soap, and gently use it to clean the frame. Distilled water should be used for both the dilution of the Murphy's Oil Soap and the cleaning off of any residue before the frame is patted with cotton paper towels and blown dry (air without heat). In addition, if the frame needs structural repair, it should be expertly repaired by a framer, or if necessary, replace an unsalvageable frame with a similar newer frame. Do not paint or refinish the frame; do minor touch-up at most. If the frame is beyond repair, it can be replaced with a frame recycled from the period. As the value of vintage hand-painted photographs escalates, the amateur repairs of today will prove very costly tomorrow.

Step 5) Dry clean the mat, using an archival-quality document cleaning pad.

Step 6) With a soft hairbrush, gently brush any remaining particles off the mat. Do not use a hair dryer on the mat, because this could damage the painted photograph.

Step 7) Take the cleaned frame and lightly brush off the back and interior glides of the frame, to make sure no loose pieces of paper or dust are present. Then place the clean glass back into the frame.

Step 8) Place the hand-painted photograph, whether mat-mounted or open-framed, back into the frame. Carefully turn the image over to make sure no flecks of debris have slipped between the glass and the image.

Step 9) Do not reuse the original wood slat, cardboard, or hard paperboard backing (save these only if they carry markings). Discard this original material, as it is too high in acid content. In its place, use a cut-to-size piece of acid-free matboard or acid-free corrugated cardboard, depending on the depth of the frame. This material is readily available at art supply stores.

Step 10) With the foam core holding the mat-mounted or close-framed image against the glass in the frame, turn the picture over one last time to make sure that debris has not found its way between the glass and the image. If all is well at this point, turn the framed image over and replace the original nails in the original nail holes, to hold in the foam core board.

Step 11) Take the original backing paper and salvage any labels, stamps or other markings. Leaving margins, cut the labels, stamps, and other reusable markings from the old backing paper. Although the stamps, labels, and other markings may be glued (with water soluble white glue, like school glue) to new backing paper, an alternative technique is to cut a window the size of the stamp to be reused, and then take the original stamp, with margins, and reverse glue the stamp to the backing paper, so that when the backing paper is placed on the back of the image, the stamp shows, as if a television screen, through the window cut in the backing paper. However the labels, stamps, or other markings are affixed to the backing paper, it is now time to apply the backing paper to the frame.

Step 12) Place an appropriate glue (water soluble white glue, like school glue) around the perimeter of the back of the frame. Take the oversized backing paper and stretch it across the back of the frame. Place a lightweight object (e.g. a book) over the backing paper until the glue has dried. Then take an X-Acto knife and trim off the excess backing paper.

Step 13) If possible, reuse the original screw eyes or other hardware mountings removed from the original frame. These should be mounted in new holds for security, as the old holes may be stripped.

Step 14) The original picture wire should be discarded. Most of the wires have grown brittle over time and may be dangerously weakened. Apply new lightweight picture wire, and you are done.

Step 15) When cleaning the glass of a framed print, never spray the glass cleaner directly onto the glass. The liquid will quickly wick under the glass and stain the mat. Always spray any cleaner onto a clean cloth and then use the dampened cloth to clean the glass.

SOME CLOSING THOUGHTS

Conservation is a key to condition, and condition is a key to value.

The cleaning and removal of acidic materials can be performed by the careful layperson. More sophisticated repairs such as mat stain treatment or image problems require the services of a professional conservator.

As the demand for early twentieth century hand-painted photography grows, prices will rise. Rising prices will begin to justify the reclamation of lower-grade pictures. At the present time, it is probably best to leave low-grade pictures untouched rather than taking the risks associated with an amateur repair.

Finally, the authors extend their appreciation to paper conservator Valerie Baas. Her review, based upon the current state of the art, strengthens our belief in the opinions we offer in this chapter.

For the names, addresses, and telephone numbers of professional conservators near you, call the American Institute of Conservation in Washington DC at 202-452-9545.

Vintage hand-painted photographs are now 60 – 100 years old. No matter how fine the image looks, it is important that every framed image be opened and conserved as outlined above.

Untended collections will decay and be diminished in value. This will increase the value of pieces that have been properly conserved. As always, rarity and condition determine value.

Sophisticated corrections and repairs, such as treating water stains to mat and image, deserve professional conservation. Amateur attempts to bleach water stains from mats, or paint in and correct water stains on images, are always apparent. This is especially true now that we understand the benefits of black-light testing.

About the Authors

Michael & Susan Ivankovich

Michael Ivankovich has been collecting and researching early twentieth century hand-painted photographs for over 30 years and today is generally considered to be the country's leading authority on the subject. Through Michael's love of seeking out these treasures, his wife, Susan, has caught the collecting bug as well, and together they have built their full time antique and auction company upon early twentieth century hand-painted photography. Together they have been conducting live auctions since 1988 that feature the works of Wallace Nutting, David Davidson, Fred Thompson, Charles Sawyer, and many other photographers of the genre.

Michael's specialization led to his first book, *The Price Guide to Wallace Nutting Pictures*, in 1984. Three additional self-published editions of that book were released between 1986 and 1991. He has also authored and/or self-published six other books in this field, including *The Alphabetical and Numerical Index to Wallace Nutting Pictures*, *The Guide to Wallace Nutting Furniture*, and *The Guide to Wallace Nutting–Like Photographers of the Early 20th Century*. And he has also reprinted Nutting's original books, which include the *Wallace Nutting Expansible Catalog*, *Wallace Nutting: The Great American Idea*, and *Wallace Nutting Windsors: Correct Windsor Furniture*.

In 1997, Michael's *Collector's Guide to Wallace Nutting Pictures: Identification and Values* was published by Collector Books, and it is generally considered to be the number one book for Wallace Nutting collectors.

In 1998, Collector Books published Michael's *Collectors Value Guide to Early 20th Century American Prints*. This book included eight separate price guides, with individual value chapters on Wallace Nutting, David Davidson, Fred Thompson, Charles Sawyer, Maxfield Parrish, Bessie Pease Gutmann, R. Atkinson Fox, and a separate chapter on all the lesser-known hand-painted picture photographers.

In 2002, Michael partnered with Carol Gray and Doug Peters for *The Hand-Painted Pictures of Charles Henry Sawyer*.

And in June of 2004, his *Collector's Guide to Wallace Nutting Furniture* was released by Collector Books.

Susan has served as Michael's right-hand person in all aspects of their business, and has had some of her own books published, although not in the antiques and collectibles field. She co-wrote and illustrated *The Not-Strictly Vegetarian Cookbook*, *The Supernatural Dessert Book*, and *Cooking with Sun-Dried Tomatoes*, all published by the Creative Arts Book Company (Berkeley CA), and most recently, *The New Not-Strictly Vegetarian Cookbook*, released by Viking Penguin Press (New York NY).

The enthusiasm generated from Michael and Susan's first live consignment auction in September 1988 led to over 60 additional such catalog auctions, which featured many photographers of early twentieth century hand-painted pictures. Today the Michael Ivankovich Auction Company conducts quarterly auctions throughout the mid-Atlantic and New England states.

These auctions have now become the national center of early twentieth century hand-colored photography activity. They provide buyers with the opportunity to compete for a wide variety of pictures, ranging from common scenes to the best and rarest pictures in the country. They provide sellers and dealers with the opportunity to place their consignments in front of the country's leading collectors, where they can be sold in a competitive bidding situation. And, since December 2003, the Ivankovich auctions are now featured on eBay Live as well.

Michael is a licensed auctioneer in Pennsylvania, New Hampshire, and Massachusetts. He is a member of the Pennsylvania Auctioneers Association and has served as the president and secretary/treasurer of the Lehigh Valley Society of Auctioneers. Michael gained special recognition when he was named the 2004 Pennsylvania Auctioneer of the Year.

Locally, Michael and Susan are members of the Bucks County Antiques Dealers Association (Susan also serves as secretary for the organization), and together they serve as show managers for the BCADA annual summer antiques show.

In 2002, Susan was inspired to use her creativity to begin designing and creating websites. She has 12 sites online now; the largest is for her and Michael's company. It features Wallace Nutting Pictures, Wallace Nutting–Like Photography, Wallace Nutting Furniture, Early 20th C. Prints, and Early 20th C. Pastels sites.

Michael and Susan reside in Doylestown, Pennsylvania, where they have five children (Nash, Megan, Jenna, Lindsey, and son-in-law Jake) and two grandchildren (Jake and Kayla). They can be reached at ivankovich@wnutting.com or P.O. Box 1536, Doylestown PA 18901.